Troubling
the Angels

Troubling the Angels

Women Living with HIV/AIDS

PATTI LATHER AND
CHRIS SMITHIES

Westview Press
A Member of Perseus Books Group

Copyright © 1997 by Westview Press, A Member of Perseus Books, L.L.C.

Published in 1997 in the United States of America by Westview Press, 5500 Central Avenue, Boulder, Colorado 80301-2877, and in the United Kingdom by Westview Press, 12 Hid's Copse Road, Cumnor Hill, Oxford OX2 9JJ

Library of Congress Cataloging-in-Publication Data
Lather, Patti, 1948–
  Troubling the angels : women living with HIV/AIDS / Patti Lather,
Chris Smithies.
     p.   cm.
  Includes bibliographic references (p.).
  ISBN 0-8133-9016-8
  1. AIDS (Disease)—Sex factors. 2. Women—Diseases.
I. Smithies, Chris   II. Title.
RC607.A26L377   1997
362.1'969792'0082—dc21   97-3989
                                                                              CIP

Internal design and typesetting: Letra Libre

The paper used in this publication meets the requirements of the American National Standard for Permanence of Paper for Printed Library Materials Z39.48-1984.

10   9

For Rex, PAL
For Elena, CSS

How do we get people who are afraid of us to hear this stuff?

—Linda B

I was going to die *before* I got HIV.

—Sandy

I have laughed more, cried more and eaten more than at any other time in my life.

—Chris

It's OK to be a positive woman.

—Joanna

(To Patti) You've grown so much and gotten a lot smarter than when I first met you at the AIDS retreat.

—Amber

When are you guys going to publish? Some of us are on deadline, you know.

—Linda B

Contents

STORY SERIES FOUR: LIVING/DYING WITH AIDS

STORY SERIES FIVE: SUPPORT GROUPS

EPILOGUE

RUNNING SUBTEXT

"Our Learning Hearts": Chris and Patti

Illustrations

Acknowledgments

We are profoundly grateful to the women whose stories we tell here. For all the obvious and many not so obvious reasons, there would be no book without them. They gave time and insight to the lengthy interview process and privileged us with the most personal aspects of their lives. We are simply and deeply touched by their trust and hope.

This research was funded through two Ohio State University sources, the Elizabeth Gee Fund for Research on Women, 1993, and the Coca Cola Grant for Research on Women, 1995. Fieldwork and interview transcription costs were supported by an Ohio State University Seed Grant, 1992, a College of Education Small Research Grant Award, 1993, and a particularly timely cash infusion from Jim Pearsol, former Director of the East Central AIDS Education and Training Center. We thank Jim, too, for introducing us to one another and launching our research partnership.

Nancy McDonald Kenworthy of Athena's Press and Jon Brooks of Letra Libre were angels of desktop publishing and Jill Rothenberg of Westview Press helped us learn to live with the twists and turns of the publishing world.

We are grateful to the artists who have let us use their work, the community service associations that sponsor the support groups, the group facilitators, and the many members of our families and friendship circles who have stood with us through the time of bringing this book to fruition.

On behalf of the women of this book, we are pledging one-third of the royalties of this publication, after production costs, to organizations that help women and their families live with HIV/AIDS.

Patti Lather
Chris Smithies

The angel handed me a book saying, "It contains everything that you could possibly wish to know." And he disappeared.

So I opened the book, which was not particularly fat.

It was written in an unknown character.

Scholars translated it, but they produced altogether different versions.

They differed even about the very senses of their own readings, agreeing upon neither the tops nor the bottoms of them, nor upon the beginnings of them nor the ends.

Toward the close of this vision it seemed to me that the book melted, until it could no longer be distinguished from this world that is about us.

(Paul Valéry, quoted in Carolyn Forché's book of poems, *The Angel of History,* 1994)

PREFACE 1

The Book

AIDS is on the rise among women in the United States, especially poor African American and Latina urban women. This book explores the cultural meanings and social ramifications of the experiences and understandings of a particular grouping of women who live with the disease. Found in support groups, they both are and are not representative of the larger population of US women infected with HIV. To listen to these women deal with the disease and their experiences of the sea changes that HIV/AIDS brings to living suggests what it means for each of us to address similar issues in meeting what we cannot know: death and the future we make present in the way we live our lives. As witnesses to the women's courage and struggle, our hope is that this book will support, inform, and trouble its various readers as well as make visible the work of living with HIV/AIDS.

By raising such emotionally charged issues as death, survival and self-determination, this book walks a fine line between making a spectacle of these women's struggles and a wanting to speak quietly, with respect for all that it means to tell the stories of people willing to put their lives on public display in the hope that it will make it better for others. Charting the journey of their struggles with the disease, from initial shock to getting on with their lives in ways that make time for what matters often results in admiration for those who are HIV+. Their vibrancy and hopeful realism are lessons in living. Their journeys from infection to symptom to sickness to wasting to death are studies in what it means to be "wise before their time."[1] Their willingness to let us into their lives as witnesses to their struggles has touched us both in ways that we will elaborate upon in what follows. But before getting into their stories and our stories of listening to and then telling their stories, we want to say a few words about this book.

The question of what this book is can be approached by talking about what it is not. This is NOT a chronicle where we as researchers record events as unobtrusively as possible. The book is laid out so that, rather than only "giving voice" to the stories of others, this is also a book about researchers both getting out of the way and getting in the way. As filters for the stories that we heard, we have written a book that is about others who both are and are not like ourselves, as we give testimony to what are our own stories and larger than our own lives. Telling of a loss beyond naming where we try to know from the inside what is our outside, a threshold between what we know and what is beyond our knowing, this book, then, is about the limits of what can be said and known about the lives of others. Doing this work as both a service and a learning, our challenge has been to risk the necessary invasions and misuses of telling other people's stories in order to bear witness with fierce but unsentimental conviction that such stories can transfix, overwhelm, linger, and compel in taking readers to the place where this research has brought us, a place where we can see all the "truth" that we can handle and be grateful for it.

For a disease not known to exist until the last decade, AIDS has become a major part of living at the end of the twentieth century. It is understood in our culture in many ways, from "a metaphor for mortality, for human fragility and vulnerability," in Susan Sontag's words,[2] to a plague wreaked by a vengeful God, according to "the un-Christian religious right,"[3] to "the battleground of moral courage," to quote AIDS activist, Cindy Patton.[4] Demographically, it is a disease of homosexual men and the Third World and, increasingly, the disadvantaged, especially of poor blacks and Hispanics, and women and children. Women, for example, now account for almost 40 percent of the 22 million people with the HIV infection worldwide, and in May 1994, the federal Centers for Disease Control and Prevention announced that women infected by male sexual partners are the fastest growing population of AIDS patients in the United States. Until recently, however, women with HIV/AIDS have been largely invisible in the epidemic. This book is designed to counter that silence as it explores what can be learned from the perspectives of HIV+ women about the cultural significance of the disease, its capacity to alter how we know ourselves and what we can do in the midst of epidemic.

Like the women we have listened to, our hope in the book is to provide support and information to women with HIV/AIDS and their friends, families and loved ones, to educate and inspire women with HIV/AIDS to advocate for themselves, one another and their communities, and to promote public awareness of women's HIV/AIDS issues and a compassionate response for all people with HIV/AIDS. The subject of AIDS is as much about categories of inside/outside, us/them, innocence/guilt, as it is about viruses and healthcare needs. As such, it is not so much a story about "some others" as it is a story of how AIDS shapes our everyday lives, whether we be "positives" or "negatives" in terms of HIV status.

According to 1996 figures from the Centers for Disease Control and Prevention:

- It is estimated that 750,000 to a million and a half Americans are infected with HIV, approximately 1 in 250. This breaks down to 1 in every 100 men and 1 in every 600 women, but the risk is distributed unevenly across race, age and sexuality.
- More than 343,000 people have died of AIDS related complications since the disease was first reported in the US in 1981, more than have died in the Gulf, Vietnam and Korean wars combined.
- Of the 548,102 reported cases of those living with AIDS, 7,296 involve children under age 13 and 78,654 are women.
- 40,000 to 50,000 Americans are infected with HIV yearly. Half are under the age of 25. Rates are leveling for men who have sex with men and for pediatric cases, but increasing for women.
- Among persons 25 to 44 years old, AIDS is the leading cause of death for men and the third leading cause for women.
- In 1995, women accounted for 19 percent of new AIDS cases and 14 percent of the cumulative number. Three out of four of these women are women of color.
- HIV/AIDS in women increased 20-fold between 1981 and 1990. Black women are sixteen times more likely than white women to be diagnosed with AIDS.
- About 46 percent of the reported cases of women with AIDS in the US is from IV drug use. About 38 percent were infected through sexual contact with an HIV+ male. In contrast, heterosexual contact was the means of transmission for only 4 percent of reported cases of men.
- Of women who contract HIV sexually, the portion who are infected by bisexual males remains 10 to twenty percent; 80 to 90 percent are infected by intravenous drug users.

In terms of the changing demographics of the infection:
- African-Americans constitute 12 percent of the United States population, but account for over half of all US women with AIDS.
- Hispanics/Latinos constitute 9 percent of the population, but account for 20 percent of 1995 AIDS cases.
- In children reported with AIDS, 84 percent were black or Hispanic.
- More than 80 percent of all youth whose mothers have died of AIDS are offspring of African-American or Hispanic/Latina women.

This is not, perhaps, the book that any of the women would write, but it is an effort to include many voices and to offer various levels of knowing and thinking through which a reader can make their own sense. While there is some effort to look for patterns as well as differences, our primary interest is in a more interactive way of doing research than is usually the case where researchers are presented as disembodied, "objective" knowers. We are very much in the book, but we have tried to put it together in such a way that our stories are situated among many voices where, accumulating layerings of meanings as the book proceeds, the story of these women goes far beyond the pages of this book as they change themselves, their worlds and researchers like us.

To look with restraint as we bear responsibility to the women who have told us their stories: this is our task as we accept the gift of witness proffered to us by this study. As such, this work has made a claim on us to not drown the poem of the other with the sound of our own voices, as the ones who know, the "experts" about how people make sense of their lives and what searching for meaning means. Hence the book is organized as layers of various kinds of information, shifts of register, turns of different faces toward the reader, in order to provide a glimpse of the vast and intricate network of the complexities of cultural information about AIDS in which we are all caught. While this book is not so much planned confusion as it might at first appear, it is, at some level, about what we see as a breakdown of clear interpretation and confidence of the ability/warrant to tell such stories in uncomplicated, non-messy ways. Wanting a book that puts things in motion versus captures them in some still-life, we walk a line between a victory story of triumph over adversity and a despairing story of loss and darkness. How, for example, are we to situate AIDS: as manageable? as fatal? As we trace the patterns and change of how the women make sense of HIV/AIDS, how they negotiate the balance between denial and obsession, how can we work to neither pathologize nor mythologize them? How can we not make the mistake of taking AIDS as an isolated event in someone's life, to place it at the level of primary identity? Such questions capture our position where, while we are hesitant about adding to the avalanche of meanings caused by AIDS, our hope is to contribute to the strength needed to continue the fight.

By moving from inside to outside, across different levels and a multiplicity and complexity of layers that unfold an event which exceeds our frames of reference, we hope to create a book that does justice to these women's lives, a book that exceeds our own understandings, some widened space to speak beyond our means. Via a format that folds both backward and forward, the book moves toward a weaving of method, the politics of interpretation, data, analysis—all embedded in the tale. Challenging any easy reading via shifting styles, the book positions the reader as thinker, willing to trouble the easily understood and the taken-for-granted. Within such a book, reading both becomes a kind of brooding over that which is beyond the word and the rational, and gestures toward the limits as well as the possibilities of knowing.

Some liberties have been taken, particularly the blending of different support group voices into one story about various aspects of living with HIV/

AIDS. Hence quotes from interview transcripts have sometimes been taken out of sequence and combined from across varied support groups for purposes of theme development, dramatic flow and to protect confidentiality. Efforts were made to not "sanitize" each woman's way of speaking and each thematic grouping of chapters includes some of the women's own writing. Each story series is followed by an intertext on angels which chronicles the social and cultural issues raised by the AIDS pandemic. The angels of the intertexts are intended to serve as both bridges and breathers as they take the reader on a journey that troubles any easy sense of what AIDS means. Across the bottom of much of the book is a continuously running commentary by us, Chris and Patti, the co-researchers, regarding our experiences in telling the women's stories that moves between autobiography and academic "Big Talk" about research methods and theoretical frameworks. Occasionally, the subtext opens out to include one of the women, as she narrates her recent changes, providing a counter-story to her earlier story at the top of the page. Finally, scattered throughout the pages are "factoid" boxes which contain information about AIDS and writings from some of the women in the form of poems, letters, speeches and e-mails.

Networking across all of these parts, the effort of the book is a work which will not be exhausted by the meaning given to it by any one person, be they readers or the authors or the women themselves. Using a kind of speaking out ahead of itself, the book addresses the beyond of what we think we believe through the multiplication of layers of meaning that trouble what we come to such a book to understand and what it means to know more than we are able to know and to write and read toward what we don't understand. It is our hope that the combination of all of this will work in ways we cannot even anticipate.

Notes

1. Ann Richardson and Dietmar Bolle (1992). *Wise Before Their Time: People From Around the World Living with AIDS and HIV Tell Their Stories.* London: HarperCollins.

2. Susan Sontag (1990). *Illness as Metaphor and AIDS and Its Metaphors.* New York: Anchor Books.

3. Phrase from former Surgeon General Joycelyn Elders, referring to opposition to educational programs in such areas as sex and AIDS (*USA Today*, June 24, 1994).

4. Cindy Patton (1991). Visualizing Safe Sex: When Pedagogy and Pornography Collide. In Diana Fuss, ed., *Inside/Out: Lesbian Theories, Gay Theories*, 373–386. New York: Routledge.

PREFACE 2

The Women and the Support Group Meetings

We begin by introducing the Ohio women whose stories are the heart of this book. Through their words, we take the reader into the experience of daily living with HIV /AIDS. The journey of each woman is uniquely her own, but marked by one common decision: to join a support group created specifically for women infected with HIV. It is through the support groups in Dayton, Columbus, Cleveland and Cincinnati that we find these women. The support group is the backbone of this project. The women are the voice, the researchers are the hands and feet. Together, we write this book.

Originally, we planned to conduct multiple individual interviews. In the autumn of 1992, we met with one of the support groups to explore what questions we should use in the interviews. The women attending this meeting were spilling over with excitement and ideas; their talk became a dialogue of issues and feelings and insights. Group process was producing a form and level of collaboration that could not be remotely duplicated in one-on-one interviews, so the decision was made to maintain the group format for most of the data collection. As feminists, we were interested in working in participatory and collaborative ways, particularly in an area where efforts toward "knowing" have often been intrusive and exploitative.

Group interviews occurred from 1992–1993. We met with groups in their usual meeting places, which ranged from a living room in a home to meeting rooms in an AIDS community center or healthcare facility. After discussion of the project and confidentiality, each woman signed a consent form. The time was generally in the early evening; the meetings were marked by laughter, tears, self-disclosures, AIDS jokes, disagreements, hugs, and breaks for pizza. In addition to formal taping sessions with each group, we spent time with various participants at holiday and birthday parties, camping trips, retreats, hospital rooms, funerals, baby showers and picnics.

In the autumn of 1994, we met with some of the women so that they could help make decisions about the actual form of the book intended to address the relative invisibility of women in AIDS discourses. In winter, 1994, several women were frank with their impatience: "Where's the book? Some of us are on deadline, you know!" We decided to desktop publish an early version, thus getting the book to the women sooner rather than yet later and beginning the process of securing a book contract. The epilogue includes the women's reactions to the desktop printed version, as well as an update on them and their support groups.

Many of the women wrote their own introduction; when this was not possible, we wrote it. Each woman also chose either to use a pseudonym or to keep her own name, if she is "out" as an HIV positive woman. After the introductions, we take the reader to a support group meeting that we pulled together across the various times and places where the women talked about why they wanted to help in the making of this book.

Persons and Places

SUPPORT GROUP 1:   Chris began her HIV/AIDS work here in 1988 when she started this group with the support of the local AIDS treatment facility. It was working with these particular women that inspired Chris to expand her AIDS work, to envision a book, and eventually to find Patti as a co-author. Chris moved in 1991 and commuted to group meetings until 1993, when she finally left the group in the hands of the current facilitator. This group meets at the local AIDS community center twice a month. We taped this group in August and October of 1992. Additionally, Chris taped with this group in July 1993 and February 1994.

CR: I am a 49 year-old African-American woman, mother of four daughters and seven grandchildren. There has always been a struggle in my life: incest, being poor and a single parent. When AIDS came into my life I had to accept it as another obstacle in my life, something I've been dealing with for years. I love myself more now but hate the disease and what it does to our bodies. As of this date, February 1995, I've been HIV positive for nine years, with an AIDS diagnosis for three years. I've met many loving people and lost them to this devastating disease. I know what's to come and, in the words of my favorite author, Maya Angelou, "And Still She Rises."

Lori: I am a 37 year old native Cincinnatian. I was diagnosed HIV+ in 1989, along with my husband who died one year later. My health held out until 1994 when my first AIDS infection hit, and I have been battling several illnesses since then. As I am no longer able to work, I have been involved in many AIDS organizations and enjoy speaking to public groups to share my experiences. [Lori died on August 8, 1996.]

Linda B: I am a 47 year old mother of two grown daughters and the grandmother of three (one girl, two boys). I was born and raised in a small northwest Ohio town. A high school graduate, I've had and still have a career in civil service—19 years. I now live in southwestern Ohio. I've been infected since my 39th birthday (8 years). I'm still asymptomatic. I'm very active in AIDS education. My mother, brothers and sisters know I'm infected. My Dad, who abused me as a child and teen, has not been told. My family is *very* supportive. Humor sustains me! I remain widowed—husband infected me.

Rosemary: Rosemary was 48 in 1992, when she attended support group meetings quite regularly, often accompanied by her young grandchild who lived with her. She described herself as "Afro-American, four kids, seven grandchildren, high school education, diagnosed in 1992, infected in 1987."

Carol X: I am a 29 year old African American female challenged with "HIV," healthy and protecting my health status. I am winning and will continue to win. I have obtained a lot in my few years of life, although there is so much more out there for me, and I will be around for the cure. Someone told me that I could do "ANYTHING THAT I SET MY MIND ON." Why did they tell me that? I am going for it. I have obtained a BS and MS in mechanical engineering, and hope to start medical school to become a physician by the year 2000. Life with the "virus" is "no different." I can say that the knowledge of living with the virus is a blessing in that there are so many people walking around without any knowledge and carrying the disease. I am blessed to have the knowledge and know that I have to take the best care of myself, to protect my health. I am LIVING.

Rita: Rita was 38 when we talked with her group. She described herself as "Caucasian with a sixteen year old child, unemployed with two years of vocational education, diagnosed in 1989, possibly infected in 1984." Rita abused heroin and other drugs, and used sex to support her habit. Since her diagnosis with HIV, she has struggled to remain drug free.

Robyn: Robyn was 26 when we talked with her group. At that time, she described herself as "a Caucasian redhead, employed with a high school degree, diagnosed in August of 1991, not sure of infection date."

Barb: I am 28 years old and have been a widow since October 8, 1993. Although Bill is no longer a physical part of my life, his memory, strength and courage will forever survive within me. I go on and live each day with the knowledge and certainty that we will be together again one day. But—until then—there are things I still need to do here. My life continues for reasons that aren't always clear to me.

SUPPORT GROUP 2: This group began in the fall of 1991. Begun by Hispanic community activists, this group met during the afternoon so that its members would not be away from husbands and children in the evenings. This group met at a community center, for about two years, and then disbanded. We met with this group in December of 1992.

Geneva: Geneva was unemployed with 14 years of education. She stated that she was "diagnosed June 21, 1991; I don't know when I was infected. I am 23 years old." Her daughter was 4 years old at the time of the interview.

Sandy: I am 29 years old and Hispanic. I welcome the idea of living with AIDS. It has taught me to love myself and to live every day to the fullest. My health is pretty good.

Maria: Maria described herself as "Hispanic, 39, no children, employed full time with some college education, diagnosed in 1987, infected in 1985. My health is fine, but emotionally it's killing me, especially dealing with the public and their crude jokes." She was a "drop-in" to the support group who agreed to be a part of the taped interview.

Ana: Ana was 40 and "out" as an HIV+ activist when we talked with her group. She described herself as "white, three children, unemployed, high school education. I was diagnosed June 14, 1989. My health is fine."

Louisa: Louisa's daughter was conceived and infected *in utero* in 1987. Louisa, a 24 year old Hispanic, received her HIV diagnosis in 1988. The child died from AIDS complications at the age of 4, in 1991. [Louisa died in June 1993 after many months of illness.]

SUPPORT GROUP 3:   This group began in 1990 and continues to meet monthly. Chris has been a co-facilitator since fall of 1991. The group has always been sponsored by the local AIDS Task Force and meets at Chris' office. We interviewed with this group in April 1993.

Diane: I'm 39 and I know I have grown so much in the past three and a half years since being diagnosed HIV. I have found an inner strength that I didn't know I had. I'm a better friend than I ever thought I could be. I've taken responsibility for my own actions instead of blaming everyone else. I like myself. I like what I am; I like what I have to offer to people. Before HIV, I never thought I did. My friend, Holley, says I've been through a metamorphosis, changing before her eyes. For myself, now that I like who I am: if other people don't, they can go to hell.

Joanna: I'm a 43 year old Gramma (three daughters and one granddaughter) with two years of college. My husband (my daughters' step-father) and I were diagnosed positive in 1989 when he was hospitalized with PCP. He passed away February 1990; I have remained asymptomatic. Yes, there is love after HIV+. The spring of 1995, my beau and I were married.

Alisha: I am 38 years old. I graduated from Gallaudet University, Washington, DC, with a BS degree in Business Administration/Accounting. I have worked as an accounting technician for the federal government for ten years. I am divorced. I was diagnosed HIV+ in November 1991. My health is stable with medication, AZT. Support group is really wonderful although it is a very difficult time to get through. My great emphasis is that you are NOT alone!

Tracy: My name is Tracy. I am a 30 year old African-American graduate student. I never thought I would ever be caught up in one of the worst tragedies of the 90's. Unfortunately I was. I was diagnosed with AIDS in the summer of 1991. The negative aspects of my situation are that I feel that I've lost my chances of living a "normal" healthy life and becoming a mother. The positive side is that I have learned to value several aspects of my life that I used to take for granted. I only wish that it hadn't taken this experience with AIDS to make me appreciate life more.

Danielle: At the interview, Danielle, 25, described herself as "white, no kids, employed with a BS degree. I was diagnosed in April of 1990, infected in 1984." In 1994 and 1995, Danielle had many health problems and a major hospitalization. She was unable to write her introduction due to poor concentration and confusion, symptoms of an AIDS-related form of dementia that are not unusual in the late stages of AIDS. [Danielle died on July 23, 1995.]

Holley: At the time of the group interview, Holley had not yet moved to this larger city, primarily to find a support group specifically for women with HIV/AIDS. Holley was settled in a new apartment, working full-time, and just married when she was diagnosed with various cancers that rapidly overtook her body. She has joined this book through her poetry. Holley's ability to discuss her impending death and say "good-byes" at a support group meeting was the first time Chris witnessed such in-the-moment courage and openness when a support group faced the loss of a member. Holley died on February 12, 1996.

SUPPORT GROUP 4: This group was an outgrowth of a retreat held for women with HIV/AIDS in May 1992. The group was facilitated by an HIV+ woman until declining health led her to turn it over to a family service counselor. It continues to meet in the local HIV/AIDS community center on a weekly basis. We taped with this group in October of 1992 when it had seven members. It now has twenty-four members.

Amber: At the interview, Amber described herself as "32, white, unemployed due to the economy, one year short of a BA, no children, married and divorced twice, diagnosed in 1991, infected perhaps in 1985."

On March 20, 1995, Amber learned that she was NOT HIV+, in spite of three tests on one sample of blood in 1991. This unusual circumstance might be due to another immuno-suppressant condition, perhaps a rheumatoid disorder. It is also possible that Amber's blood sample was mixed up with someone else's. She continues to attend group as it has become her central support network. Believing she was HIV+ for four years, she struggles to shift her identity yet again, this time to an HIV- person who should feel no "survivor guilt" when so many of her friends are sick and dying from AIDS. She has plans to write a book about this experience and has expressed hope that "Dr. Patti" might help her do so. Amber was married in 1995.

Melody: Melody was the "founding mother" of this support group. She described herself as "39, white, one child, employed 'in life' with 14 years of

Amber's unusual situation began with the usual sequence of HIV antibody tests. In 1991, she had a standard Elisa test which has the highest percentage of false positives. A second positive Elisa test was followed one week later by a confirmatory Western Blot test, all on the same blood sample, all administered through a public testing site. In March of 1995, she traveled to another town for medical care and was re-tested with the Elisa in order to gain free healthcare. When she learned of the negative results, her new hometown physician administered a second Elisa, which came back negative, and then, a week later, a PCR (Polymerase Chain Reaction) which, while expensive and not routinely offered at public testing sites, is a DNA test that is the most accurate in terms of both sensitivity and specificity to the HIV virus. The PCR also came back negative. What all of this means in terms of both any kind of certainty in testing and Amber's reaction to what happened to her is dealt with further in Story Series I: "And I Didn't Even Pay My Income Taxes."

education. I was diagnosed in 1989, infected in 1984 or '85." She was formerly a substance abuser with substantial sobriety by the time of the interview. Since then, Melody has had a grandchild. Her health is sometimes good, sometimes not so good.

Tommie: I am a 32 year old white female who, when diagnosed in 1991, was very angry and resentful. Over the last four years, I have been able to accept and learn to be grateful for my diagnosis because I now have a new wonderful husband and I found out what unconditional love really is. I have also learned that God will help in strange ways. My health is wonderful.

Tina: I'm a 29 year old African-American woman. I'm learning to deal with being HIV+, after being diagnosed May 16, 1992. I go to support group and Healing Weekends. I'm not married and I have no children. Friends, relatives and co-workers help support me. Being a positive woman is part of my life.

Iris: Iris was 32 when we interviewed her group in 1992. She described herself as "white, two children, not employed, 10 years of education. I was diagnosed in 1990." In November 1993, Iris went through alcohol and drug treatment and has remained sober.

Iris asked to be re-interviewed in June 1995 because, "I'm not the person now that I was when you interviewed me for the book. Everything has changed so much. My recovery support group is what matters now; I don't want to continue dwelling on the HIV issue. Everyday a person changes, and I'll have changed again in another year. God willing and with the help of my recovery group, I'll keep getting better, but I really like myself better now than I ever have. My girls are my focus. Now that I'm sober, it's so wonderful that it's hard to explain. We have hopes and dreams together and plan for the future.

Little things like having a good dinner together mean so much. We want to go to the Grand Canyon and the mountains. When the day comes that I pass away, the girls can take my ashes back to where we were so we can be together even in death."

Nancy: Nancy was diagnosed with HIV on July 5, 1991. She worked in the medical profession, and was deeply closeted about her HIV status at work. She had an adult son. She died in 1993, alone, except for her support group.

Sarah: I am a 42 year old assistant professor at a community college. I love to travel and be outdoors, camping, hiking, and relaxing in nature. I believe in using herbs, yoga and meditation for emotional and physical well-being and healing. I appreciate the loving support of my partner, family, and support group members. Where am I now? My current struggle is to cut way back on drinking alcohol and eating food compulsively. I believe stopping drinking is something that will bring direct benefits in slowing down the spread of HIV in my body, but it's also the toughest challenge I've ever faced. For me, alcohol has always been connected to socializing and good times with friends, and it's difficult to break the drinking habit and have fun without it. I'm gaining more excess weight (I'm already overweight) as I cut back on drinking; I seem to be exchanging an alcohol dependence for a food addiction. And as I gain weight, my self esteem drops and my sexuality declines. Also, my partner, who is HIV-challenged too, has begun to discover some health problems, and I worry about the impact of HIV on his life and our lives together. We've been blessed with a very special love and life together that supports me in my day-to-day living. I don't want to see him suffer; I don't want to lose our lives together; and experiencing his decline in health foreshadows my own yet to come. The HIV certainly heightens the preciousness of our time together in a very bittersweet way.

Co-Researchers

Patti: This project has come along at a time when I was asking myself hard questions about how social research could be of use to communities outside the academy. Responding to the same sorts of demographic questions that Chris and I asked of the women we interviewed, I am 48 years old, white, no children, with a Ph.D. in education and women's studies, and not yet, to my knowledge, HIV positive. Long interested in research *with* people, instead of the more typical research *on* people, what I have learned from being invited into this project has already greatly influenced my teaching and writing on issues of qualitative research in education and feminist research methodologies at Ohio State University.

Chris: I am 45 years old, I have a Ph.D. in counseling, and work as a feminist psychologist in private practice in Columbus. Since 1988, I have organized support groups, workshops, and weekend retreats especially for women living with HIV/AIDS. I never ever thought that I would co-author a book. But then, who could foresee the AIDS pandemic? Frequently, I witness how "the VIRUS," as it is called by the initiated, is a catalyst for finding what is really important in life. I guess this must rub off, because I credit my HIV+ friends and clients for inspiring me to become a mother to my daughter, Elena.

"Statistics Are Human Beings with the Tears Wiped Off" (Linda B)

Twenty-five women with HIV/AIDS, ages 23–49, have participated in this project. Four are Hispanic, five are African-American, and sixteen are white. Thirteen are mothers and six are grandmothers. At the time of the support group interviews, in 1992, seventeen held jobs across varying professional and service sectors and eight were not employed. Twenty-three women have completed high school, and sixteen have some post secondary education. One is pursuing doctoral study, and another is preparing to take the MCAT examination for entry into medical school.

Dates of HIV+ diagnosis range from 1987–1992. By September 1996, over half of the women are living with an AIDS diagnosis and four are dead. Demographic charts are included in the Appendix, including a summary table that allows the reader to track individual women across their comments in the book.

Why are these women willing to open up their lives to strangers? No other disease is associated with so many stigmas. To identify as HIV+ is to invite the most personal of questions, spoken and unspoken. It also risks loss of relationships with family and friends, sexual intimacy, jobs and, with that, insurance and financial security, housing, identity and self-esteem. Illness and mortality may assume center stage in one's life. Denial makes sense in such a scenario, but it often results in a high price being paid in terms of attending to healthcare needs and changing risk-related behaviors. The fol-

---

According to current diagnostic criteria, adopted in 1993, the line between HIV+ and AIDS is determined by a T cell count of less than 200 or the onset of two or more of the numerous opportunistic infections that characterize AIDS, e.g., thrush, kaposi sarcoma (rare in women), herpes simplex with an ulcer that lasts more than a month, diarrhea that lasts more than a month, PML (affects nervous system), lymphoma, and, specific to women, vaginal candidiasis that is recurring and resistant to treatment and/or invasive cervical cancer. The criteria themselves have shifted over the fifteen plus years of the pandemic, representing the changing nature of knowledge about AIDS.

lowing presents some of what these women intend by their participation in this project. It is assembled across various support groups at various times and places.

"It's OK to Be a Positive Woman"

Chris: Winding down our interview, is there any feedback on what this evening has been like?

Melody: It was like after the retreat weekend. Tonight I feel is one of the times I can say I feel lucky that I am HIV+. I feel blessed with something special, that I can be bonded with so many special women. I feel special to be involved, with the women and the love.

Linda B: How else do we get the people who are afraid of us to hear this stuff?

Lori: I'm really excited about you guys writing this book and I want you to get it published right away. That's just where I'm at right now. I want to do something. I think we've all had this feeling, why did this happen to me? And I keep thinking that there's something there, there's some message, there's something that I need to be doing. Maybe it's connected with going public, and that's a struggle I'm going through and then this book is coming up at the same time. And maybe this is the sign that I've been waiting for, that things are going to change, we have to make them change, and I think the book is really good. Going through the interviews and hearing everyone's story, a lot of this stuff, we don't talk about in group, we don't talk about like how do you really feel about that stuff. I think it's good that these interviews let us do that.

CR: I'm glad about our meetings and the book because if the interviewers would have been doctors, especially men, I would have felt exploited. But I know there are women just like us all over, and hopefully other women and some doctors will read this.

Rita: I go to the library a lot. There is not one book about women. The closest it comes is a woman writing about her husband with AIDS. Everything I've found out about me and what I can expect comes from the women in this group.

Sandy: The one thing I wanted to stress whether in the book or not, is how important it is for them to give more to research on women, to help women get tested earlier, to find out earlier.

Chris: Any other comments on the process, how it's felt being here and doing this?

Diane: I think it's good to have a forum, to be able to talk about it. And to know that what we're talking about is really going to go out and maybe make a difference somehow.

Patti: Why did you participate?

Danielle: Well, I think, if at all possible, I would like to reach certain people like government people and say "help us." And to reach other women or other people who are infected and say "don't give up."

Alisha: Also, try to reach out to the few deaf women who are HIV+. I don't think that they have really stepped out and I would like to reach them. Maybe deaf people are very afraid of it, and they are hiding from it The deaf community is very, very small. And they wouldn't want to step out because everybody would know. It is like one big family. And I want to encourage deaf women to do that and for them to know that there is nothing wrong with it. It is OK to take those steps. I want to help them, but who they are exactly, I don't know. I feel like at this point that I am the only one in the world who is deaf and has HIV although I know that I am not. I want to encourage them to come out so that we can help each other.

Joanna: I want this book to get in the right hands so that people will do something about it, take some kind of action, get more people involved, to open the door for other people, let them know that it is OK to say that I am HIV+. It's OK to be a positive woman.

On July 1, 1994, Being Alive in Los Angeles became the first HIV/AIDS organization to comply with the Americans with Disabilities Act of 1990 by opening its programs to the deaf community. Services include an ongoing deaf support group, a phone line for deaf callers, sign language interpreters at all social and program events and the formation of a Deaf/HIV Issues Advisory Board. *Being Alive*, 3626 Sunset Blvd., LA CA 90026. *Listen to the Hands of Our People* is a documentary film about seven deaf people living with AIDS, directed by Ann Marie "Jade" Bryan, 1990.

Positive Attitude: Keep in Mind the Following Things

1. New treatments are becoming more rapidly available.
2. Support networks are available at no or little cost.
3. Quality of life can be maintained and enhanced.
4. Developing and maintaining a positive attitude can have a strong beneficial impact on your health.
5. Remember that most people who test positive remain symptom-free and healthy for many years (*The Positive Woman* newsletter, see Resources).

David Adams, *Flying Woman: And She Still Rises,* 1995, linocut. Used by permission of the artist.

Life After Diagnosis

"I'm Gonna Die from Stress, Not HIV"

Chris: How has HIV changed your life?

Linda B: I have a whole completely different outlook on life than before I was diagnosed. Some days it's good and some days it's bad. I don't look that far into the future anymore. I don't think about retirement. I don't think about getting old. I want to. I want to see the year 2000, but I just don't look that far ahead. I feel cheated. I feel really cheated that there's a possibility that I'm not going to get to see and do what I would normally.

Barb: I think some of what you said is how I feel. I am 26 and there's goals that I want to pursue and things that I feel like I've held back from, like children or law school. At this time it's not my choice. I don't have the energy or the money. I can't quit work because I can't lose my insurance for myself or my husband. I can't move to where my family is because I can't lose my

---

Our Learning Hearts: Chris and Patti

". . . somehow with a confidence that this very dreadfulness may be something completely *ours*, though something that is just now too great, too vast, too incomprehensible for our learning hearts" (Rilke, 1989, p. 317).

Chris: In 1988, I started a support group for women with HIV/AIDS. It was soon apparent that the impact of HIV on their lives was so much more than I had anticipated, and having recently survived graduate school, this work helped me get back to my heart. As a psychologist, I became interested in how facing this crisis became a catalyst for change and growth for these women. The support group expanded, in numbers and in mission. I wanted to better understand what was happening in the support group, but it was impractical to do research by myself. I was very nervous about using their illness and my already existent relation-

insurance. I don't really get angry about it, but sometimes I feel stuck a lot. But other than that I don't feel angry, you know. It was my choice to have sex without a condom. And I knew what risks I was taking and decided well it won't happen to me. So I don't feel that anyone is to blame for it. I don't really blame myself either. I don't blame anyone.

Chris: What is the worst aspect?

Linda B: Wondering what's going to happen if I have to quit [work], just going through the bullshit you have to go through: where am I going to land? I like where I am now. It's taken me a long time to get where I am. I've had men that were just absolutely anchors on my butt. Now I've finally got to the place where I can enjoy myself and have the things I want, and I know that I don't get to keep them. I'll have to go through a lot of government rhetoric and bullshit just to live. CR and I have talked about this just the last couple of days, it's scary.

Diane: Also it is hard when you are a woman, because with the diagnosis you are either promiscuous, or labeled as not normal.

Patti: What did you mean by label?

Diane: Well, I mean, like people stereotype people who are infected with the virus. I mean we are very stereotyped. We are gay. We are uneducated. We are, you know, sleeping around. I mean it is terrible and I find myself to

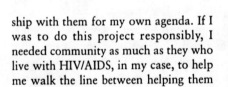

ship with them for my own agenda. If I was to do this project responsibly, I needed community as much as they who live with HIV/AIDS, in my case, to help me walk the line between helping them and researching them.

I approached James Pearsol, director of the East Central AIDS Education and Training Center, about a feminist research partner who could serve as a "chronicler" for the stories I was hearing from women living with HIV/AIDS. Jim felt he knew just the right colleague for me! He arranged a meeting with Patti Lather, who became quite interested in how such a project might push her ideas about doing research that could be of use in struggles for social justice. Thus, this research project began in January 1992.

A month later Patti presented some possible research designs. As I was orga-nizing a weekend retreat at a rural convent for Ohio women living with HIV/AIDS, I invited Patti to attend the retreat so that we could present a research opportunity to the women. In retrospect, I was quite protective of these women, and was undoubtedly testing whether Patti was the right woman for the job. I stipulated: 1) the feminist research partner must agree to be a sympathetic, full participant at the upcoming retreat; 2) she must be experienced in dealing with qualitative and feminist research, especially the ethical and political issues involved; 3) she must agree to me as co-researcher with final say in order to honor the women's concerns regarding right treatment; 4) confidentiality issues must be carefully honored; and 5) factors of sickness and depression must be taken into account in what is asked of the women in terms of

be very average, normal. I don't want anybody to be labeled. I think that is wrong.

Joanna: I sit on panels sometimes and do speaking engagements and there will always be people sitting in the audience wanting to know how I got infected.

Patti: How does that question make you feel?

Joanna: Well, it depends on my time of the month. And it depends on my general mood. And it depends on the nature of the audience. Sometimes I'll just come out and say, you know it is really just none of your business. Or, it doesn't really matter, the point is I am HIV+ now and I am living with it. And this shouldn't happen to other people and hopefully we can educate. And usually I will tell them that I became infected probably through my husband who died. But that doesn't matter. Because if he had known I wouldn't be positive. He didn't know; I just knew shortly after he knew. Nothing changes. The fact is we all are positive and we all are living with it.

Chris: What's it like to live with such a secret?

Rita: That's why I am thinking about moving even though I feel pretty good right now, my count is up and everything. But just for that reason— to take off the pressure of living with a bunch of women that if one day you just don't feel like getting up, you've been up all night long with

participation. Needless to say, Patti passed my inspection. She understood my protectiveness and honored these requirements. We began to create a partnership.

Notes from drive to Women and AIDS retreat, Chris and Patti, May 22, 1992

Chris: I want this research to fill a void: there is very little psychosocial research on HIV+ women, and even fewer opportunities for these women to express their own views and feelings. We have the skills and training to get their voices out there: we are a conduit for these women, and they are our opportunity to create new research design and presentation. There's so much about these women that inspires me. Personally and professionally, I want to better understand them and I want others to not fear them. Most of what is written is about dying and I want to fore-

ground what incredible examples of living HIV+ folks are. I want to hear them talk about how this has changed them: relations with women, the disease, themselves, the world. For some, the support group is the first experience of closeness with women outside their families. In this work, I can apply what I've learned in the feminist trenches but in a context that is heart-centered. This is unlike a lot of other feminist space nowadays.

These women search to find meaning in being HIV+. This project could really help. A while back a romance writer presented her view on living with HIV/AIDS to the Cincinnati support group, who challenged her narrative considerably. Her manuscript contained a thanks to the group; they were energized by this and decided then to publish their own stories. That was the seedling for this project.

night sweats, you've changed the damn bed three times, and you don't want to get up—you don't have to make up a BIG LIE, and a hundred and one other stupid things that go with living with people that don't know.

Geneva: I was at this wedding after I first found out. The photographer was sitting there and telling somebody that she had just bought this apartment, and she said guess what, after I paid my down payment they told me that the guy that lived there had died of AIDS. We had it disinfected, we had a scrub it down party. And it was like, "oh you poor thing, they didn't tell you." And then just the other night, I was at my best friend's house and she knew that I am HIV+, but her mother doesn't know, and they were talking about Magic [Johnson], and her mother was making the same kind of comments, like put them out on an island, and my friend just went crazy, in tears, defending. It was just a really weird position to be in. They got in this big argument.

Linda B: It's a double life, it's an absolute double life. You cannot imagine ever in your whole life what it's like. Somebody has cancer, you go and tell them you have cancer, it's oh you poor thing. You say you have AIDS or you're HIV+ and they can't jump backwards fast enough or far enough.

Chris: What does that feel like?

🐚   🐚   🐚   🐚   🐚   🐚   🐚

Their participation will be maximized if participation helps the women construct meaning out of the HIV experience. The project must not lose sight of the marvel of how they do this, particularly the spiritual dimensions of this process. We need to be realistic about the time, energy, skills, and patience of these women as we move toward more participatory research designs. They do like to TALK, especially in groups! As far as using photographs, they were bruised by a newspaper reporter, so there is no good taste in their mouth on this. They felt betrayed. Perhaps we can construct anonymous representations, that are not within the usual terrorist images of the horrors of AIDS. There are few images of people *living* their lives in all of their infinite variety and dignity.

From Patti's research journal

I was introduced at the retreat as NOT there to gather data, but rather to participate in the workshops so that the women could get to know me and decide whether to join in the research. I deliberately took neither a tape recorder nor a notepad. It was an immersion experience; it was awkward; the touchy feelingness of it was all too much for me sometimes. I had a lot of struggles with voyeurism. I took a lot of walks by myself.

A big memory from the May retreat was the effects of not identifying myself as a researcher until Saturday lunch. Somehow thinking that they already knew my researcher status, I remember my discomfort with Rosemary on the smoking porch; she was crying and saying how important it was to cry and how she could only let herself go with some-

Linda B: I think it's amusing sometimes. You do a lot of: I wonder what they would say if they really knew about me. Oh if you only knew about me, honey; you think you've got it bad.

Rosemary: When they be talking about it, like me, I work in a place where I'm subject to [germs]. I should be more afraid of them than they are of me. I'm so afraid a lot of the time I spray so much Lysol and stuff, somebody come in coughing or whatever. I'm the one trying to jump back; I get real tight and scared that I'm going to catch it. But I can't say anything. Somebody come in there with cuts and whatever, I panic. It's hell trying to be two people. I wish I could go public, I really do. That's what I told the doctor. I wish I could go public so people would know. It would release that tight tension inside of hiding, like you're hiding behind a wall. And if you come out, everybody is going to look at you, that's how I feel inside.

Chris: If you feel any anger at being cheated, where do you direct the anger?

Lori: President Bush.

Linda B: When I get really mad, I get mad at my husband whose philandering gave it to me. But I just get mad in general. Lately I notice I stay mad. That's one of the problems I have to deal with, I have got to figure out some way to unload this. I got into it with my supervisor the other night. She

one in the same boat with her. At which point I stated, "but I don't have AIDS." She mumbled something about "It doesn't matter. You're here supporting us," but it hit me that I was undercover. At lunch, Tracy asked that "facilitators" stand and identify themselves. While uncomfortable, this unintended "undercover" status resulted in a window where I was NOT perceived as an expert or an outsider. I was "them" for awhile, demonstrating the thin line that is crossed between "them" and "us." Some of the women warmed to my not rushing to declare myself not one of "them," while others wanted clarity as to who was who.

I did not have a good time at this retreat. The chance construction of my "undercover" researcher identity slapped me in the face with issues around researcher/ researched relations. Chris had antici-pated that I would be overwhelmed and hoped that I would see the honor of being around these women and hearing their stories. It was important for her that our relationship grow out of my support for her commitment to her work and the tensions of her doubled role as helper/researcher. That my car broke down and we ended up riding to the retreat together was fortuitous as it enabled us to establish a comfort zone with one another in our fledgling relationship; it also enabled me to ride Chris's coattails in terms of the women's willingness to trust me.

My strongest memory of the retreat is from the closing "sistercelebration" where we were lighting candles for those who had died from AIDS and the Dayton women ended up all crying together in a configuration that looked like the statue of Iwo Jima. I remember a particu-

probably carries Lysol in her purse. She asked me what in the world is wrong with you. And I wanted to tell her. Everybody senses a change in me. I'm sick of it. It gets old. It's a big burden too; I don't want this burden anymore. I've got enough to deal with, I don't want to protect anybody else anymore. I think a lot of us feel that way. When we finally all make up our mind to do it, expose ourselves, open the closet door. . . but I just, you know, I just feel absolutely cheated.

Chris: What keeps you going?

Linda B: I keep thinking tomorrow is going to be different. And when it isn't different, that's when it starts getting raggedy. Magic Johnson was hell day.

Robyn: I don't think about it unless I want to date someone. But now I know someone who died. I wonder how I'd afford AZT. With my insurance, I have to pay first and then be reimbursed.

Tina: I told a friend, and it was like I'd given her this big burden. Now that she knows, I can just tell that everything has changed. Now she is trying to take care of me. I don't really want that. I can't tell them at work. That's the worst thing for me, tension around work. And insurance, because I'm not gonna be at this job forever. I go to the doctors and I say to them, "Please don't put down the diagnosis, HIV+," and I know it is going to mess up somewhere, and I won't have any medical insurance. That's a big issue for me. It even makes it hard to go to a counselor because I don't want it in their records. It's all sort of job related.

❀   ❀   ❀   ❀   ❀   ❀   ❀

larly small woman looked HUGE to me as she circled the group of four with her arms. Some angel image jarred in my mind, some image from my own Catholic past and present post-Wiccan spiritual sensibility. Across multiple differences of race, class, age and health, the women seemed angels in their love for one another and in their wanting to be "messengers" to other women about HIV/AIDS. Not too much later, as I puzzled over how to situate myself in relation to the women, the concept of "standing with" impressed itself upon me, which segued into standing with angels—and a world opened up. Chris had told me to expect a spiritual experience in this work, but I had not expected it to announce itself in the form of angels, angels who troubled any comfortable familiarity with their very availability.

Notes from drive to conduct first support group interviews, October 3, 1992

Chris: It's difficult to narrow down a focus. I want to blend current feminist psychology with feminist research, particularly studies of the relational aspects of women's lives. What can be learned from the perspective of HIV-challenged women: how being in relation enhances,

Carol X: Some people don't have an easy time of knowing my HIV status. Everything becomes "because you're HIV+." Damn it, I have a life and no I don't want to go out with this clown, because he's a clown, not because I have HIV [laughter]. A lot of people will play God with you and say, "She's not smiling today so maybe that's because of HIV."

Patti: So your whole life gets reduced to that one thing.

Carol X: Right.

Rosemary: I think about them trying to take my grandson away, especially as rotten as his mother is. On the job, I've been going to several doctors so it's on my record. In a sneaky way I guess my subconscious really wants to let everyone know so it would be a relief from this strain. I've told several of my friends and some at work and they've been a crutch for me.

Chris: How do you decide who to trust?

Rita: (who moved from a different state where she was "out" as a positive woman) Being out brings you more peace of mind, but it's still hard. I worry about the stigma on my son, especially. I was like a freak when I was out as HIV+. That's part of the reason I moved. I choose very carefully who I tell. You might be able to handle it, but what about your family? You can't really think about you wanting to tell the world. You have to stop and think how this will affect your family.

Chris: Bad days?

Lori: Going through my husband's death and becoming a widow. I didn't expect any of that stuff to happen in my life. Dealing with that was the first

adds complexity to life versus more masculinist theories of loss of self and need for separation in relationship?

I made a formal presentation a week or so ago to a group of university staff people. I was the last speaker, after three medical doctors. The program was running behind schedule by the time it was my turn to speak. I dropped all of my anecdotes and humor and was "too grim." I don't know yet how to talk about this. My intention was to accomplish an alliance, a concern and appreciation for those living with HIV/AIDS, but instead, I ended up shaking my finger at them and over-emphasizing the tragic part of HIV/AIDS. The picture I created was truthful, but plain, drab, objectifying. I hate to give a bad talk.

Patti: Maybe it's good that we don't know how we want to talk about this. Are we talking *about* these women? *for* them? *with* them? We *should* be uncomfortable with these issues of telling other people's stories. I'm having a similar problem in terms of a conference paper I'm writing. Part of me wants to begin sharing the stories we are hearing; part of me wants to move softly, with restraint, being careful to not pounce too quickly in thinking I understand their lives well enough to tell their stories to others.

thing I had to get over. I still don't think of myself as being sick, I don't really think about it, my healthy denial. But it's made me a better person, not that I would ask for it, but there are some positive things that come out of going through a tragedy. Look at this room full of wonderful people that I'd never have in my life and that's really important to me. But the way I look at this, and I think things are really going to change if I ever get sick, but so far, my saying has always been everybody has a crisis in their lives and this just happens to be mine. I've been really lucky with who I've told. I've been in two relationships since I've been a widow and been infected and they've both worked out really well. I don't know, I think that in some ways, you get back the vibes that you put out. I'm not saying this to tell anybody that they're wrong, but I think what worked for me was to put the expectation on people that I'm giving you a gift, I'm sharing something with you that's really, really important to me and don't take it lightly [tears] and I haven't been let down. I've told everyone except the people in my new job. No one has ever betrayed my trust. The only bad experience I've had has been within the medical community. I don't know, there's some reason why this happened. I don't know why; I'm not angry at my husband for infecting me. I'm not really angry about being infected at all, but I get angry about situations that happen. It's so wearing; which circle are you going to walk today? Are you allowed to be real?

Linda B: You have to lie so much.

Joanna: Hope, that is what keeps us going.

Patti: What does that hope look like?

Joanna: Some days it is very good. You meet someone who has lived for so long and it's like, they did it, I can do it too.

Chris: So survivor stories?

Joanna: Yeah. Sometimes, it's, like, even though I know we don't trust our government and stuff, you know that every time there is a conference, you are busy flipping through those magazines, hoping to hear something good. So, I guess, it is mostly other people who have beaten the odds, gone against the odds.

Tracy: I think the media tends to impact us negatively about it a lot. They put these people on TV who are on their last breath instead of empowering us by saying this person is around still, they are still going, we are getting somewhere. So I think we need to tune out a lot of what the media is talking about, because they need ratings and dying people are going to get a lot of attention.

Linda B: Group is one place you don't have to be a phony. You don't have to ask: Which face do I put on today? "Bond" is inadequate. No word can describe the love you get in this group. My family doesn't understand my

forgiveness. I call this "front-pew-itis," selective Christianity. If this is such a Christian country, why do I have to hide?

Rosemary: I'm gonna die from stress, not HIV.

Characteristics of *Positive* Living

Some while back, the *Annals of the New York Academy of Science* presented the results of a study of the common attributes of "long term survivors." Long term survivors:

- are able to communicate openly about their concerns
- are sensitive to their bodies' physical and psychological needs
- practice the ability to withdraw from taxing involvements and to nurture themselves
- are assertive and able to say "no"
- have a personalized means of active coping they believe has healing effects
- accept the reality of their diagnoses and refuse to perceive the condition as a "death sentence"
- are altruistically involved with other HIV+ persons
- derived useful information from and maintained supportive contact with a person having the same diagnosis shortly after their own diagnosis
- are actively involved in physical fitness (exercise and dietary work)
- found a new meaning in life as a result of the diagnosis itself
- consider their lives to have great meaning and purpose, which they are focused upon and invested in
- are committed to life in terms of "unfinished business," unmet goals, or as yet unfulfilled experiences and wishes
- are influencing their own health outcome
- are assuming personal responsibility for their health

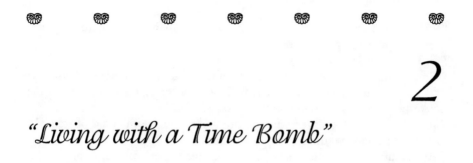
"Living with a Time Bomb"

Chris: What's been helpful to you, what gets in the way, what is a really bad day?

Danielle: Obviously, the HIV virus makes it incredibly difficult, living with fear all the time. Getting sick, having a lot of fatigue, a lot of uncertainty about the future. Should I pursue a Master's degree, should I go for some career move, am I wasting my time? Should I just lay at home and wait to die? I mean, what about relationships? You are **living with a time bomb** now. That's a drastic change, and a miserable one.

Chris: How is it miserable?

Tracy: Well, I'd say my misery stems from the stress of it all. If I wake up not feeling well, I am afraid. God, could this be the end? That's incredibly stressful. I remember the very first time I met Chris. She said, "It's like sitting on a time bomb and never knowing when it is going to go off." For me that is the worst thing about this situation. There are some days when I can believe that I am invincible and I don't even think about HIV. And then there are those days that I can't forget it and I am just. . . . *why me?*

Diane: I don't know. Maybe I am naive, but I *don't* see myself sitting on a time bomb. If you look at it rationally, everybody is sitting on a time bomb. Nobody knows for sure when the end is. When I first found out I couldn't sleep for months. I was afraid I wasn't going to wake up in the morning. And then once enough time goes by, and you are still there, and things are still functioning, you think, "Oh, maybe I am going to live." Then you just get back on with living again. Most of the time I don't think about HIV, though I have started reading more, where I didn't want to know anything before. Now I am reading, taking an interest. I talk to other HIV+ women and ask them questions and get feedback, so it has changed.

CR: When I found out, I had never heard of HIV so I didn't think I had that long to live. If someone would ask me to go somewhere, I was like,

"Well, I don't think I'll be alive." I thought I'd be sick. I am here and I am doing fine and I'm glad I came to the group.

Patti: So there is life after the diagnosis?

CR: Yeah. So I am real proud of myself. I realize it's a manageable disease and you just don't die within a year. It took a lot of guts to come to the meetings, to read stuff and admit you are HIV+.

Patti: That raises an interesting question. Are there some kind of stages?

Chris: Anybody want to take a stab at that?

CR: Denial, shock, numbness, paranoia, reality, education, coping, freedom. At first, a paranoia about everything that goes wrong with your body. Now I'm in the coping stage. The stages I went through were: first denial, second, shock—when I got the results. And then numbness—just like, don't sneeze because you don't want to shake up anything in your body. I'd take a shower and I wouldn't look at my body because I was afraid that something else would show up. And then reality. And then education comes next. Now I am in the coping stage.

Tina: I'm getting used to it, adjusted to it more since I found out June 12. I started coming to the group in July. At first it was always on my mind, but now I don't think about it as much. Like today, coming to the group, I just figured a bunch of girls to talk with and then I can go home. I work at the library and get all these books about AIDS. I get all of them and read them so it's getting better now.

Chris: How would you name the stages?

Tommie: Shock, numbness, denial, anger, grief, cover-up the feelings because they are just too powerful. I've been diagnosed almost two years now and I've watched the new girls go through their stages. Some I see going through the same stages that I went through, having to use alcohol or drugs, to cry out and scream. It's OK; I had to learn how to give myself permission, to allow myself to go through those stages, and to feel certain ways.

Lori: I've been diagnosed for almost two years and now there is this numbness. Sometimes I've accepted my HIV status. I'm OK with it most of time. Sometimes it "Oh, I'm HIV+," but the numbness is still there.

Ana: I'm better now. I'm not on drugs anymore. I don't use alcohol. I think about what's a year from now; I am not thinking about dying. Half the time it doesn't even cross my mind. It took some time to get here. I used to worry about my kids; now I just don't worry. When I was first diagnosed, the hurt was like when a baby dies. I had one that died and that's how I can tell.

"Hugging That Dragon Within Me"

Chris: How do you take care of yourself?

Amber: I'm trying to quit smoking more often, but I'm not successful. I'm taking a bunch of vitamins and stuff. I go through that, like eating all the

The first generation of AIDS drugs seemed to delay symptoms, but did not prolong survival. Those who waited to take AZT until they had full-blown AIDS lived about a year longer than those who started taking the drug as soon as they knew they were infected. Those who were treated earlier suffered fewer AIDS-related infections. Yet, once they got sick, they died, on average, a year sooner than those who did not take any drugs until severe symptoms began (*Columbus Dispatch*, July 14, 1995). This captures some of the difficulties of both doctors and Persons With AIDS (PWA's) in making treatment decisions when available information is uncertain and constantly changing.

All of this is even more complicated with the new generation of drugs that has come on the scene in 1996. Called protease inhibitors, they are combined with earlier drugs like AZT into three or four drug "cocktails" which combine to form the most potent treatment yet. Early indications are that these drugs slow and perhaps stall the disease, but many questions remain, especially whether HIV will develop immunities to these treatments, given the tendencies of the virus to quickly mutate. There is a new optimism around these drugs as side effects seem to be minimal and the new treatments appear to hold the virus at bay. But the AIDS crisis is by no means over. Cost is a problem (the three-drug regime presently costs $18,000 a year) and administration of the drugs is not easy, sometimes involving as many as twenty pills a day which must be taken at exact times in exact combinations, maybe over a lifetime. There are questions as to whether prolonged early treatment is best or, if the drugs quickly lose their punch, whether they should be saved for later stages of infection. And while the new viral load tests assess the presence of the virus in the blood, it is difficult to find out if the virus is being harbored in the lymph nodes, brain and/or spinal fluid. Hence while hope is high that AIDS will become a chronic rather than a lethal condition, the disease is still untamed and many worry that prevention efforts will fall on deaf ears as people assume that AIDS is now curable (*Newsweek*, February 12, 1996).

stuff that's right for me and everything. And then I go through other times where I don't take my vitamins and I smoke a lot and eat a half gallon of ice cream.

Melody: You want to read up on how to improve your health and take better care of yourself, but it can become really overwhelming. Everyone has to find their own happy medium. For me, I had to learn about my body. What is causing the physical pain that I'm experiencing? Is it a situation that I've been through? Is it something that I'm allergic to? Is it something I ate? Is it emotional or physical? I've had to tune in and really listen to the symptoms that my body was giving me. Which has helped when it comes to dealing with life on life's terms, how my mind and my soul are all connected together. I want to do everything I can now, so down the line a doctor doesn't say, "Well, if you would have done this or that." I want to read and do everything right.

Sarah: I think that's hard. I'm not at the point of AZT, but all the medical possibilities out there ranging from nutritional macrobiotic and acupuncture over to AZT and things like that. It's all a big question mark. What would be best? It's hard to decide. Things are scarier. The stakes are higher. The virus propels you to health and doing good things for yourself. But on the other hand, everything has got this sorta little jab to it. There is always this little jab in your back.

Chris: Have you made any changes?

Sarah: Something I've had to deal with body wise is stress. I really do believe that stress can have a huge impact on everything, especially how your body does. And I have a lot of stress with my job. My job is so important to me, so that elevates it. I've had to deal with ways to de-stress. A lot of that is trying to change my thinking about things. One good thing I've done for my body is I meditate twenty minutes almost everyday. I didn't use to do that. That's a wonderful thing I do to help myself deal with stress specifically.

Iris: I don't know what's gonna happen to my kids. I haven't handled it very well. I am working on it now. I always used to get high, get drunk. Now, I am seeing a therapist.

Tommie: I'm going more with the untraditional methods with my body. I have had experiences . . . tell me if my pronunciation is right . . . with the metaphysical reasons for why my body hurts. I'm just learning these new ways of healing myself. The relaxation is something I depend on now every week.

Melody: I have to tell myself it's OK to get fatigued. I have to reach that level of acceptance and tolerance of what my body is going through. I have to take a moment and do a light meditation and **hug that dragon** that is within me, and tell him "It's OK."

Patti: Who is that dragon?

Melody: That's the HIV or if it's not the HIV, then it is the medicines that I am on. I never have liked medicines. The medicine I'm on is very toxic and it makes my body go through changes I do not appreciate. I've just been grasping at straws to relieve the symptoms of the toxic side effects and nothing's working. It can make a person tired. That's when I have to get out of myself and go and help someone else, or get busy with nature or do something I enjoy doing so that it just kind of pulls me away, so it doesn't overwhelm me or overcome me.

CR: One thing that's scary for me now: it was OK to say I am HIV+ in some groups, but it's harder to say "I have AIDS." If I say I'm HIV+, lots of people have that, but when I say the word AIDS, I see sickness and illness. When I was first tested, I was real frightened, but then over a few months it kind of smoothed out, and I said I can live with this. Then J died; that hit

> While the virus was previously assumed to lay dormant for as much as ten years, new research suggests that it works aggressively from the beginning of infection. The virus infects immune cells called CD4 lymphocytes, using their machinery to duplicate itself. After an initial period of great activity, the virus forms a stable relationship with the host body as it develops an immune response, with CD4 counts changing slowly over the next few years. Finally, on the average of ten years into the infection, the immune system crashes (*Newsweek*, January 23, 1995).

hard. She was the first person in the group to die. But the word AIDS is hard to get used to. From what the reports say, my T-cells are below 200 and I do have a cervical problem. When I was HIV+ I said they'll come up with a cure, it's gonna be OK, T-cells were up 400 or 500. But now I'm being taken off some of the medications. They're doing more harm than good, my liver especially.

Tracy: The other thing that is scaring everybody is that we really want to believe so much in the drugs, but we do get disappointed. We have seen other people who have taken one drug, shifted to the next one because this one lost its effectiveness, shifted to the next one, and died in front of our very own eyes. We tell ourselves no, we are different, we are going to be able to do better than they were. Then someone else goes. That is kind of scary when you feel that there is nothing that you can absolutely trust. You want to believe in something so badly, yet the only thing you can believe in is *yourself*.

Patti: Where did you learn that, to trust in your own mental power?

Tracy: Well, just reading a lot, and speaking with others. And just becoming pretty disgusted with the whole medical society. And just thinking, like, for example the other day, when they mentioned on CNN that there are a lot of long term survivors who are doing well, even after 14–15 years of the disease. And these people don't believe in the medication, most of them. This one particular doctor said that those who feel that they can survive for a long time tend to do a lot better than those that don't. To me that makes sense.

Joanna: Well, I may have gotten some of this from my mom and dad, who have never thought of doctors as gods or next to God. You really know your body better than another person, even if he examines you and listens to your history. And quite often, I'll take a weekend off of drugs. I don't even take my heart medications. Maybe I'll take some vitamins, but maybe not. If I just don't feel like dealing with it for the weekend, I don't, even when I have been in drug studies. My doctor says, "Just don't tell me about it; whatever

Many HIV+ people participate in clinical drug trials. Recently, for example, there are experiments around viral load testing which measure the quantity of HIV in the blood. While still experimental, results indicate that viral load may be a better predictor of the course of HIV infection than the CD4 (T cell) count. This has the practical value of letting people know quickly if an antiviral regime is working or not. New antivirals are being tested, with indications that viral strains develop resistance fairly quickly. HIV+ people participate in such trials in order to contribute to finding a cure and to obtain free supplies of experimental drugs and blood work. An interesting outcome is the changes in experimental drug trials in terms of opening up to community input and dialogue. For example, a Clinical Trial Forum was held in June of 1995 by the AIDS Project Los Angeles with clinical trial representatives from over fifteen clinical trial sites in Los Angeles. Here HIV+ people could learn about patient rights and clinical trial experiences, with a focus on viral load testing, protease inhibitors, and studies of women and children.

you are doing, it seems to be working." So that is my attitude about all of that.

"I Don't Have a Butt Anymore": Body Image

Chris: What about your relationship with your body? How has it changed since HIV?

CR: I used to like my body, but now, I don't care too much. I take care of it, I bathe it, but that's the extent of it. When I was first diagnosed, I was afraid to even look at my body. I would take a shower, I would wash and get out in a hurry and put clothes on. I didn't want to see. Now if I see someone and they say "you've lost weight," that puts me back in that same groove of not looking at my body.

Chris: What's happening with your body?

Melody: It was bad enough before menopause, but the HIV intensifies it. It's like, everything was bad before but now it's worse because I am HIV positive and I don't know what is going to happen.

CR: Me too. I am going through menopause, and then I have the virus. It's like, I don't know, you know? And then some people look at women and they say women are supposed to bear children, and women are supposed to be pretty. I just feel like a shell sometimes, a warm, empty shell. I don't feel no self worth from my body, other than my hands. If I produce work, if I work, that's the only thing I feel I can do to help. I wouldn't feel comfortable having a sexual relationship with anyone; I don't feel comfortable telling people I have the virus. I have AIDS, so I'm limited. I don't have a Ph.D. degree so I can't sit and talk theory and science and all that, so I just feel limited. I feel detached. I know that there's something inside of me, growing; it's just there. If I could take the AIDS virus out, I would feel different about my body.

Chris: Does your body feel like home or has your body betrayed you?

CR: I feel more like I betrayed my body when I got the virus.

Lori: I guess because I am involved in a physical relationship, I don't really feel like I've lost my body. It's different and it's a struggle, but it's not like I've gotten completely away from it. I do remember after I was first diagnosed having really weird feelings seeing my own blood. And I still sometimes have that. Does anybody else have that? My relationship hasn't changed with my body but I do feel detached to things a lot of the time and it has to do with the virus. I don't know how to put it into words. It's like people hug me and I don't really feel it.

Robyn: I never cared much for my body before the virus or now. I do tend to notice things more, like: was that mole always there?

Chris: Rita, you've been through so much. How do you feel about your body?

Rita: I used to hate it because being young and nice looking and being in that business, it was just the money, that's all it was. The nicer you looked, the more money you had, the more drugs you could buy. I knew I had to look OK. It was like an endless cycle. I got hurt real bad by one of the guys and I had to have surgery. When the guy got done with me, he said, "I have AIDS." I felt like saying—I couldn't say anything I was hurt too bad, but I felt like saying—"If you don't, you do now, you asshole."

Chris: So you knew you were HIV+, and you continued?

Rita: I had to. I was a drug addict. I mean I practiced safe sex. I tried as much as I could. It was part of the rules of the house to use condoms. But this guy who hurt me, he did it on the way home from work. He abducted me. The police could have had his fingerprints. I had never gotten charged with prostitution, but they came rolling up the street one day and said, "Going to work?" I just looked at them and I said, "Did you find him?" They said, "Why? You won't go to court if we do." It's like no, I just wanted to know his name, but they wouldn't give that to me. So I knew where I stood; they weren't going to do anything about it. And I said, "Oh, by the way, he said he had AIDS." Five months later I went to treatment. I was tired of going to jail. I did four months of a six month sentence and then called my mom to get a ticket to come back here.

Chris: What does your body feel like now, off drugs?

Rita: Kinda like Robyn, looking in the mirror all the time, looking for things—spots, lumps, bruises, all this stuff. It's not really a friend to me. It's a shell.

CR: A lot of black women have big butts, and I don't have a butt anymore.
I was thinking of going to Frederick's of Hollywood to get one!

Infection via injecting drugs is now a driving force of the epidemic in the
United States which has an estimated one million injection drug users. In
1996, forty percent of all new AIDS cases in New York City were injection
drug related. Injection drug use is a major form of infection for US women. Of
the 13,838 cases of women diagnosed with AIDS between July 94–June 95,
39 percent were infected through injecting drugs and 38 percent from heterosexual intercourse. Over 20 percent had no reported or identified risk which
often turns out to be sex with injecting drug user as the mode of transmission.
Over three quarters are women of color: 57 percent African American, 20
percent Latinas, .3 percent American Indians, .3 percent Asians, 22 percent
whites. (*World*, December 1995).

3

"Full Blown AIDS Had Come": Lori

Having HIV is like living near a war. You know that battles are being fought nearby, lives are being lost. You have not yet heard a shot fired or seen a bomb explode. But you know the front line is moving closer to you.

I lived four and a half years far from the battle zone. There were periods of time that I almost completely forgot about my illness. Not having any health problems makes for a very difficult place to be—you don't fit in any of the categories. You are living with a big weight on your shoulders, but you aren't sick, so you try to live a normal life, which is not possible. You're not among the healthy, but since you're not sick, you're not exactly a PLWA. You don't want a sick person to feel that you're flaunting your healthiness, and it's also difficult for you to see sick people—how you might be "someday." And you must carry a big secret around like a ball and chain.

Then this past winter I got sick. Miserable from the cold, thinking I had the flu, I had a routine checkup at the clinic. Calling the clinic after being up all night with nausea from, I thought, the prescription, I noticed a change in the nurse's voice. She told me the doctor wanted to see me that day. I asked her what was going on, and she told me that my lab results were back and my T-cells had dropped to 190, so they wanted to run tests for PCP. Full blown AIDS had come.

I got to the clinic and was met by several of my regular team. They all seemed to know that something was going on. After several tests were run, the results were inconclusive on the PCP, but the doctor decided to treat me with a heavy dose of Bactrim. I improved dramatically over the next few days of bed rest, so I returned to work part-time. I don't remember feeling hysterical over the AIDS diagnosis, but I know that it was on my mind.

I did decide to protect myself at work against any job situation that might cause me to lose my precious benefits. I went to my human resources manager with a letter from my doctor that announced my medical condition as a matter of record only. It quoted the confidentiality laws, and stated my prognosis for continuing to work as good. I did this so that my records showed that I was in a "protected" group and would have to be handled gingerly if there was ever a question about my performance. She was very supportive and asked to be kept informed.

The second day after returning to work full-time, I developed red blotches all over my body. The clinic explained that this was a common reaction to Bactrim, if I could just ride it out. Then I developed a fever that began calmly, climbing between normal and 100 for a week, with a general malaise. I took two weeks off from work. It was a huge relief to concentrate only on my health and not have to push myself to work.

The next few weeks get foggy for me. I remember the fevers coming and going. By the end of the second week, the clinic thought the Bactrim reaction had peaked. But by the end of the next week, the fever went to 104. In addition to the fevers were body-wrenching chills and shortness of breath. I was worried about the PCP coming back, but was told that these symptoms were normal for a severe drug reaction. I could not easily walk without getting winded and had congestion in my lungs. A few days later, I woke up and couldn't move. My fever was 106. I was taken to the clinic for more tests. The high fever and fatigue knocked me out, and I fell into a semi-coma. I have a few memories of this day—my dad and friends had been called, and rushed over to the clinic. I remember people coming in and out of the exam room, and I remember being wheeled around in a wheelchair for the first time in my life. As the day wore on, the tests were coming back negative, so the doctor decided not to admit me to the hospital. I was sent to my parents' home for a few days, but I got worse so I was hospitalized for two days.

While in the hospital I was subjected to several nasty procedures that I have dreaded for years—a lung biopsy, spinal tap, and bone marrow test to name the worst. Fortunately I don't remember a thing. As the fever broke, I was released to my parents' home and started recovering slowly. I still couldn't breath easily or get around—even going to the bathroom was a huge effort, so I wasn't drinking the fluids I needed. I had lost six to seven pounds from the fever so I was told to eat high calorie foods, but my appetite was gone and I was too fatigued to eat or drink. This was my life for the next week or so as I gained strength daily. By the end of the week, I was able to visit my home and my beloved cats.

In clinic visits over the next few weeks, it was decided that this was a Bactrim reaction and, finally, I was given the thumbs up to go back to my own home. It was such a great feeling to walk in my door and be in my own space. I still felt very weak, but I was able to perform necessary daily tasks.

Although I was improving and feeling stronger every day, I was forever changed by this experience. How had an illness slipped through? What does this mean? When would I get sick again? What would my life be like now?

I don't have all the answers. I don't think I'm even looking for them now. I have learned to live in the present. My energy is spent in healing, life-affirming activities with people who I cherish. I made one of the biggest decisions of my life—to stop working. Although I knew this was the only choice I could make for my health, it was very difficult to close the door on the only life I have ever known. I feel so lucky that my first illness left me in a position to still enjoy life and do what's important to me. My challenge now is to explore my new identity and find out who I am. The person I was for 36 years is gone—no more career, no more husband, no opportunity for children, no good health, and no clear self-image. These were things that I spent my life either working toward or taking for granted. Having this illness made me realize years ago that my life would not meet my earlier expectations, but without being sick, it's difficult to feel the full impact of the changes. None of us knows what our future holds, but I am looking forward to *my* future in good health and serenity.

Typical health problems of AIDS include disabling fatigue and weakness, severe nutritional problems, pneumonia, chronic diarrhea and the associated skin breakdown, wasting syndrome, severe fever, dementia, depression, anxiety, edema, loss of vision, pain, night sweats and the constant threat of yet another opportunistic infection.

4

"I Got Another Wake-Up Call": Linda B

I got another wake-up call in July of 1995 when I got PCP.[1] I stared death in the face. I didn't like what I saw. It is odd how you receive things like "you have a 50-50 chance of surviving this" or "You are going to get worse before you get better" or "If your body accepts the medicine, you'll survive." I was dumb-founded. I was, once again, saying "It won't happen to me." Such a cocky bitch!

I am still one of those people who has to address the problem immediately. I tried to think of ways I could get my lungs to heal. I only had 33 percent of my lungs that was not involved with the pneumonia. How do you strengthen your lungs? Running was out of the question (my hospital room was too small). So at night I sang. I sang LOUD! I sang hymns. I sang every Sunday School song I could remember. I prayed. I visualized my granddad, who was a carpenter, fixing my lungs. Rebuilding the walls.

What do you think about when you're in this situation? At first, many things race through your mind as you try to digest all that has been told to you. As it sunk in, I became very frightened. Die? Me? Die? It can't be. I'm not done. What about my grandsons? What about my girls? Shit! What am I going to do? I knew at that point that I had to get my mental faculties calmed down. I called a nurse to come and talk to me. I told them if I didn't get this dying thing out of my mind that I would surely die. They brought in one of the residents and she assured me that I was responding very well to treatment. I then called Kathryn, our facilitator. She came right over. The same day, both of my daughters came.

The thing I thought of the most about the prospect of death was all the unspoken words. Not good-byes, but the "I love you" one more time. The words of encouragement to my children and grandchildren. To tell my parents, brothers and sisters that I love them, I'm sorry if I hurt you, the thoughts

I've held inside me because the time was never right. I talked on the phone to all of them at some point in my stay. I managed to relay my thoughts to everyone.

I went back to work half days ten days after I got out of the hospital. Death? Ha! I went in the hospital on July 6th and was back to work full time by the last week of July.

Since then it has been tough. I was having a hard time getting my strength back. I wanted the old me back. The Linda that created great flower arrangements, the Linda that could read a WHOLE book. The Linda that enjoyed sewing. I let my apartment go. I had moved in April before I got sick in July. In November, I still hadn't arranged it the way I really wanted it. I knew I was getting depressed. I couldn't figure out why. I tried to get out of the funk I was in but couldn't. The winter was horrible. The study I was trying to get in at the clinic kept getting snagged by government red tape. I was running out of money to buy drugs. I made an appointment to see the shrink at the clinic.

I prayed.

In the meantime, my friend ____ started showing signs of AIDS. Trouble was, he had never got tested and he refused to believe he, too, was infected. We have been friends since 1986, as co-workers. I finally convinced him to get tested. He was more compromised than I. So, I saw him through the first steps of getting treatment.

It was February. Promises that the study with AZT, 3TC and the Protease was coming together. By then I was getting up at 10 AM, going back to bed at 11 AM and sleeping until 1 PM, getting up and going to work from 2:30 PM until 1 AM. I was off on Wednesdays. I would sleep most of Wednesdays. It was awful. I thought, why am I alive?

Alas, the government ran out of red tape!! The study started. It was a miracle. After two weeks on the study drugs I had arranged my apartment the way I wanted it. I was no longer depressed! I had so much energy that I was getting up at 9 in the morning and staying up! My T-cells had fallen to 98. In two weeks on the protease inhibitor they doubled. Two weeks after that they went up over 200. I feel really great. I even started putting money into a supplementary retirement fund at work. Because of all this returned energy, I've not been seeing much of the group which, sadly, continues to grow. I have so much to do. I was so excited about feeling "normal" again that I wouldn't go to bed. I was like a bad little girl. It was really weird. I've settled down a little. However, I walk about two miles a day, having lost only six damn pounds. My muscle tone is still weak. I rode my "new" bicycle for the first time. They say you get your muscle tone back with this new drug. I hope so. I truly think it's only fat that is holding my bones together.

My friend is on the same drug therapy. He looks great. He feels great. We walk about two miles every day on our breaks, about a mile each break. We feel so good. It's almost a miracle.

I see a lot of controversy coming down the road now that we have these new drugs and new frontiers challenging the virus. Will Social Security now be denied because of the drugs? Will they rewrite the criteria they use to consider disability? Will the price of these drugs ever come down? And, most of all, is this a cure?

Life IS short. Life IS what you make it. Our bodies are the car our souls ride around in. It is up to each individual to take good care of that "car." The saying "Drive SAFE" has new meaning.

Yes, it's been a wake-up call for me, and I've finally quit hitting the snooze button.

Note

1. E-mail, July 1996.

"I See Things Getting Even More Complicated with the New Drugs"

Linda B, e-mail, August 1996: Did you see where the guys who buy life insurance policies from people with AIDS are backing up because of the new drugs? They are seeing that we are living longer, which makes their business less profitable. So even if you need the money to buy the drugs to keep you well, they don't want your business because they can't make enough money. Sick people. They'll never get MY policy. I see a lot of changes coming down the road rather quickly because of the new drugs. For openers, you'll have the fools who will now regard the disease the same way they do syphilis. You know, as just go get a shot! Then they'll take the disability away from us because we will be well enough to work even though you still have people getting disability for a pain in their shoulder. I know someone like that. Been on the dole since she was 18. Anyway, because this disease has been controversial from the start, **I see things getting even more complicated with the new drugs.** The life insurance thing is an example.

CR, phone call, September 1996: The path of the virus in the next five to ten years, I worry that doctors can choose not to give the new drugs to people they think won't use them right, especially drug abusers. The medicine is so expensive. If the new drugs mean the disease is chronic, then people need job training so they're not on "welfare as we know it." Plus state control of drugs is scary. I'm the only infected person on the local AIDS board, so I hear these things and try to speak up, but sometimes I just have to leave the room. My questions come from my soul, not statistics. The social servicey types talk about funds and statistics, and I am one of the statistics.

5

"I've Got Some Stories That Would Curl Your Hair"

"Have a Seat, You're Positive": Getting Tested

Amber: I went to get the HIV test because I had a miscarriage and the biological clock was ticking. And I decided to take the test. I didn't want to end up with the baby being HIV+. And I do feel a big loss because I always did want to have a child.

Sandy: I think how you get your results can really make a difference in how you are going to take it. The lady who gave me my results, I swear, she doesn't need to be working at this. I walked in and she said, **"Have a seat, you're positive."** I knew my daughter's father had just passed away from AIDS. And I knew my best friend in New York was dying. So I just went to get my results, because I just knew it was not me. But she told me and actually turned her back, and I freaked and said "What the fuck are you talking about?" And she went up and got [a counselor], and that man, I mean, he's wonderful.

> The most frequent way women find out that they are HIV+ is through test results after either an ill male partner or an ill child tests positive. Amber's case of being tested prior to the decision to get pregnant is both unusual and a goal of many policy makers—that every woman would be so tested, ideally prior to conception. Whether this is to be through voluntary or mandatory testing is a source of great controversy, a controversy heating up due to recent advances in treating pregnant HIV+ women with AZT which can reduce the risk of transmitting the virus to the fetus from 33 percent to 8 percent. See "I Don't Have Fifty Years to Be a Mother" in Story Series II for more on perinatal transmission.

Ana: I want to comment on that real quick. I took a friend of mine to get tested and this person turned out to be negative and the guy said you're lucky you're negative, because if you were positive you would die. My friend didn't know that I was positive.

Geneva: I was 20 when I found out. I was going through the nursing program at the community college. I had to go through Job Corp for them to pay for it and I had to take all these tests, including a mandatory AIDS test. So when they called me up, first I waited in this clinic for a good hour, me and three guys. Then I started panicking because I knew they had done an AIDS test. Then they had us each come in and told us we were positive. It was really cold, kind of "legally we have to inform you." I was crying so hard. The way you find out can be devastating.

Maria: I wanted to mention real quickly how I found out. This was back in '87. It was my birthday and I thought it would be nice to find out that I was negative. I didn't want to drive back to the testing place, so I called. And there was one particular person I asked for and I said, "It's my birthday and I don't want to drive into the city; can you just tell me?" He goes, "I can't do that, you have to come in." I was pleading so he told me over the phone. And I just stayed quiet for a minute. And I was at work and I was looking around and all of a sudden I thought I was going to pass out.

☙☙   ☙☙   ☙☙   ☙☙   ☙☙   ☙☙   ☙☙

Patti: In a September 30, 1993 *Rolling Stone* interview, Randy Shilts, author of *And the Band Played On*, revealed that he found out he was HIV positive as he finished writing the book. I knew early on that my own HIV status was an important factor in my positioning in this study. I was tested on August 12 of 1993 and received the results of my negative status on September 8. Going through the tension of getting the test and, especially, waiting to hear the results, I learned that part of me didn't want to know if I was positive, but that I wanted very much to know if I was negative. It meant that I was "safe" somehow and could stop worrying that every skin spot, every tiredness was some sign, a situation I hadn't given much thought to until I had the test. The most important thing was to realize how easily I could have been positive, how much of it is sheer luck. It's like a poker hand you get dealt, caught up in history's net, one way or the other. I remember thinking that if I were negative, I would be grateful and, I promised, I would be CAREFUL, if allowed to escape this time, this 1993, at the end of this first decade of the epidemic.

If positive, I thought of how my identity would shift and the world would be so very different, including the perspective I would bring to this project. I would be much more like Francisco Ibañez-Carrasco in his 1992 study of gay men in Vancouver and Chile: one of, studying across, instead of "down" or, as I seem to be doing, "up." Or maybe not. Maybe the angelizing move has something to do with creating equivalencies: we are all angels, or all not angels, or all angels not, or all near angels. It blurs up the distinc-

And I had to go back to work and smile at the customers. It was a long time ago.

Robyn: I never knew about lymph glands. This one that I felt prompted me to get tested and it isn't even a lymph node. I saw something on TV, the women were positive and the lady asked the girl, what prompted you to get tested? My doctor told me I had enlarged lymph glands. Then I went to my regular doctor and he said he didn't think it was anything. And he was so sure I didn't have anything to worry about and it took the test results so long to come back, two weeks. He seemed more stressed than I did when he told me. He wanted me to come in to talk about it. I knew.

CR: They had messed my test up and they had to do it again.

Rita: I went to three different places. See, I went to detox and I left detox and was out running around and I went to exchange needles. This guy in a van who worked for the health department said "Let's go for a ride," and it freaked me out. I love him to death, he is a good friend of mine. But he is gay, and he said, "Come on, wreck my reputation." And I was like, oh, something is up. And he said, "You haven't listened to me for the last five years. Come on." So I knew, I just knew what he was going to tell me, and sure enough. He's the one that put me in detox 1001 times.

Chris: He cared about you?

tions, between we/they, researcher/researched, reader/writer.

If positive, I thought of Carol X's story about going off for six months: to not have to face it, to have some time of being her old self, her self without HIV, to not have to tell others and, in the telling, become "this HIV+ person." This is about stealing some time from being swallowed up in the identity of an HIV+ person: the stigma, the reduction of one's identity, the forced encounters with the medical world, the horrors of a wasting death in the prime of life. "Who would have thought that we would come to this," as my friend Rex said, when he gave me the news of Randy's deathwatch.

Finding out that I was HIV–, "negative women," as Chris said to me after I got the results, we jumped up and down with the joy of it. Now I knew what she learned from her dream of June 18 where she dreamed she had AIDS: the distance between someone who "helps" and someone who is in it. Three days after getting the results, it already seemed distant, even melodramatic, but it is a marker of our positioning in this study: non HIV+ women telling stories which are not ours. Such a position cannot escape being, to some extent, part of the traditional spectator-narrator, purveying the less fortunate, parading our good will.

Reflexive Coda: Confessional writing is not my cup of tea, but I was fairly satisfied that the preceding was useful in moving toward some emotional shape for this work. Then I received Francisco Ibañez-Carrasco's MA thesis in the mail and was brought up short by how symptomatic my "confessional narrative" is in terms of my limits in the context of this study.

Rita: You see, I left detox to go out and get high and they contacted him and he knew I would show up down there. I told him he was a liar. I was "sick" so he gave me money to "go get well" and then took me to a hospital to get back into detox.

Patti: What happened next?

Rita: You can't be out on the streets if . . . they got a law, if you're a convicted prostitute and you have two condoms on you, you go to jail, directly to jail. And they threatened me when they found out that I was HIV. Just for us to walk down there to get our drugs and stuff, we wouldn't be working necessarily, but if they would see us. . . . They had our pictures in a notebook with AIDS written across the front of my face with red ink. When I come into jail that time it was like they put plastic gloves on and it turned into a circus. They started bringing cops back there, saying, "Look at her, look at her face, you see her, get her." They were just parading people. They had me in there for 18 hours, no charges or anything. I had to leave there and come back to Ohio.

An HIV+ gay man, Ibañez-Carrasco's study of the translations between official safer sex discourse and the lived experience of men who have sex with men positions him as an "insider" in contrast to my "outsider" status. His ability to speak "of 'us' rather than 'them,'" to speak from and through as well as for, helps me to see how easily I fall back into what he terms "the infamous HIV+/HIV– dichotomy." We all live with HIV labels, he says; be they positive or negative, we are all caught up in this crisis. Rather than the either/or of HIV+ or HIV–, he posits an HIV continuum where, culturally speaking, everyone is at risk and we are all involved because sexuality is a collective phenomenon.

Yet, too, it is the HIV positive who are "described and prescribed to exhaustion . . . before we even get to tell our own stories." Quoting Paula Treichler on AIDS as "'an epidemic of signification,'" he writes of how "Those of us living with HIV/AIDS twitch in terror every time someone writes a new magazine column, shoots a new video, or gives yet another 'enlightened workshop.'" Particularly worried about how the lives of PWA's are "represented only as sad testimonials," his work fleshes out "the intricate architecture of this HIV positive identity" that is about so much more than being HIV+.

Much of the literature treats an HIV diagnosis as "a point of clearance [if positive] or death [if negative]." "Does it really matter if one is HIV negative? I believe the answer is no." To have to live out the operations of labeling means to be nomads amidst a politics of fear and containment which has evolved into a paternalistic "politics of care" in which

"Is Anybody Going to Take Care of Me?"
Insurance and Medical Services

Danielle: My insurance is going to be running out in December and at that point my only option is to try and get Medicaid. And in order to get it, I am going to not have an income. So it is a total vicious cycle. I *want* to continue working, I *don't* want to sit at home and have Medicaid, but I am going to be stuck. As far as the medication is concerned, I think the doctors are still really iffy. AZT is the only thing they have to offer us, so they are offering it,

AIDS testing is sometimes referred to as the "commitment ceremony of the 90's." The July 1994 issue of *Positively Aware* announced that the Centers for Disease Control had determined that, for adults, the time from HIV infection to the production of detectable HIV antibodies can be anywhere from 45 days to six months, with an average of three months. Hence the current recommendation is testing at three months after the last possible exposure.

Deciding which tests to get and at what times depends on risk behavior factors. If the window period of three months after the last possible exposure has been followed and the test is negative, there is no need for a second test. But if the window period has not been followed or if high risk related behaviors have occurred, a second test should be administered three months after the first. For adults, risk related behaviors include unprotected sexual activity that involves the exchange of bodily fluids and sharing needles. In terms of sexual transmission, unprotected anal intercourse is the highest risk behavior, with unprotected vaginal intercourse the next riskiest, followed by unprotected oral intercourse as the least risky, with the fluid-receiving partner at most risk due to the release of fluids during both arousal (pre-ejaculate or cervical fluid) and orgasm. Menstruation is a particularly vulnerable time for women as the cervix opens, increasing the chances of infection for the menstruating woman as well as her sexual partner.

Cities with Public Health Departments provide free and anonymous testing for those who do not want to go through a family physician or health clinic where, even given norms of confidentiality, names and test results are recorded. Most states have a hotline number for information on HIV testing site locations. In Ohio: 800-332-AIDS. The Centers for Disease Control has a 24 hour hotline: 800-342-AIDS.

A new development is home testing which became available in 1996. Many people who test positive never return for their results, and of the over one million Americans with the virus, as many as half don't know they are infected. The $40.00 home testing kit could help with this. Blood from a finger prick is sent in to a laboratory which deals with the results in a manner that assures confidentiality. Home Access Express test 800-HIV-TEST. Johnson and Johnson's test: 800-THE-TEST.

regardless of the severe toxic side effects. And that concerns me; I think a lot of people are getting sick from that medication. I don't take it anymore and I strongly don't believe in it. And the latest international conference has also said that AZT is pretty ineffective.

Chris: How did you make the decision to discontinue AZT?

Danielle: Regardless of the medication, my counts were still dropping, the disease was still progressing. So, what was it really doing, besides suppressing my white and red blood cells, making me feel like shit and costing a lot of money? I had taken it for quite some time and I was getting the numbness and pain in my feet. I thought this is just not worth it! The medication is not even saving me. So that is when I said *forget it.*

Chris: Is your physician supportive?

Danielle: Actually, he believes pretty strongly in AZT. But I think that is because he doesn't know what else to say.

Patti: Are you cleaning out by stopping all medications?

Danielle: Well, I still do my one medicine three times a week because pneumonia is the number one killer. So I continue doing that. And the peripheral neuropathy is mild, it is not severe. At this point I can still live with it and tolerate it.

Alisha: I had no idea what they were giving me. I wasn't familiar with doctors and medications. I just took it, because that is what they said to do. There were three medications I was taking. After a week, I realized that they

---

we are all accomplices. But, as Francisco's final words note, some are paying a much higher price than others.

In 1993, Randy Shilts spoke of his plans to not write any more about AIDS: "To live it and to write about it is just too much." This, perhaps, creates some space for "outsiders" to be of use. But where is the outside of this pandemic? Who is this we/they? In French feminist Luce Irigaray's concept of the "We-you/I" there is no "they," only some we of us that joins some you/ I (Game, 1991). When asked about my HIV status, I thought I had learned to say, "I am not yet to my knowledge HIV positive." But my confessional narrative, written on the heels of getting

tested, reverted unproblematically to expected binaries.

What is to be done with me? Can I protect the research from myself? How can such research protect those who offer their tragedies for public scrutiny given the inevitable interpretive weight of a researcher in telling data stories? Is it enough to include in our research plan having some of the women read the manuscript and write themselves into the text with their reactions to our storying of their lives? What kind of a text can capture how such research as this is about the paths to finding, the unfolding of the research itself, rethinking the meaning and the implications of the advent of its own unfolding?

were making me viciously ill and I was throwing up, incredibly sick most of the time.

Chris: What happened next?

Alisha: So I went back to the doctor and said that I wasn't feeling good and asked if I could stop. And they said no, that I had to try and put up with it for three months. So I did put up with it, for two or three months. At the end of that I thought, "No more of this, this is enough!" I decided that I didn't want to take it anymore. And I went to the doctor and said I wasn't going to take it anymore. I am sick of being sick! I stopped it myself without the doctor knowing it.

Chris: You made a big decision. Did the doctor find out?

Alisha: When I told the doctor, the doctor said fine. But then I decided to find another doctor. I borrowed the records. A specialist was looking through them and said, "Oh my God, you were taking three medications! No wonder. They should have stopped them immediately." It was like I didn't know what I was doing.

Patti: Did you feel better?

In January of 1993, more than ten years into the epidemic, the Centers for Disease Control and Prevention formally recognized that HIV+ women experience gender-specific medical problems. Possible correlates of seropositivity include invasive cervical cancer, severe and recurrent vaginal yeast infections, and pelvic inflammatory disease. Women continue to get such opportunistic infections that are misdiagnosed or not immediately identified because it is not suspected that a woman might be HIV positive. Fissures or lesions in the body increase viral passage, e.g. herpes simplex, genital ulcers. Sperm and blood are the major carriers of the virus, and women are 10–12 times more likely to contract HIV from men than the other way around. Approximately 38 percent of women have contracted the disease from male partners: 14,165 from sex with injecting drug user; 2,425 from sex with a bisexual male; 312 from sex with a person with hemophilia; 482 from sex with a transfusion recipient with HIV infection; and 12,328 from sex with an HIV-infected person, "risk not specified." The fastest growing segment of HIV infected women is the transmission from injecting drugs, 46 percent of all female cases as of June, 1996. Female-to-female transmission remains an unknown area, particularly given the classifying of all women who have had sex with men even once since 1978 as heterosexuals by the Centers for Disease Control. For a reading list about HIV and women, including a resource list, send a self-addressed stamped envelope to *Positively Aware*, 1340 West Irving Park Road, Box 259, Chicago, IL 60613. See, also, Patton, 1994.

Alisha: After about a month, I felt so much better with no medication, I felt excellent! I decided that I didn't want to go back to that. My doctor, however, said, "We need to check your T-cell count." I was so excited to find that I had a high count! But then about four months after that, my count went down. The doctor said I had to take something and I really didn't want to, because I thought that I was going to have to go through that whole experience again. But the doctor said this time that I would take only one medication. So the doctor gave me AZT five times a day and I got sick *again*. I wanted to stop again, but I just went to a lower dosage. And it has been gradually increasing, which actually seems to be working out pretty well.

Chris: It sounds like this doctor works with you as a partner. How is your T-cell count?

Alisha: My count went up again and has stayed pretty steady. So I have been taking the medication two times a day and doing fine. We are just keeping a real close eye on it. I go to the doctor monthly and if I get sick at all again, I am going to do something about it. But I don't understand why the first doctor gave me these three medications and told me that I just had to put up with it! I don't want to go through it ever again. That was just awful!

Rita: I was in Indiana and I started breaking out. So I called my doctor who said it sounded like shingles and called in a prescription to Indiana. But they wouldn't take the medical card, so I had to pay for it. $200.97 for thirty pills. No way. I came back to Ohio and went over to the pharmacy and they said we can't do no call-in orders. You have to go to the emergency room. So I went to emergency and the doctor called to say, "will you give her a prescription? We've been doing this since 8 AM, and she's come all the way from Indiana for these pills." But the pharmacy said, "Well, we still have to process her." I finally got all the way through and he said, "Do you want a pain shot?" Knock me out, I didn't care. So finally at 11:30 at night, I got a prescription.

Tracy: One time about a year ago, when I had a pap smear at my general practitioner, her nurses were not real cool. She is a fine doctor, she is very understanding of HIV, she has no problem with that. It could have been they were busy that day, but I thought it was strange. I had to get radical.

Patti: What does that mean, get radical?

Tracy: Well, you go out in the hall with your paper gown on and say "Is anybody going to take care of me?" and slam the door. I'll do that, I have no problem doing that. I mean, I am paying her, even if it is my insurance that is doing it, I pay my insurance.

Chris: What about normal health problems?

CR: One thing that cracked me up is that I got a cold a few weeks ago and went to the walk-in clinic because I couldn't get hold of my doctor. I was about ready to freak. Everything, PCP, every kind of pneumonia was coming to my mind. It is just a cold, a "*normal* person's cold," they said. Everytime there is something that happens to you doesn't mean it's HIV related. It's like instant paranoia.

Chris:　Yours or theirs?

CR:　Both. Saturday, I laid in bed and I just felt terrible. My period had started, but I'm so wrapped in this virus and AIDS, I can't get normal cramps without thinking I'm real sick. The medical profession also clumps everything with the virus. It's like when I had those headaches from the gas fumes from the furnace. I had two MRI's and spinal taps and medicines! Sometimes I get so angry, I wish I would get sick and die or they find a cure because this living in limbo is shit! It takes all your energy to try to keep a positive outlook toward life.

Linda B:　My doctor got sick of me. I used to call him everyday. They say, "Well, what's wrong?" I said "I'm sick and you don't even care." I aggravate them so much and **I've got some stories that would curl your hair.** I sat and sweated over this bill, this $638 bill. It's been mis-billed by this insurance company and they are wanting to put it in collection. So I sat and worked this bill over and took it down there to her and she tried to tell me that I didn't know what I was talking about. I finally told her it's obvious you don't know who you are talking to because I said I had worked this bill over, and I do this for a living, I know what I am talking about and it's gonna get fixed today. And it was on its way to getting fixed when I walked out of there.

Fear that AIDS is a new genocide against the black race is fed by African-American distrust of white medicine, partly due to the heritage of the Tuskegee experiment. *In Bad Blood: The Tuskegee Syphilis Experiment,* James Jones (1981) chronicles how black sharecroppers were lied to and denied appropriate treatment during the forty years of the research, conducted by the US Public Health Services, into what happens to untreated syphilis. In 1932, looking for a maximally controllable sample, government health officials enlisted 412 rural black men in Alabama who were recruited through institutions that they trusted, church and school, under promises of free medical care and burial money. Subjected to painful spinal tap tests that they thought were treatments for their "bad blood," the worst horror was the denial of penicillin once it was discovered a decade or so into the research study. A February 6 1992 segment of ABC's Primetime covered the Tuskegee experiment, interviewing survivors and drawing connections to its continued legacy of mistrust, especially regarding sexually transmitted diseases. This distrust on the part of the black community has stymied AIDS prevention efforts and fueled conspiracy theories of the origin of the HIV virus, such as AIDS as a US military plot to destroy developing countries and black people worldwide. For more information, see Hammonds (1992) and Farmer (1992) in Resources.

Rita: They just sent me to a collection agency, for $15.00.

Chris: How is your experience, particularly as being HIV and women? Do you think it has effected the quality of care?

Tracy: I want things to be getting better for women. I feel like with the white heterosexuals and the gay community, even though AIDS is still hush hush, they come out more openly, they are getting treated. But my biggest concern is that black people, black women, are diagnosed right at the *last stage*. People still don't talk about it, even though the black community has the highest rate of infection right now. Every group I go to, I just don't find my people there. And I know that black people are infected and it is a concern to me because I really want to know where they are. I've seen people on TV. I've heard black women who are taking care of people who are dying. So I know that there is some activism in the black community. But at the same time, people look at it like they look at drugs, because it is probably going to have the same devastating effect. If people could talk about it in church, because in the black community the church is very effective. I feel that maybe we are still in denial.

Chris: It seems that in the black community it is considered a particularly degrading disease because black men who get it are considered to have a "white fag" disease.

Tracy: I have never heard it rationalized like that. I have heard it rationalized in terms of a gay men's disease. That is why Magic Johnson was so busy trying to ruin his life, by trying to justify that he had AIDS without being a homosexual. At the same time, we are always talking about America. What about South American? What about Africa? In the rest of the world it is not perceived as a white gay disease. Only in America because in America so much is sexual. Everything in our society has a sexual context to it of some sort, especially advertising. And there are a lot of people out there, you can stand on a street corner and ask people what their true feelings are about HIV/AIDS and they would say it is a gay white disease. That is how they still see it.

As of 1996, AIDS is the leading cause of death for black men, ages 25–44. Over half of AIDS cases among black men are injection drug related, with black men five times more likely to contract HIV than white drug injectors. Hence, legal obstacles to clean needle and harm reduction programs hit black communities harder, given that they are often targeted for tougher drug law enforcement. The needle crisis affects whole families, putting unaware groups at risk. For women, particularly black women, this growing incidence of HIV+ male drug injectors is a growing threat (*Vibe*, August 1996).

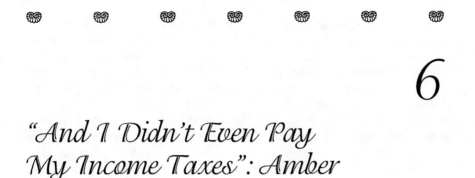

6

"And I Didn't Even Pay My Income Taxes": Amber

Amber: On April 2, 1991, I was tested for HIV and on April 5, I received positive results from two different Elisa tests on the same blood sample. One week later I got confirmatory results of a positive Western Blot. On January 2, 1995, my results from another Elisa test came back negative. I said how can this be? I had already scheduled an appointment for the next day with a new doctor in my hometown. He had the records showing I was HIV+. So when I went in there, I showed him the new records and said what do you make of this? He did another Elisa test which was negative also, so then we did a PCR, which is an HIV DNA test. I got the negative results of that the end of March. Then he wrote a letter saying I never had been positive. He couldn't really explain it. I had rheumatoid arthritis, but he said that wouldn't effect the Western Blot. Someone had to make a mistake and test someone else's blood. Accidents do happen in the lab. I've been through a lot of turmoil and was thinking about a lawsuit. It's a really hard thing; now I have to watch all my friends get sick.

Iris: It's like an emotional roller coaster, now she doesn't know where she's standing. She like came to grips and was learning how not to die of HIV but how to live with HIV; now she has to learn all over again how to live not being HIV, but she's been so touched and so affected by it. HIV touches your life and affects your life like we can't really explain, but I can understand where she's coming from. Because if someone told me I wasn't positive now, it would be like, now what do I do? The positive part is that you know you're not going to die of AIDS and can make long term plans. I'm making long term plans too, but like getting a job and being insurable, those are so hard.

Amber: I'm worried that I might still be seen as in a high risk group and will have trouble getting insured. That's why I have copies of all these letters.

I'm going to mail one to every doctor and dentist I've ever been to and to all my family members who said I couldn't come around the kids, that they didn't want to see me anymore, or that maybe I was making this up, just wanting attention. Now they're really saying that. I told our support group leader about sending them this letter from my doctor, and she said you don't owe them a damn thing. They didn't stand by you through any of this, why do you want anything to do with them now? Now my family has started calling me. I told them the reason I hadn't sent the letter was because I was mad and I'm still mad at them. Supposedly they're happy that I'm not HIV, but my stepfather always adds onto the end of it that there has been some discussion among family members that I was making it all up and, if that is the case, I'm forgiven for that. But that would be a hell of a thing to do to your family, he always says. They're acting like that would be a bigger crime than the way that they treated me when they thought I had it.

Believe it or not, the same lab that did the first tests did the second. I mean, it makes you feel like, what can you believe? So now I'm afraid to have a sexual relationship, because if I don't have HIV now, I could get it. The kind of people I'm attracted to and tend to have relationships with, I have come to see a pattern. And it's almost like it seems inevitable. When I first thought I was positive, I didn't talk to anybody about it. I went through taking care of someone who was sick with AIDS to expose myself to what AIDS looked like. That was really hard for me and I went through that and I thought, if I can go through this, I can handle anything. He passed away and it was really hard. Now that I know I'm not positive, I've developed

❀   ❀   ❀   ❀   ❀   ❀   ❀

Patti: In June of 1995, I met with Amber who had just found out that she had received false positives on her original HIV tests. Amber comes from a family with a history of diabetes, lupus, rheumatoid arthritis and connective tissue disorders, some of which may have influenced the outcome of HIV test results. Amber's story of thinking she was HIV+ for four years, while unusual, is not unheard of. A San Antonio woman was recently reported as going eight years assuming she was positive, losing her health, her marriage and her two young sons in the process (*Columbus Dispatch*, June 27, 1995). Unlike Amber who never received any medical treatment for HIV, the San Antonio woman, Grace Mireles, was prescribed powerful and toxic doses of anti-AIDS drugs including AZT and DDI. In 1993, Mireles stopped taking the medication, ready to die. She began feeling better and underwent acupuncture and massage therapy. Watching a *60 Minutes* program on a Connecticut woman who had been misdiagnosed with HIV, Mireles was re-tested, with negative results. She is suing dozens of San Antonio healthcare providers.

Such stories raise many issues: the uncertainty of testing, where both false positives and false negatives are not unheard of, the toxic effects of anti-HIV

another relationship with someone with substance abuse problems who just found out they're HIV+. I want to be supportive and helpful, but it takes so much out of you. You can't get away from it; you wouldn't want to because you want to help, but it is so draining.

Iris: Now that you're not HIV, how do you feel about being around HIV people? Are there other people in this situation? If I was in this situation, I would want to talk to other people in the same situation, but how would you find them?

Amber: My doctor said there are three documented cases in the world of people who had it and have no signs of it now. There are more tests that can be done to see if my cells have been affected by HIV, because it changes the shape of your cells. So I could be the fourth such person in the world. Or maybe they mixed up my blood sample in the lab. Which means there's some positive person running around out there who thinks they're negative. Or maybe my other health problems caused a false positive. The Columbus doctor said the Western Blot couldn't have been wrong because it tests for specific antigens for HIV. My local doctor said the same thing, although then he backed away from this and thought maybe it was the rheumatoid arthritis and related collagen tissue disorder that caused the false positive. My T cells have always been high, so that gives some support to that theory.

Iris: Maybe I should go get re-tested.

Patti: That's why we want to report Amber's story as fully as possible, so we don't feed false hope in lots of positive people. How are you doing in your head, girl?

⁂　　　⁂　　　⁂　　　⁂　　　⁂　　　⁂　　　⁂

drugs that are routinely prescribed, and the psychological effects of such misdiagnosis.

Chris: On first thought, a false positive HIV test result should only be good news, but it turned out more complicated than this. Several years ago I received a call from a colleague requesting that I see a young woman, Jenny, age 19, whose only sexual experience was rape at age 15. She had just tested HIV+. She wanted to protect her family, adamant that only the closest members know her HIV status. Her world turned upside-down as she began questioning her role with friends, her education, her future. She felt profoundly isolated, alone with this unusual experience. She began medical treatment at the AIDS clinic. About six weeks later, we both learned that she was HIV negative. Probably the error occurred at the original test site or the lab. Rather than feeling joy and relief, Jenny was a mess. Now who does she talk to and what does she say?

Misdiagnosis has been rare; most test sites and labs have been highly reliable, but when a mistake like this has occurred, it seriously impacted the individual who was misdiagnosed. This probably also meant that someone who was HIV+ did not know to seek medical treatment and that they could infect others. ☸

The difficulty of establishing certain knowledge about HIV is related to the nature of the virus itself. As an RNA-based virus, it mutates quickly, allowing it to adapt at a rate that overwhelms the body's immune reactions. Especially in circumstances of frequent transmission from person to person, the rapid rate of evolution is bad news for diagnostic tests as well as treatment and prevention. In terms of diagnostic tests, new variants of HIV not detectable by common tests were discussed at the 1994 International AIDS conference in Japan. While very rare even in the areas of the world where they are found (1 percent of HIV infections in Guinea and Cameron), they demonstrate how the virus shifts its essential molecules to thwart treatment and vaccine, and represent how complicated the family of RNA viruses is and the consequent likelihood of new patterns of HIV. The presence of diverse strains of the virus began to be noted in the US in 1996, raising worries that current tests cannot detect all types of the virus. This is particularly problematic in terms of a safe blood supply although people at highest risk are immigrants whose blood donations are already restricted (*Columbus Dispatch*, October 8, 1996).

In terms of routine testing, the standard test for HIV, the Elisa, is not specific for HIV and, hence, provides the highest rate of false positives, given the presence of other immunosuppressant processes. If the first Elisa test is positive, a second is quickly conducted and, if positive, a confirmatory Western Blot or, increasingly, IFA (Immuno Fluorescent Assay) is administered, all using the same blood sample. The Western Blot is not specific to HIV, resulting in a too-high rate of false positives and indeterminate results. The IFA is better at detecting false positives, and it is equal in cost to the Western Blot. The PCR, a highly sensitive HIV-1 DNA test, costs $200.00 or more and picks up infinitesimal amounts of HIV. While not 100 percent reliable either, it narrows the window of detection (from time of infection) to two weeks, whereas three months is the typical detectable window using the less expensive tests.

The PCR was not available for clinical use at the time of Amber's first tests and continues to be used very seldomly due to expense. It is not unusual, however, for long term asymptomatic people to have an IFA and/or PCR test, especially when T cells remain high (normal count is 1100). Amber's T cell count, for example, was 1164 when she was first tested and was up to 1590 two years later, the contrary of the decrease in CD4 counts (T cells) that would be expected. Her doctor has two theories: either her blood sample was mixed up in the original laboratory findings or she had a false positive due to her other auto immune processes (lupus and rheumatoid arthritis).

Amber: Crazy. I probably just took a big chance last week, going to bed with someone without a condom. I even thought about it, told the person I was now negative but that I wanted to use a condom until he had a test and even then I couldn't be that sure. So what is the difference between thinking all this time that you have it, I mean, it's too much to think about. Later on, another night, I ended up going to bed with him. We started using a condom but he said he couldn't handle it and it just happened, we had unprotected sex. Now, I'm like I don't want to think about it. You have to face so much rejection, it's easier just to forget about sex and not go out with very many people. Also this caused me to get in a relationship for eight months with someone who was HIV negative but sick with cirrhosis of the liver and the girl he lived with before me had AIDS and hepatitis and I thought, well, I've got it anyway. I could so easily have gotten involved with someone who did have it.

Iris: There's so many strains that even if you both have it, you need to practice safer sex. I don't want to get their strain.[1]

Amber: So I could very well have gotten infected. I know a lot of positive bi-sexual men who might be more accepting of a woman who is positive. I don't like the real masculine type of guy who is going to slap me up against the wall. I mean, I've had that. Been there, done that. I don't want to be beat around anymore. So I just don't know what I'm going to do.

Patti: You've had less than three months to rethink yourself. Do you think about it all the time?

Amber: I don't think about it much except when I'm talking to someone whose count is really low. A friend and I were hoping it was some kind of miracle that was keeping my blood count so high and we would laugh that I could give her some of my miracle blood. But now we know that my blood is just like everyone else's, just worthless. There's nothing special about me that is keeping me healthy as far as HIV. I'm not invincible, I'm not special, I can get sick from this and die like everyone else. I'm just as vulnerable as anybody else out there now. I'm even more vulnerable in a way. I got tested to begin with because I had gotten my life pretty well together and wanted to have a baby and I wanted to do the responsible thing. Then I found out I was positive and I figured I couldn't have a baby. But I was headed in the right direction and then it kind of put my life at a standstill these four years. I haven't done that much with my life. I didn't even pay my income taxes. I worried that I was getting laid off at work because they knew my HIV status; every time my name was called over a speaker, I thought, oh, no, this is it. Then I'd get called back to work part-time, and you don't have taxes taken out. So you get to the end of the year and you don't have the money, so what do you do? If you figure you're going to die soon anyway, you just pretend it doesn't exist. So now I have to write the IRS and Social Security and start to get that straightened out.

Iris: Congratulations. What does it feel like? I mean the whole gamut of emotions you go through when you find out you're positive and then one day you find out, oh it was a mistake. What does it feel like, to feel for four years you're HIV positive?

Amber: It's pretty hard when you think what it means to think there's no tomorrow. I had totally accepted it and was even looking forward to dying;

this is no kind of life. I try to be happy but I'm not afraid of death. I'm disappointed that I'm not going out.

Patti: Why?

Amber: Because I have had a rotten life. I alway have had; I just got dealt a crappy hand. Death was my reward to look forward to. I haven't been as careful as I might have been if I hadn't thought I was HIV, like I've been in two car accidents since I was diagnosed positive four years ago. I'm just not real thrilled about it, because now I can't blame my arthritis and my anxiety and my whatever on HIV. Now I have to realize I'm responsible for my own health, like losing weight. I can't use that cushion of saying, why lose weight, I may need it later.

Iris: You still have us; we understand.

Patti: Why?

Iris: She's still like a pioneer. She knows how we feel. She's had a really shitty injustice done to her, maybe not purposely, but for four years, she thought she was positive.

Amber: I would never have been through all the problems and made the decisions I have if I hadn't thought I was HIV. Just one little thing can change so many things in your life, you know—if if if. It's like dominoes, things just fall a certain way and it affects something else that affects something else. Who knows where I might have been if I hadn't thought I was HIV for four years.

Iris: You know, maybe Amber's just an angel put in people's lives, like ___, because he died without anyone but Amber.

Amber: I tried so hard the whole time I thought I was HIV+ to keep it separate from my real life, you know using a different name and keeping people from finding out. I would just say, that's not me, Amber Lee has HIV, not me. That's how I've kept my sanity through this whole thing, I could separate it to a certain extent. Now I don't know. HIV takes up so much of your life.

I'm so glad I didn't go tell everyone I slept with. If I had called all those people and affected their lives, you know, some people go and kill themselves when they think they have HIV. I carried with me all this guilt, in the beginning. Then I found out it's not so easy to transmit from women to men. That relieved me a little bit, but still you have this burden on you. And that is the best thing that's happened out of this. I have this feeling about myself that's so bad; I'm so used to having so much guilt. I have to remind myself I didn't give HIV to anyone. I've been punishing myself. I didn't like to look in the mirror. Now I feel like I don't even look the same. There's something inside you that changes; I can look myself in the mirror better now.

Patti: Thanks so much for coming in and setting me straight. I feel a lot more confident now that I can get the right stuff in here. This has been a complication in the book, but it's also just a really rich layer.

Amber: I've talked to a couple of lawyers. The first was both a M.D. and a lawyer and he was all for taking the case. But I talked to a second lawyer and he said I'd have to be ready to have my life put on trial. He said you would be on trial like women who get raped. I might be on the front page of the local newspaper and then everyone would know my business. Even the IRS would get on me.

Note

1. In addition to the presence of so many different strains of the disease, any two HIV+ people risk infection with more virulent forms, or what is called higher viral loads, if safer sex is not practiced.

AIDS and Angels: A Cloudy Place

No interpretation and no remembrance could clarify this cloudy place, for what is covered by it is nothing that was ever understood and could thus be encountered in memory. It would be that bodily gesture which, associated with death, is just as impossible to understand as death 'itself' . . . the cloudy place from which it issues is just that place where doctrine is not (Hamacher, 1988).[1]

What it means to take angels seriously in the AIDS crisis will be pursued across the angel intertexts of this book. The pursuit begins with a conversation staged between Reader and Authors regarding the work of the angels in this book that includes an assembling of angel portrayals across time, particularly the uses of angels in relation to AIDS. Writing under this, Patti traces her interest in angels as a space of use, "a tangled web of meanings" in which to read out "the weight of hard-borne history."[2] In subsequent intertexts, a certain "angelology" is elaborated via a survey of angels as a theological concept and their metamorphosis into a popular one. This detour into angels is intended both as a breathing space from the women's stories and as a place to bring snapshots from poetry, fiction, sociology, history, art, and philosophy together to bear on understanding the work of living with HIV/AIDS.

The Work of the Angels in This Book[3]

Reader: *Why the emphasis on angels in a book on women living with HIV/ AIDS?*

Authors: *The angels of the intertexts are intended to serve as both bridges and breathers as they take the reader on a journey that troubles any easy* *sense of what AIDS means for our living in the world. By juxtaposing angel intertexts with individual testimony from the women, the angels serve as messengers between the women's stories and the social implications of the AIDS crisis via short engagements with slices from both "high" and popular culture, returning again to the women's stories. They are, hence, bridges between worlds, but they are also breathers in the face of what gets ignited in the writing and reading of the women's stories. A way to address what the poet, Rilke, terms the "Too Big," the "too great," the work of the angels in this book is to mobilize the familiar image of angels, but then to undercut it, trouble it.*

Believing that HIV/AIDS exceeds our ability to "master" it through knowledge, we wanted a book that used a "flood" of too much too fast, data flows of trauma, shock and everydayness juxtaposed with asides of angel breathers to break down the usual codes we bring to reading. Hence the book "works" by not working the way we expect a book to work: a linear unfolding of information that builds toward a sense of "being on top" of a situation through knowledge.

Reader: *Before getting on to things quite so scholarly, I wonder whether you could provide me with a key, in order to make it easier for me to read your book.*

Authors: *The angels provide many keys. As this project began, they were intended to provide a reversal of the "demonizing" attitudes that many have toward people with HIV/AIDS who are often treated like lepers. Traditionally, angels serve as messengers and these women have a keen sense of want-*

Patti: It is important to note that everything I've learned about angels in the last few years was all new to me. I didn't even know the word angelology, the longtime study of angels in Talmudic, Gnostic, Christian, and Islamic traditions.

I did not expect to get into such a vast and diversified esoterics when I began this project on women and HIV/AIDS. As was pointed out to me at a small research retreat in Wisconsin, the metaphor of angel is so excessive that it raises red flags of caution. What we came to call there "angelizing" is dangerous business, tied to romanticizing and otherwising as it is, resonant with images of

vacuous cherubs. But I seek different angels, angels who exceed our categories of angels as I struggle to know what I want from and bring to my encounters with these women with/for/to whom I am doing this inquiry.

The first sign of my adult interest in angels was somewhere in the mid-1980's wanting a copy of the Guardian Angel with Children picture that had hung in my room as a child. My mother was put on alert; she came through with a mini plastic 25 cent version that I keep by my computer as I write. A professor colleague rounded up a holy card version, left over from a Catholic Trivial

ing to get their story out to help other women like themselves. They also want to reach a larger audience about the work of living with HIV/AIDS.

As the project developed, the angels assumed the weight of researcher interpretation in the study. Instead of analyzing the women's stories, we wanted to give pride of place to those stories, uninterrupted by our coming in and saying

---

Angels Through Time

Historically, the conception of angels grows from efforts of the early Jewish and Christian traditions to appropriate pagan traditions into a monotheistic religion. Much at the center of Gnostic and, later, medieval theological thinking, especially St. Thomas Aquinas, who was called the Angelic Doctor, angels fell out of favor toward the end of the Middle Ages. This was due partly to their failure to intervene in the Black Death that gripped Europe in the thirteenth and fourteenth centuries, the bubonic plague which resulted in the death of a quarter of Europe's population. While angels were replaced in Catholic theology by an interest in devils, saints and the Virgin Mary, their idea lived on in the art of the Renaissance until the Reformation of Martin Luther shifted attention to Jesus as the only mediator needed between the human and sacred realms. Now, at the end of the millennium, angels have returned with a force, inspiring a *New York Daily News* columnist to headline her column on publishing trends, "Enough with angels, already!" (Sherryl Connelly, January 1, 1995).

Pursuit party. These all seemed some post-Christian harkening back to childhood favorite images, with goddess overtones (these were Raphaelite guardian angels: large milky women with cascades of golden tresses, opulent robes and wings, and a single star over their motherly visages). I called them "my girls" and they brought me a sense of ironic comfort. Until writing this I never zoned in on the prayer on the back of the holy card:

> Angel of God, my
> guardian dear,
> To whom His love

commits me here;
Ever this day be
at my side,
To light and guard,
to rule and guide.
Amen.

God as male and angels as rulers are both distasteful concepts to me, but the singsong of the prayer is an old rhythm in my head, the rhythm of a young Catholic girl known to do novenas and rosaries in the walk-in closet before going to bed at night; who grew up to hate the Church for, first, its stand on birth control and, later, its fueling/funding of anti-

what the women's words "really meant," as is typical of academic research. So the angel intertexts provided a place where we could bring to bear the socio-logical and historical layers of the AIDS crisis on the women's stories, without having to insert those layers directly into their stories.

Reader: *But isn't there a danger that the angels will take over the women's stories?*

Authors: *Yes, the risk of the angels is that they will displace the "real" with a mythos. Intended to evoke what Rilke called a "wider space to speak be-yond our means," they may, in fact, be an error. But it seemed a greater risk to tell a "simple" tale, a "realist" tale about the AIDS pandemic. We take the risk to point out that there is no "simple" way to tell the story of women living with HIV/AIDS, that having to negotiate layers of constantly chang-ing, often contradictory information is a hallmark of the pandemic.*

Angels at the Millennium

At the end of 1993, both *Time* and *Newsweek* featured stories relating the return of angels in American popular imagination to desperate times in the face of war, hunger, AIDS, drugs, sorrow and fear. In this resurgence of inter-est, everything angel sells: perfume, books, music, icons, jewelry, napkin rings, plates and thank-you notes. The articles report that many traditional church leaders are skeptical, seeing the turn to angels as looking for simple answers in a time of disaster.

---

choice efforts. And more complicatedly, its misogyny and imperialism and bureau-craticizing of spirituality.

Feminism and then marxism and, more recently, something called "theory" have been my adult religions, my frame-works for making sense and nurturing hope in what I saw as a never-ending struggle for social justice. Angels began popping into this nexus in the summer of 1991, first through a book entitled *An Angel's Guide to Spiritual Development* that I was turned onto by some friends at the feminist bookstore in Mankato, Min-nesota. I was especially enamoured of their tales of angel dinner parties of femi-

nists who would share their expanding collections of angel paraphernalia. This caught my post-Wiccan sense of humor and I began exploring the possibilities of angel lawn ornaments. I started seeking out angel gifts for Solstice and birthdays. My 1991 Solstice letter xeroxed to my network of friends ended with a hope that we could all "stand with the angels" in the coming year.

This had something to do with the hoped for end of the Reagan/Bush years, but it was also about some yearning that I didn't understand until I read about Walter Benjamin and his angel, the An-gel of History, some marxist messianic

Reader: *Were the angels your idea or did they come from the women?*
Authors: *The angels were very much Patti's idea. Everyone else, Chris in-cluded, expected a much more straight ahead story. Somewhat obsessed with angels as a means to trouble familiar categories and logics, Patti wanted to work against the "comfort text" that would provide the consolations of cer-tain meaning and knowing, the romance of knowledge as cure. Through its very dangers, the angel was a way to steer the book away from the melo-drama or easy sentiment attendant upon the stories that the women tell about living with HIV/AIDS. These women deserve better than sentimentality, and part of the work of the angels is to interrupt the kind of easy empathy or*

The Gnosis of Angels

"The angelic world, whether it be metaphor or reality, is a giant image in which we may see and study ourselves, even as we move towards what may be the end of our time." Harold Bloom's book on angels, dreams and the millennium complicates the New Age revival of angels by focusing on angel menace, power and otherness. Bloom bases his arguments on Talmudic, Gnos-tic and Mormon ideas and argues that we debase this tradition when we do not know the long history of angels. Angels become insipid, "pressed into service as philosophy or prophecy," by "angel enthusiasts."*

* Harold Bloom (1996) *Omens of Millennium: The Gnosis of Angels, Dreams, and Resurrection.* New York: Riverhead Books.

---

yearning for grace and apocalypse amidst the debris of history.

Knowing angels would be important to this project and searching for a way out of the romanticized, sentimentalized, trivialized angels that have long domi-nated popular conceptions, I searched the library. In addition to Benjamin's Angel of History, I found Paul Klee's fifty angel images that he produced among his 8000 drawings and etchings. I found the an-gels of various poets, particularly Rilke's "Terrible Angels" and Valéry's "Broken Angel." I found angels in AIDS discourses such as Tony Kushner's play, *Angels in America.* It was cooling comfort to es-cape from the intensity of field-work to the library stacks. But my search for an-gels was also about working the angels, using the angels as a way to move be-tween and among the layers of meaning and levels of knowing involved in living with HIV/AIDS.

In terms of the logic of invoking an-gels in a book on women living with HIV/AIDS, clearly the angel is my investment in this project, a sign of the inevitable in-terpretive weight a researcher carries in telling other people's stories. Speaking to/from me as a way to negotiate a relation-ship to loss, perhaps the angel is an error. Holding on to the notion of error, my

---

Angels Across Cultures

Much elaborated upon in Jewish, Islamic and Christian traditions, angels or angel-like creatures are part of spiritual traditions around the world. In *Angels* by Peter Lamborn Wilson (1980), winged creatures who move between realms are traced across global contexts.

"downward directed sympathy" that readers often fall into when reading about the tragedies of others. The hope is that the very fragmentation of the book, its detours and delays, will unsettle readers into a sort of stammering knowing about the work of living with HIV/AIDS, a knowing not so sure of itself.

Reader: *Well, I guess I'll just have to see for myself how this works as I still don't exactly understand what you are about here.*

Authors: *Our hope is that each reader will work through the accumulating layers of information in the book and decide for themselves how it all comes together. Or, more exactly, how the various layers of information about HIV/AIDS, researcher reflections and the women's stories interrupt one another into some place of not making any easy sense. At some level, the book is about getting lost across these various layers and registers, about not finding one's way into making a sense that maps easily onto our usual ways of making sense. Here we all get lost: the women, the researchers, the readers, the angels, in order to open up present frames of knowing to the possibilities of thinking differently.*

Reader: *But why would you WANT a reader to get lost and disoriented in reading the book?*

Authors: *AIDS is not the only crisis in our times, and we all face death. But AIDS combines sex, blood and untimely death within a particular moment*

approach risks sentimentality and romanticization in order to exceed and expand our ability to think history differently, outside of a victory narrative, but in a way that is still enspiriting as we try to live beyond despair in the historical space in which we find ourselves.

Here the angels stage how we make sense within past ways of making meaning, ways that are often inadequate in the face of changing conditions. These, then, are troubling angels who use the seduction of angels to undo the very claims that are associated with angels. Carrying messages so that something might be seen regarding the registers in which we live out the weight of history, the work of the angels is to ask questions of our comfort spaces in an economy so marked by loss as the place of AIDS.

Rilke's Terrifying Angels

The German poet, Rainer Maria Rilke (1875–1926), in *Duino Elegies*, uses angels to interrupt any easy idea of transcendence. In Rilke, the "longing for the angel" is desire for the end of limit. Angels are produced by a human yearning that is about being in the world with the knowledge of death:

> But this: that one can contain
> death, the whole of death, even before
> life has begun, can hold it to one's heart
> gently, and not refuse to go on living,
> is inexpressible.

For Rilke, angels are an "in-seeing" in regards to death in all its wonder and life in all its pain and passion. The angel is about giving full consent to the dreadfulness of life in order for "our learning hearts" to possess abundance and power in our existence. In the world in which the angels are at home, human longing is a storm in which to shrink from what is heaviest, what is "too large, too dangerous, too many-sided . . . an excess of meaning" is to miss learning from life and, especially, death, "an intuition of blessedness [that] will open up for us and, at this cost, be ours."

---

in history. Instead of the comfort text that maps easily onto our usual way of making sense of crisis, this book is written out of a kind of knowing through not knowing, knowing both too little and too much about that historical situation. Hence, unlike the sanitized Hallmark angels of Christmas cards, the angels of this book are troubling angels, trickster angels that both mark that something Too Big is going on and render it elusive, ambiguous, outside easily available ways of making sense. Such trickster angels are a register of ruin, unable to make whole what has been smashed in a book involved in telling other people's stories in the shadow places of history as loss.

Notes

1. Hamacher, Werner (1988). The Word *Wolke*—If It Is One. In *Benjamin's Ground: New Readings of Walter Benjamin*, Rainer Nagele, editor. Detroit: Wayne State University Press, 147–175.

2. Michel Serres (1995). *Angels: A Modern Myth*, trans., Francis Cowper. Paris: Flammarion.

3. This staged conversation is modeled after Michel Serres' *Angels: A Modern Myth* (1995) where, at the end of the book, he has a dialogue between "The Reader" and "The Author" that begins with "Why should we be interested in angels nowadays?" (p. 293).

Benjamin's Angel of History

Based on Klee's painting *Angelus Novus* or *New Angel*, Walter Benjamin's (1892–1940) Angel of History is blown into the future backwards. The old angels were messengers with news of war and pestilence. The new angel is a lamenting, accusing angel, "blown away" by the storms of the world, staring eyes widened with terror at the shock of the twentieth century. About survival in the midst of historical catastrophe, for Benjamin, the angel became the vehicle for dealing with what Rilke, called "the Too Big" or "*too* great" in our lives.[*] Rilke's Too Big is about confronting issues of loss and the immensities of the ordinary: birth, change, death. Faced with the Too Big, we turn to available ways of making sense, especially through religion. Benjamin's angel challenges the kind of comfort angels that we have come to expect, what someone has called "the universe's social workers." The Angel of History is a symbol for the exhausted strength of religious traditions in the face of the shock of the twentieth century which make it impossible for the angel to carry out its mission of redemption. Benjamin hoped to capture the resonant familiarity of angels in order to move our hope for change from some Almighty to history as a human responsibility. This is about thinking our way out of rather than into the angel, as the angel is incapable of action in the face of the scandal of the world.

[*] Rainer Maria Rilke (1969). *Letters of Rainer Maria Rilke, 1910–1926,* Vol. 2, trans. Jane Bannard Greene and M.D. Norton, p. 300.

Laurie Anderson's *Strange Angels*

Performance artist and musician Laurie Anderson's album *Strange Angels* (1988) includes a song for Walter Benjamin. One stanza reads:

> She said: What is history?
> And he said: History is an angel
> being blown backwards into the future
> He said: History is a pile of debris
> And the Angel wants to go back and fix things
> To repair the things that have been broken
> But there is a storm blowing from paradise
> and the storm keeps blowing the angel
> backwards into the future
> and this storm, this storm
> is called
> progress.

Tony Kushner's Angels in America

Kushner's 1993 Pulitzer Prize and Tony award winning play, *Angels in America: A Gay Fantasia on National Themes: Part One: Millennium Approaches* and *Perestroika (Part Two)*, draws on Benjamin's Angel of History to focus on the human struggle to live worthwhile lives in a world of inhuman catastrophe. Spread out over two nights and seven hours, the play brings together a married Mormon couple, infamous Cold War lawyer Roy Cohn, a homosexual couple, the ghost of Ethel Rosenberg and the world's oldest Bolshevik who mourns the death of Grand Theories to explore Reagan-era ethics, the fall of the Right, and the possibilities of multiculturalism. Angels, deserted by God, add an apocalyptic tone as both part of such calamities as AIDS and as some unclear place between hope and despair. Here, Kushner uses the end of the Cold War and the growing political clout of the gay movement to ponder the limits of tolerance, particularly our tendencies to "demonize and other-ize." Writing about what was closest and most frightening to him, Kushner's play is about trying to devise a relevant ethics in a time when, "everywhere, things are collapsing, lies surfacing. . . . History is about to crack wide open. Millennium approaches."

Valéry's Broken Angel

The French poet, Valéry (1871–1945), a close friend of Rilke's, also used angels in his work. In Valéry, the angel is used as an expression of the tension between presence and absence and as a remainder from a former age, a universal order now fragmented and secularized where the angel is terrible and frail. This broken angel marks the human fall into knowledge that troubles the ability to believe in transcendence. Where the angels of St. Thomas Aquinas were pure intelligences, each one a species onto itself, Valéry's angel interrupts the traditional celestial hierarchy that puts angels above humans. His angel is a play of multiple polarities, a speaking angel, a split angel, broken away from being a species onto itself, fallen into time and speech, less than human because still outside the knowledge of sadness that separates humans from either beast or angel, the sadness that marks the distance of earth from Eden. In Valéry, angels do not have the last word, constructed as they are out of the very vulnerability of human existence.[*]

[*] Ursula Franklin (1983). The Angel in Valéry and Rilke. *Comparative Literature*, 35, 215–246.

Angels and AIDS

- from Peter Adair's 1991 *Absolutely + Positive* video: "the amazing angels they are" in their love for friends
- the Angel Food project in Los Angeles that delivers food to homebound AIDS survivors
- "Heaven Can Wait" T-shirts with angel image used as a fund-raiser by the Danish AIDS coalition
- Eve van Grafhorst died of AIDS in November 1993 at the age of 11 in New Zealand after being shunned in Australia. The Angel Eve foundation was set up to respond to educational and service needs of HIV+ children and their families.
- Tom Hanks's 1994 Oscar acceptance speech for best actor, playing a gay man with AIDS in the movie, *Philadelphia*: "I know that my work in this case is magnified with the fact that the streets of heaven are too crowded with angels. We know their names. They number a thousand for each one of the red (AIDS awareness) ribbons that we wear here tonight."
- John Killacky writes of his stint with the National Endowment for the Humanities under the Republicans. He speaks of 72 "angels" who have died of AIDS who inspire him to speak up and out, "demanding clarity in both my private and public actions" (*Utne Reader*, November/December, 1992:).

Angels and AIDS Books

- Mary Fisher, *Sleep With the Angels: A Mother Challenges AIDS* (Moyer Bell Publishers, 1994).
- Elizabeth Glaser and Laura Palmer, *In the Absence of Angels: A Hollywood Family's Courageous Story* (Berkeley Books, 1991).
- Philip Kayal's, *Bearing Witness: Gay Men's Health Crisis and the Politics of AIDS*, originally entitled *Angels at War* (Westview Press, 1993).

The Sex of the Angels

Catherine Millot positions those who exceed the traditional categories of sexuality as "The Sex of the Angels." Quoting one of the people she interviewed, "Gabriel": "'transsexuals are neither men nor women, but something else.'" As an "outsidesex," for transsexuals, surgery incarnates them as pure difference, "an attempt to join the abstract being beyond sex, the angel-being of the pure spirits."[*]

[*] Catherine Millot (1990). *Horsexe: Essay on Transsexuality*. Brooklyn, New York: Autonomedia.

Angel Breathers

Women and Men: A Novel, by Joseph McElroy, is organized around inter-chapters that are the postmodern or *"angelology"* sections, *"between"* spaces, as their titles announce, inserts that get out of hand, growing longer and longer as the 1000+ page novel progresses until they eventually are longer than the chapters. Somewhat ironically called "breathers," the inter-chapters introduce the novel's chorus, *"this voice which utters the discourse of the 'breathers,' which uses the first-person plural pronouns, belongs to—angels"* (p. 200). Brought ingloriously down to earth in the face of God's desertion of the world, McElroy's angels call attention to the plurality of worlds and the blurring of levels.[*]

[*] Joseph McElroy (1987). *Women and Men: A Novel.* New York: Knopf.

Postmodern Angelology

Literary critic, Brian McHale, in *Constructing Postmodernism* (1992), chronicles the "strange kind of come-back" of angels in late twentieth century fiction. McHale speaks of the "enduring angel-function" where, throughout history, angels have served various roles as dictated by their times. McHale positions the "revival of angelology" as a strategy to raise issues about the plurality of world-visions, a world where there are multiple ways of making sense.

Klee's Angels

German painter, Paul Klee (1879–1940), used angels more than any other major twentieth century artist, producing drawings and paintings of angels that carry such names as *Unfinished Angel, Forgetful Angel, Angel Still Female, Angel Still Groping, Angel as Yet Untrained in Walking,* and *Angel Delivering a Light Breakfast.* With changing forms and meanings, from the dawn of creation to birth and death and other states of becoming or intermediate zones, Klee's angels were more about an ironic reflection of facing the ordinary terrors of the here and now than about an afterlife. Hopeful but uncertain, his angels occupy a position between life and death, the poignancy of departures, the mysteries and vagaries of life, and the possibilities of transformation within a context of human frailties. In a poem from his youth, Klee wrote, "One day I will not be anywhere, lying next to some angel or other."

The Angel of Philosophy of Science

French philosopher Michel Serres argues for the angel as a way to think ourselves into a different kind of science. In *Angels: A Modern Myth* (1995), Serres see angelology as key to moving from static models of knowing to chaos and turbulent relations outside of defined concepts. We are accustomed to thinking in a way that organizes stabilities, but the new science is about fuzziness and fluctuation as we head "toward a different organization of knowledge on the wings of angels, who are its workers" (p. 295). French historian Michel de Certeau, exploring how humanities and social science based knowledges are more alike than different, writes of the "'language of the angels'" in the search for dialogue after the language of certainty has been shattered.*

* Michel de Certeau (1986). *Heterologies: Discourse on the Other.* Translated by Brian Massumi. Minneapolis: University of Minnesota Press.

Angel Punks

Elegies for Angels, Punks and Raging Queens brings the AIDS Quilt project to the theater stage. "The intense theatrical scrutiny afforded the AIDS crisis for more than a decade renders almost any tack on the subject dated and cliched. This is particularly true of this paean to the AIDS Quilt. . . . This major reservation not withstanding, one cannot help but admire the heartfelt emotions of the 34 devoted singers and actors . . . as they depict the pain, suffering and remarkable unity that comes from adversity" (*LA Weekly*, 6–9 1995).

Angel Condom

An International Center for Research on Women project on women and AIDS in the developing world uses a picture of a condom with wings, an Angel Condom, to recode condoms as a "good thing" that "good girls" can use. Seeing the education of girls and women about their bodies and sexuality and the development of culturally appropriate interventions as part of the fight against AIDS, this study of Thai female adolescents uses the story of an invisible flying condom that whispers to young women how to negotiate with a boyfriend about condom use in a way that reflects the high value that Thai culture places on sanuk or humor.*

* Materials are available through the International Center for Research on Women, Women and AIDS Research Program, 1717 Massachusetts Avenue, NW, Suite 302, Washington, DC 20036. 202-797-0007. e-mail: icrw@igc.apc.org

Angels as a Limit Space

French feminist philosopher, Luce Irigaray writes of "the between and the angel," with love as the vehicle which permits the passage over not an abyss but a threshold. Passing between boundaries, always in movement, a messenger between heaven and earth, the angel is a limit space, the link between the flesh and the spirit that is not about a return to traditional religion but a change in the economy of desire that accompanies the transition to a new age. Here, angels mediate what has not yet taken place or what is heralded, opening up closed notions of the world, identity, action and history.*

* Luce Irigaray (1991). *The Irigaray Reader*, Margaret Whitford, ed. London: Basil Blackwell.

Whispers of Angels

David Roussever and his dance company present an in-process work, "Whispers of Angels," at the Walker Art Center in Minneapolis, that explores black fantasies and dreams and faith, with a focus on the relationships between fathers and sons. "I'm looking for hope in a time when death is omnipresent—AIDS, violence" (*Star and Tribune*, August 6, 1995).

Will There Be Angels?

In a series of cards expressing the challenge of living with HIV/AIDS "and the pain and hope of those left behind by death," HIV+ poet, Jim Chalgren, writes:

> **Will** there be angels
> when I open the door
> walk through
> to the other side?
> **Will** they take my hand?
> walk beside me
> in the light?
> **Will** I close my eyes
> and dream of angels?
> will they take me
> in their arms?
> **Will** there be angels? (1994)*

* Cards are available through Air San Francisco Aviation Group, Box 14317, San Francisco, CA 94114.

Elsa Flores, *Angel,* 1992. From Journey/Journals, 1994 show, New Gallery, Santa Monica, California. Used by permission of the artist, whose husband, Carlos Almaraz, died of AIDS on December 11, 1989.

Relationships

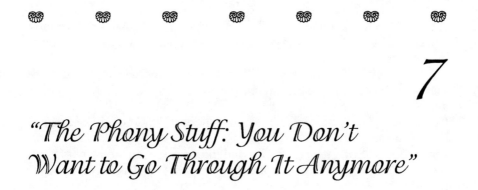

7

"The Phony Stuff: You Don't Want to Go Through It Anymore"

Chris: Even with people who do know, do you have to fake it?

Carol X: Even when you're not even thinking about it, all of a sudden your mom will be like, well, you know, you need to keep that job, you need that insurance. How are you feeling? Everything is fine. I'm fine, I'm fine. I'm feeling great, nothing's wrong, and inside you're feeling the opposite.

Lori: I've had the opposite experience, everybody lies to me that they're fine because they don't want to upset me. My family keeps everything from me now because "I have enough to deal with." They don't want to upset me.

Carol X: Only my parents know and a sister who happened to be in the city. And to be honest I probably wouldn't have told her; she has had a hard time with it. I don't have to stand for this just because I need insurance. My family feels it's a terminal disease and you need your insurance if something were to happen. It's not going to be tomorrow that I am going to keel over; if I need help I'll ask for help. One of the last conversations I had with my mom she got real weird on me. My youngest brother was visiting and she said I should tell my best friend and her husband and my little brother. And I am like where is this coming from? And mom says, "well you don't have too many people in your life and no one to support you," and I was like, what is with you? Yes I do!

Attitude and Prayers

T's went up again they said
The reason they can't conclude
All my friends are happy
They say it's attitude.

But when I call my Mother
She said, "It's so wonderful everyone cares.
But it's not just attitude, honey,
It's all your Mother's prayers."

—Linda B, 6-93

Linda B: You're supposed to tell them so they can all come and be phony and get mad at each other and go away and wish they had never been told in the first place.

Carol X: Right. I mean they don't quite understand and then you think that your mother is your friend at one point and then she turns into a mother again.

Chris: Are you saying that with some people, once they know, it does change the relationship?

Carol X: Yeah and it's smothering and more stress than family not knowing. I don't want any relationships to have to change because of them knowing.

Rosemary: Me I have to hide all this so I can keep a job and insurance.

Linda B: The phony stuff you don't want to go through it anymore. I don't care about the fancy furniture and the fancy cars; give me someplace to park it, give me something to drive in, something to cook a hamburger on, wash my arm pits. I don't care.

Carol X: My mother drives me crazy because she knows and everything has to be relative to HIV and I am sorry, it's not; it's a crazy feeling. I worked ten hours today and I don't feel like getting up and driving to Dayton to go bowling! It's just a simple fact. But because I have HIV—I am tired and

---

Chris: How would I *ever* tell my parents, *I am HIV+* or *I have AIDS?* Every family that hears this news has its own history, scripts, roles, strengths, and weaknesses that impact how they respond to riding the waves of unpredictability that go with living with HIV/AIDS. While some family members are remarkably able to handle even the first wave, more typically, a family learns to deal with HIV/AIDS over time.

In the early AIDS epidemic, due to more rapid progression of HIV disease, I met family members for the first time at the hospital. I knew little about them, and most had not had much opportunity to prepare for an AIDS related death in their family. And they brought their own tangled web of resentments, fears, conflicts, shame, and blame. These were evident in my very first family experience.

Lori's husband, Jack, was rapidly dying of mystery complications from AIDS, and the family was gathering for his death. When Jack married Lori, he converted to Judaism. This angered his southern Baptist parents, who blamed Lori for generating the downfall of their son (never mind that he infected her with HIV). In the hospital, Jack's mother tried to give me a letter sent to her some years ago by Lori, in an effort to swing me to their side. And Lori's emotionally distraught parents were spilling over with feelings, but unable at that time to express them. Tension, anger, old resentments surrounded Jack's death, a disappointing contradiction for a man who had been loving, silly, and accepting of other people. Even though Jack was primarily comatose, I wondered about *his* experience of the tense and conflicted family situation.

maybe that's the reason and because my sister doesn't know that I have HIV, then that explains it, according to my mother.

Linda B: I hate being by myself; I hate going home after work. I am just a big baby, but the thing is that in the long run you're better off by yourself because you can come and go as you please. If you don't want to deal with anybody, you can cut everybody out.

CR: I love living by myself. When I was rooming with my cousin and I had a bad day at work and didn't feel like talking, she'd go on and on.

Amber: Only a few people know: this group, a handful of friends, my cousin. Nobody else counts. I don't let myself get close. My roommate, who is my ex-sister in law, she knows, but her mama doesn't know. Her kid comes over so I have to hide everything in my room so no one finds out so the whole family doesn't decide to hang me on a telephone pole like Jesus or something. I am serious. When they have parties, I don't go because I am not able to share this with them. They'll look back and say, after they find out, she was at my house all the time, she used the bathroom. My sister-in-law won't let me go back to her house. Maybe someday, when I have to tell these people, I can say, maybe you had the right to know, but I couldn't hack telling you, so I didn't come around. I am sure I am not giving them enough credit, but I just can't take the risk.

I also recall Caroline, formerly a nun, who had had only one sexual relationship. She became infected with HIV, and after caring for her partner until his death, she rapidly became ill herself. Her Midwestern farm family gathered around her deathbed. They were confused, angry, grievous. They could do little to comfort their daughter who had somehow ended up with AIDS. In a lucid moment, Caroline had extracted a promise that I would not disclose that her boyfriend was African American. Why? Perhaps she was offering her parents some final protection from knowledge that they would find embarrassing or shameful, or perhaps she feared that they would forevermore blame all black people for their daughter's death.

I sit in the hospital room, alone with Caroline's father, while Caroline is hav-ing a CAT scan. He asks me to tell him about Michael, the man who infected his daughter. And then the phone rings, and it's Michael's sister. She wants to visit Caroline in the hospital. What do I do? Her visit will give away the secret. I am saved by Caroline's death several hours later. Michael's family members are "lost" among the many people of color who attend Caroline's funeral. This is a sterling example of the difficult and surprising issues that are encountered by families, friends, and caregivers.

Thanks to earlier diagnosis and better medical management, people with HIV infection now live for many years. This also means that a family is "HIV affected" for many years. With this gift of time, many families are remarkable in their capacity to change and adapt to the situation. As Melody states, her adoptive

Melody: My parents are real supportive. These people adopted me when I was six and they've been fantastic throughout my life. They went through their own reactionary period. Like my daughter had gone over to do the wash, like we had always done, and the first time after my diagnosis, they had plastic on everything in the washroom. My daughter, being in the denial and anger stage that she was in, just threw it all out and said, my mother has it, I don't and these are my clothes. When I first was coming out with the newspaper article they did not want me to use my name or have a picture in there and this was their own fear. I knew when I went to them, out of respect, to let them know that I was going public, I said mom, I got to do what I got to do and right now part of my healing is to be able to go that public. And if my picture and my name being in the paper can help one person, then it's been worth it for me. When I can look at someone and say, yes, I am Melody, I am alcoholic, I'm an addict, I'm HIV, but I am still me.

Chris: What did she say?

Melody: She said, don't do it. If you die tomorrow, your daughter and us are left with that stigma. Well they did some growth. The day the article came out, they were afraid of their church friends, they were afraid of their club, they were fearful of their friends rejecting them. Mom called me and said her senior minister called and said how much he respected me and ad-

parents "did some growth," especially when she "came out" as HIV positive in her local newspaper. Rather than harassment, the parents receive respect and admiration for their courage and openness (which certainly encourages one to behave with courage and openness!). Rita reunites with her family after years of drug addiction and prostitution. Barb's parents become AIDS activists and educators in their small, Catholic hometown. Lori's parents participate in AIDS related activities, and learn to talk more openly about their feelings and experiences. Lori's mother always brings something special to support group holiday celebrations.

Today the notion of "family" has a very broad definition. *Who* is family to the women living with HIV/AIDS? These family members may be white and middle class, or members of groups that are typically devalued and oppressed: gays, minorities, poor people, substance abusers, people who sell sex. Approximately 76 percent of women diagnosed with AIDS are nonwhite, economically disadvantaged, and 46 percent are IV drug users. Often, AIDS is just one more problem for a family with depleted financial and emotional resources. On the other hand, these families already possess the skills of survivorship.

When I work with families, I always explore family history, to identify what has already been survived: racism, the Holocaust, poverty, job loss, divorce, domestic violence, death of a child, single parenthood, substance abuse, disease. Few families are unscathed by at least some of these challenges regardless of the family's class and race.

mired me. They've gone through a lot of growth and I've gone through a lot of growth with them. Our relationship is so close now; they are starting to let me be me instead of being parent-child. It's like I am me and they're them and we are not so closed, we hug. When I grew up, we didn't express emotions. Now we hug, we cry and it's great. They are in their 70's and they are going through this spiritual awakening with me and my daughter too who is 17 and pregnant. She wanted to give me a grandchild before I died. I have mixed emotions, she doesn't realize how it changes your life. So I'm sad and happy, but it's changing her; she's getting more responsible; she's got to lead her own life.

Iris: My immediate family, they all know. I didn't tell them right away, just a year ago. They accept me. They are still trying to deal with me being the alcoholic addict, so it's not real easy for me to deal with. And my kids, two girls, 12 and 9, I told my girls a year ago. My 12 year old is in denial and she doesn't want to talk about it. The 9 year old, she said oh I am sad. They are my rocks. There are times when I wanted to give up and I would have gone to a motel room and taken a bunch of sleeping pills and just took the big nap, but I've felt like I dealt them enough of a bummer hand, being alcoholic and an addict and now their mommy's HIV+. I want them to learn all they can. They are pretty smart to the fact. I am real proud of the oldest. She's

❀   ❀   ❀   ❀   ❀   ❀   ❀

While every family situation is unique, I observe several phases related to family adjustment. The first phase is *pre-disclosure*, when the woman has not yet disclosed her HIV status. A woman who immediately discloses to her entire family is either very brave and sure of her family, or she is panicked. Immediate disclosure may mean anger and rejection, or it may bring an outpouring of love and support. Even in this latter situation, the woman is forever compromising her privacy, and may be endlessly responding to well-intentioned inquiries about her health. Generally, I encourage newly diagnosed women to be slow and deliberate in making disclosure to family, especially extended family. It is important to remember, too, that each person told will likely need to talk with another, extending the circle of people who know.

Whether a woman waits days, months or years to tell some or all of her family, the family is already affected by her diagnosis. Despite every effort to maintain normal behavior and relationships, a woman may inexplicably withdraw from the family. Perhaps she visits less often, makes excuses, or even lies to protect her family from the burden of HIV. She may try to give children as long as possible before facing the potential loss of their mother. Linda B waited one year before telling her daughter, until the daughter completed her Master's degree [Linda B's letter to her daughter is included later in this section.] The family may wonder why their member frequently sees the doctor, or perhaps they notice subtle physical or personality changes. Intuitively, they suspect "something is wrong," while the woman is declaring "I'm just fine" but

getting to the stage where her friends are starting to get sexually active, and she said something that made me real proud. She's like all I want to do is find one boyfriend, only have sex with him and marry him and have kids. My kids keep me as stable as Iris can be right now.

Nancy: I don't have anybody. These people around here are more family than anybody I have, we can talk. I've got a son, he's 22. He knows, but we don't discuss it at all. He's just like that; any time there is something on the TV about AIDS, he'll change the channel. He doesn't accept it at all. I don't accept it at all either.

Lord, my God, help me to tell my family about the virus. Give me strength, Lord, to handle the response, pro or con that I will get from my family. Guide them Lord. Help my family to understand that my survival hinges on their love and support. Thank you Lord for this life I live. Though my life seems to be filled with many trials and tribulations, I am alive. I fully realize I am an instrument. Lead me Lord. And, when it's time for me to rest, I pray my soul is nestled in your loving arms, Lord. AMEN

—Linda B, 1-3-91

---

hiding medication before family visits. The woman faces a tough decision: living in fear and secrecy is highly stressful, though some women find it safer than disclosure. I gently remind clients that eventually the family will know that she is infected, so how much control does she want regarding telling them?

The next phase is *disclosure*, when HIV+ status is disclosed to at least some family members. This may be a very emotional time, marked by anxiety, fear, guilt, and sorrow. The woman needs support (friends, support group, pastor, rabbi, counselor) to guide her through this process, and provide emotional and/or physical refuge if necessary. It is better to tell family members while the woman is still quite healthy, and she may want to provide information on AIDS resources, such as a parents' support group.

Disclosure to the family is at best a transition, at worst, a crisis. Family members differ in their knowledge about the HIV virus. Some fear contagion, sometimes to an obsessive degree. Rosemary's family buys Lysol to clean the bathroom every time she uses it. The family may withdraw, refusing to allow visitors in the home. Some family members, especially sexual partners, may engage in sexual abstinence and/or frequently repeated AIDS testing.

Family members vary tremendously in the type and intensity of their emotional reactions. Some are "right there," accepting, loving, and positive. More often, there is shock: "*not you*," "not in *our* family." Anger: "How could you let this happen?" "How could he do this to you?" Fear: "I drank from the same cup as you last week," "Can the children catch this from

Ana: I have been very open with HIV and my oldest son has been very open; he has accepted it. My fifteen-year-old daughter, for her it's off limits to talk about it. Like when I did this TV show yesterday, I am always

---

Unlike Africa, where AIDS has always been considered a disease that affects entire families, the US response to the disease has virtually ignored children orphaned by AIDS. Most of these orphans will be the children of poor black and Hispanic women whose families are already dealing with stresses like inadequate housing and health care and a stigma that plays out in many ways. While there is no comprehensive national policy or resources, some local programs have been developed. In New York City, for example, the Permanency Planning Project through Child Welfare matches foster parents with HIV+ mothers and their children well before the parent dies. In Los Angeles, Tanya's Children is a foundation that helps parents with AIDS arrange custody for their children. The program encourages parents to create a "Legacy Project" that includes art, tapes and memorabilia for their children as a farewell. And magazines like *McCall's* (November 1993) carry stories on the families that AIDS has made. But many HIV negative children go into regular foster care and receive no special resources like counseling.

---

you?" Anticipatory grief: "You're going to die," "I don't want to lose you." Shame: "What will other people think?" Fear of family stigmatization leads some members to withdraw, deny, and refuse education or support services.

Disclosure always creates some kind of change within the family. It seems that life will never be the same, that HIV/AIDS will never leave one's mind. However, as the family begins the next phase, *adjustment,* members may be surprised that birthdays still come and go, and that the family establishes a new homeostasis. This homeostasis is marked by "healthy denial," which the family can maintain as long as the HIV+ woman stays healthy.

It is important for the family to develop and maintain a support system to help with the next phase, *crisis,* marked by the woman's first major illness or hos-

pitalization. Denial dissolves, and secrecy is difficult to maintain. With this or subsequent illnesses, there may be impairment, job loss, applications for social services and disability, concern for surviving children, frustration with the medical and insurance systems, anger at God. Often it is simply necessary to sit down and cry and scream with an understanding friend.

There will likely be long stretches of healthy time between illnesses, with the re-establishment of routine and homeostasis. Eventually, as illnesses occur more frequently, the family is stressed by the ups and downs. Unpredictability of health makes it difficult to plan vacations or anticipate the future. Family members are at risk for depression and burnout, and must have breaks from AIDS. Unfortunately, the woman with AIDS cannot take

protecting the kids, but when he asked me if I had children, I just said yes. And then I thought, how is my daughter going to take this, how is this going to affect her? My attitude was not that I don't care, but I can't keep protecting her because she is not ready to deal with it. And I told her, you're going to have to learn to deal with this. First she said she was not too happy, that everyone is going to know that I am her mother. And then she said, well do what you want to. I am not co-dependent, worrying about her feelings. I would rather educate and I want my kids to know what I said.

Amber: I had a situation where I was getting very close to a person. There were different times when he'd be going out of town, and both of us, when we would see each other would have the urge to hug, to greet each other, but we never did. And I think it was mostly on my part that we never did because it was like I didn't want to get close to that person because I had already seen how much hurt he had gone through by being close to people with AIDS. It was like I don't want to be that kind of burden on him. I don't want to put that in his court. And I also felt protective towards me; I already had enough people in my life that I cared so much about and I was already missing them, even though I wasn't dead.

a break. She may experience depression, and eventually, as she accepts her impending death, she talks about funeral plans, living wills, and arrangements for children. These constructive activities may seem disheartening to family members who want to remain hopeful. Other family members may privately wish for the end to come soon.

When death is near, the strain on the family is overwhelming. They struggle to keep her comfortable, and face difficult decisions about hospice care. She may rally briefly, for a day or two, and then decline again. Who should visit? What to tell people? How to find a private moment? Time drags along, yet whips by. This is the time to clearly state one's needs, to accept all help that is offered, to try to eat and sleep regularly, and to make time for spiritual practices. Even so, there will be temper flare-ups, exhaustion, misunderstandings, anxiety, and grief. Each family does their best but cannot do this perfectly. If your family is simply with your family member, you are doing at least OK.

After death has occurred, there are the immediate tasks of funeral arrangements, the obituary (what to say about cause of death?), decisions about personal belongings, management of the estate, if there is one. Surviving children need special attention. It may be weeks or months before family members and friends can truly grieve their loss. Support groups, memorial services, and the Names Project Quilt provide support, ritual, and community. While some families are done with AIDS, it surprises me how many family members remain involved in AIDS related activities, helping those still living with AIDS. This underscores that usually we do not want to forget, and seek opportunity to remember, to give back to the disease that stole from us.

Danielle: I want to talk about my father. I am very close to my dad. We can hardly talk about this issue without breaking down, and I am worried about how he is going to handle it. It is terrible for us.

Chris: What is most painful about it?

Danielle: Well, I think he feels so helpless. And it just breaks my heart to see him suffering the pain. So he stays busy 24 hours a day so he doesn't have to think about things going on.

Chris: Have you talked about what is going to happen if you do get sick or die?

Danielle: No. We can barely talk about it. I try to cover it up all the time. I am doing great, I say. Let him think that I am still going fine. A lot of times, I am not. And I just need to keep it that way, because there is no reason for him to be bummed out, up until the last minute, you know.

Alisha: My mother knows that I am HIV+ and of course was devastated. Almost immediately she became very quiet. Last month I went to visit her. We have communication problems, but I just wanted to give her as much input as I could so that we could establish a better relationship. She had a wall up and was not going to listen to me. It was really hard and I felt badly about that. I wanted my mother to understand my feelings, and my feeling

🦪 　　🦪 　　🦪 　　🦪 　　🦪 　　🦪 　　🦪

Holley was dying as we finished the desktop version of this book. She struggled all her life, with a difficult childhood, early motherhood, drugs, poverty, and finally, education, employment, a loving relationship. Facing AIDS and, rather soon in the disease, a virulent cancer threatened her life. Holley accepted this with equanimity, and a very short list of things to do. But some of her friends and family wondered where was the fighter, the survivor? What, no chemotherapy and hospice already coming to the home?

And then there was Allison, a friend Holley met just a year ago, a large, strong woman originally from Guyana. She dedicated her summer to helping Holley die with comfort and dignity. Keeping Holley's apartment spotless, she swung my daughter around in the air, tended to her own three children, and found renewal through her faith. Holley's mother visited once, her father, once or twice. Her adult daughter didn't make it at all. I suspect her daughter was afraid, but Holley said she was always self-centered. Holley left her poetry to her daughter, a belated opportunity to know her mother, rather than the household items anticipated by the daughter.

Diane, an HIV+ friend from support group, visited several times a week, even though this meant watching an AIDS death. I took Allison's kids to a movie, and the dog to be spayed. Holley's husband worked many hours, and bought her a gold wedding band that she showed off like a youngster. We tripped over the oxygen tubing and wondered why the landlord would not fix the air conditioning. Holley lit yet another cigarette, drank another cup of coffee, waiting, waiting, waiting, and confided to me that she was doing "just fine." 🦪

for her, not only about my situation. But she had this protective armor up and it was very difficult to get in there. So as of right now, I have kind of given up on my mother. I just figure I will let her go. It is very hard on me.

CR: I'm angry at my children. I find myself being more angry because one is very dependent on me. If she asks me to do something, or she comes and eats, because it's between pay periods, which I can understand, but I feel myself getting angry and saying what the hell is she going to do when I'm not here. And they're still selfish, I don't understand. I was sort of feeling her out and I said, you know, ____ asked me to come and stay with her and she said, what will I do? Am I just supposed to keep going and giving to them until I'm just used up? I was disappointed in her. I was like what am I gonna do? I don't know if it's the change in my physical condition in the last few months, but they don't come around much, except for the one who needs so much. I could probably look like Twiggy and she would still come.

Patti: What is your theory on what's happening there?

CR: As long as they don't see me, they don't have to deal with me. Even the one who comes often, if I'm not feeling good, she gets the hell out of there quickly. The other night I asked her to give me a back rub and she said, oh mama I am so tired. I guess I'll just have to make sure that I'm somewhere safe if I'm unable to do for myself. I did my best in raising them, maybe it's something I missed out on that they are so, you know. But I would never want to live with none of them. I mean if I really had to put the skids on and if I had to live on much less it would be better to live with someone. Since I was 12 I've been a mother, and this is the first time that I'm just responsible for myself and I'm enjoying it. I find myself not wanting to be too close to my grandchildren. I burst out crying one day. My granddaughter said grandma do you think you could get me that, and it was just like something went over me, like I don't know if grandma is gonna be here one day and if I got sick or when I die, I wouldn't want the stigma. I mean kids can be so cruel. They're 4–13 and I have six.

Chris: What would you do if the motherhood script could be different?

CR: I would possibly maybe have two but much later, certainly not at 12. A long time ago it was like you wasn't a person unless you had children and you had to have this no good husband and you had to have these no good kids. My identity has always been being a mother.

Rita: It's the same way with me. It's the first year I've been on my own. Sometimes it's scary, but other times it's so great. I'm not even interested in dating. Even though I have the virus and I'm not feeling so good, I'm trying to do some things I should have done back before I had the kid. It's always taking care of someone. I grew up with my son, I was a young 18 when I had him. I grew up protected in a small town, no drugs, no blacks, no gays. When I got out of the service, it was like BOOM. I asked my dad one time, why didn't you tell us about this stuff?

Chris: CR you weren't protected in childhood. Here Rita was over-protected. Yet you end up at the same place.

CR: I think that's why I'm so adamant about education, be it condoms, be it sex, especially AIDS. Kids are going to sample everything.

Maria: My family doesn't know. I've heard my boss make comments about people with AIDS and if he thought that his insurance . . . I mean I wouldn't even go to a doctor, I am so afraid that somehow he could find out. He would destroy me. He would. I haven't been to a doctor. People just don't know and the comments they make are so cruel; it's a big joke to them. They joke at work about how everyone with AIDS, they all should be killed.

Sandy: You know my father-in-law thinks like that. He's Puerto Rican and he's back in the 30's, I guess. And they were getting on the Spanish program about how this man has AIDS and he is still having sex and not saying, so his comment was—now I am sitting here, and I think my mother-in-law knows although I haven't told her—and my father-in-law says that they should all be put away. I just looked over at my husband. I just thought, shit maybe I should be put away too. It's like I am dying to explode and tell them and maybe scare them and let them know because I do eat there and I drink out of their cups. The guy next door died. He had those sores all over and I would go and take him out and he was selling his car, a beautiful Corvette. He knew he was dying. My father-in-law wanted this car, but he didn't buy it because the guy died of AIDS. So I said one day, he died of AIDS but his car wasn't infected. I don't know; are they stupid? I wish I could tell them and invite them over for dinner and explain to them, but I don't have the time to want to sit there and explain and tell them that my husband still doesn't want to use condoms. And I don't even have the time to fight with him about it either, but I feel like telling his mother and father so maybe they could see that you just don't get this easily.

Geneva: The relationship I've been in is very supportive, as far as my HIV, and it has helped me tremendously. Because I felt like no one would want me. I noticed like my mother and other people will say, oh you're fine, you're fine. Because maybe in a way they are trying to convince themselves that you're not gonna die or you are fine. They want to be in denial about it too. So you sometimes do have to convince them—I am really sick. But I think it has to do with their denial. My mother is in extreme denial about it.

Patti: Who do you get your support from?

Geneva: For the longest time I told my best friend I had leukemia and she read up on everything and wanted to go to the doctor with me. And then I started to avoid her. And finally, we went out to dinner one time and she was like I want to know what kind of leukemia you have. And I said I don't want to talk about it, I came to talk about positive things. She told me, if you have AIDS, I want you to tell me. She figured me out. And I said no, why would you think that? And she said you know I will be there. Three days later I called her and decided to tell her. But the relationship I was in, it was really bad because I was deceitful for about the first two months. I didn't know what I was going to do. But I wasn't having risky sex. Well, when I first told my friend, the one thing that made me feel the best was when I went to her house after I told her on the phone, and she was drinking something and it was like, here have a sip. And it was just like a symbolic thing to me. We both started to cry. And I said, no you don't have to do that. She was like, no I want to, and to me it just like symbolized everything.

Lori: I think relationships are richer than they might have been if HIV wasn't a factor. I know with some of my friends that we had kind of a superficial, let's get together on Friday night kind of relationship, you know. We were friends but there really wasn't any meat to it. Now there's more, and that's what I think is part of "THE GIFT." It involves everybody that knows you. So I think when you are ready, there are good, accepting people out there.

Tracy: I guess some of the things that keep me going are Danielle, for one.

Chris: How does she do that?

Tracy: Well, she just tries to let me know that I can empower myself in certain ways. Like maybe through nutrition. I can make myself a little bit healthier. A lot of it is mental, I think, and if you feel you can survive for a long time, then I think that is really powerful, if you feel like there is no way that this is going to kill me. So we remind each other of that. And we call each other to complain a lot about our daily aches and pains. And that helps us.

Chris: You became friends after you were both HIV?

Tracy: Right. We say that we are like two grandmothers, we call each other at 10 in the morning to see whether we survived the night. Of course I'll call her and she will be like, oh, I feel kind of tired. Well let me see, have you had breakfast, have you had your cereal? You will probably feel better after you eat. I think that keeps us going, because sometimes . . .

Chris: What about you CR, friendships with women in your life?

CR: The women I've had friendships with, our friendship has grown since I've had the virus. Sometimes I get scared; they call and while I like our friendship, I know they know my health is deteriorating. But I have to honor them and I do love to eat! I've told my women friends that I had before about the virus, but my man friends, I wouldn't tell. I don't know why.

Chris: Do women feel safer?

CR: Yes, they feel safer. When I told Debbie, she said, it could have been me. Because she had had a risky relationship and I just think women understand and don't pass judgment. But men can be such *jerks*, and I am angry. They can be such scum; I don't know. I associate men with the virus, all of them can have the virus. I feel more angry at men since I've met women like D who had a husband that was bisexual and you know she was. . . I mean me, I can see, I knew my boyfriend was probably running around. That was a risk that I took, but I think when a woman is in a marriage, I mean the virus is the same whether in Lori or whoever, but it's different if you just don't know and you get sick and go to the doctor and they tell you. There's so much betrayal. I was devastated when I found out.

Chris: Your partner wasn't pretending to be something he wasn't?

CR: Yeah, he wasn't pretending to be a family man. I found out later he was an IV-drug user. I remember one night he was telling me about the shooting galleries. If I think back on it now, my life was taken in one of those shooting galleries somewhere in New York City and I'm sitting there listening to it, and it was my death sentence being read to me.

Patti: And you didn't know that at the time. So your life post-virus, most of your friendship energy has been women?

CR: Yeah, it feels safer. And I find myself living almost two, maybe three lives. This group is one; here I can say I have AIDS. My family is another where I might be really feeling bad but I say oh I just feel fine, however, get the hell out of here so I can go to bed. I put a pretense on for now. And then when I meet people on the bus, it's just like chatter, about weather, how slow the buses are. I can be one of them.

Chris: You got your mask on.

AIDS brings unexpected groups together. For example, with seemingly little in common but the virus, gay men and poor women do not necessarily mesh well in public clinics or automatically respect one another's lives. For many women of color, AIDS is often "just another problem," and not necessarily the most pressing, in a life full of poverty and violence. Ideas of "post-AIDS spirituality" or "eroticizing safer sex" are not necessarily shared problems. But AIDS does forge new relationships and recast our experience of the social. Such restructuring is unpredictable in terms of whether it will bring forth the best or the worst kind of response, as it redraws the lines and the face of politics in both small and large ways. For a philosophical take on this, see Derrida 1995. For a more narrative account, see *My Own Country: A Doctor's Story*, by Abraham Verghese (Vintage Books, 1994), which deals with the plague years in the Smoky Mountains of eastern Tennessee. Verghese writes movingly of his learning experiences of working with the disease in a town where no one expected it to occur. The book demonstrates how AIDS reaches into all corners of America and changes everything it touches through a kind of alchemy of emergency that challenges deeply felt prejudices and fear in bringing different kinds of people together. It is also quite useful in teaching the basic facts, treatment conditions, and psychological dimensions of the disease for the HIV+ and those who care for and about them.

CR: Yeah, it's OK until someone says something stupid about AIDS.

Danielle: I have a boyfriend who is HIV negative, and he has been incredibly supportive. I feel lucky in the sense that I know other women who think that there's no way guys are going to be involved, but that's not true. It's going to be more difficult obviously but that's not true. I am very lucky for that and I am very lucky for my father, because he is like, oh I'll take you anywhere in the world to get any kind of treatment. Everybody is really supportive in that sense.

Joanna: I've made a lot of friends that I probably wouldn't have had before, and I have been able to do a lot more volunteer work. I do get tired, I get real exhausted sometimes. It's so hard to get out of bed. I kind of let myself be lazy. There are two friendships in particular. One is with a guy we call the perfect male, if he wasn't gay.

Chris: Would you have had gay male friends before this?

Joanna: Not as many. Throughout my life there have always been one or two people who were gay or bisexual and I have always gotten along with them very well, but now we have the same kind of problems, fears and relationships. And when their partner dies they grieve and mourn. They are widows too.

8

"I'm Not Close-Mouthed at All": A Daughter

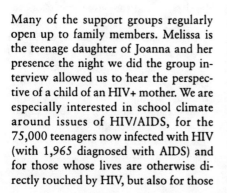

Melissa: Me, living with this, there's a lot of times I feel like her mom. I don't know if she knows that, but it has turned me to like fifty years old on the inside.

Chris: Why is that? Do you have to take care of her sometimes?

Melissa: Just worry (crying).

Chris: Can you tell us?

Melissa: Well, I lost my step dad to AIDS. The whole thing just sucks.

Patti: Can you talk about this at school?[1]

Melissa: I am not close-mouthed at all. They can even talk about me, I don't care. I am easy to get along with; I'll be your friend until you disrespect me. I ain't trying to mess with you, so don't try to mess with me. Once I let it be known, they tend to see how mature I must be to let them know that I

Many of the support groups regularly open up to family members. Melissa is the teenage daughter of Joanna and her presence the night we did the group interview allowed us to hear the perspective of a child of an HIV+ mother. We are especially interested in school climate around issues of HIV/AIDS, for the 75,000 teenagers now infected with HIV (with 1,965 diagnosed with AIDS) and for those whose lives are otherwise directly touched by HIV, but also for those who think they are not affected, that "it can't happen to me." In terms of schools and HIV/AIDS education, 15–24 year olds currently count for five percent of AIDS cases nationally, but their high incidence of risk-taking behavior places them at risk for rapid growth of the disease. Condom availability, creation of confidential AIDS testing centers for adolescents, and intense education efforts with special attention to homosexual and bisexual youths, runaways and minority

confront people who talk behind my back because I don't care what nobody thinks, what anybody says. At school, any chance I get to talk about a subject that I want to talk about, it will always be this.

Patti: So you are educating other kids?

Melissa: Yeah. And I am about the only one in the school, plus the fact that I am a kid, and half of them are my friends anyway, that's also another factor. The teachers aren't going to tell the kids. The only people that kids will listen to is the kids. The teachers don't want no part in the topic anyways. But if they tell me to write an essay about anything you want, I am like, O.K. That is always my topic. And I save all my writings. Within the first year of me going to a school, everybody knows, and I am fine with that. At first I wasn't. It started in middle school. I had confided in a teacher. Then she went and told the school counselor who is required to tell the principal of the school. And then the teacher announced it in a teachers meeting. So then the whole schools knows. The teachers are talking about it. Then the kids know. Within a week of me confiding in her, the whole school knew. And that's what started me not caring about who knew. I am not gonna let something that people think bring me down. Plus, there are a lot of people who think that this is the beginning of the end. You should look at it like it is the end of the beginning. We weren't here before we were born. This is just the beginning. After we leave this life, well my religious preference personally, I know where I am going, my mom knows where she is going, we got people there, I can't wait to go, to get away from this hell hole. So I am just looking forward to it. Live to the limit. Make sure I do all while I am here.

Note

1. For a discussion of the ways AIDS education for children is shaped by the "passion for ignorance" of parents, teachers, popular culture and policy makers, see Silin, 1995, in Resources.

adolescents with different cultures and languages are all overdue. Elementary school curriculums usually focus on health classes where the subject of AIDS is formally introduced around the fifth and sixth grades as part of choosing wellness-oriented behaviors. Knowledge bases include understanding how the virus enters the body and what occurs as a result. Students are usually taught to identify risk situations and demonstrate re-fusal skills and the development of self-esteem. A curriculum entitled, "Reducing the Risk: Building Skills to Prevent Pregnancy, STD and HIV" was developed in California and is now being tested in several Ohio public schools. For evaluation of California results, see Douglas Kirby et al., "Reducing the Risk: Impact of a New Curriculum on Sexual Risk-Taking," *Family Planning Perspectives*, 23(6), 1991.

9

"I Don't Have Fifty Years to Be a Mother": Lisa

Chris: How did Alex come into your life?

Lisa: I was living in Houston after graduating from high school and met Alex's father and I guess I was at that stage of my life when you look for the worst men you can find. He certainly had a lot of charming things about him and there was potential, but I don't know if it's the Florence Nightingale syndrome or what, but you want to save them. And he did pretty well for awhile. We got along real well for about two years, in the middle of which I took a trip to Greece, the first time we'd been apart since we'd started dating. I got really sick the day I got there, got deathly ill and they didn't know what it was, except we knew I was not pregnant. I finally had to come home I was so sick. I went to doctors in Greece and here who said it was a virus, just a virus. I had been home a couple of months when I got pregnant, so I went through my whole pregnancy not knowing.

Chris: I interviewed Lisa on August 15, 1996, two months after her three year old son died of AIDS. While Lisa was not in the original group of 25 women that we interviewed in the support groups, we thought her story was important in understanding how the disease affects women in terms of being an HIV+ mom of an HIV+ child. Lisa is white, 22, with two years of college. She was diagnosed HIV+ in 1994 and is asymptomatic in terms of her health.

When friends of mine recently became parents to an infant with Down Syndrome, reactions were heartfelt and supportive. But most discussions included "didn't they have amniocentesis?" The implicit message: screening technologies and abortion hand parents the ability, and perhaps even the responsibility, to produce only normal offspring. Certainly, most people tell me that they believe HIV+ women should never become pregnant: the risk of an HIV+ baby and/or

About half of adults who become infected with HIV will become very sick and get flu-like or mono-like symptoms shortly after infection. This illness, called "Primary HIV Infection," usually occurs two-twelve weeks after infection and ends within one to two weeks. Symptoms include fever, swollen glands, skin rash, sore throat, mouth ulcers, pain in joints or muscles, nausea and vomiting, diarrhea, weight loss of more than five pounds in one week, yeast infection in the throat, pain in feet or fingers, extreme fatigue and bad headache and stiff neck. HIV tests won't tell if you are newly infected as HIV antibodies form three to six months after infection. To find out if you're newly infected you can take a special blood test that looks for p24, a protein present in large amounts during the first six weeks of infection. This is especially important for pregnant women in terms of making choices about abortion (*World*, February 1995).

Chris: Looking back now, you think you were probably infected the whole time you were pregnant?

Lisa: Yeah, I know that illness in Greece was the initial illness of infection. When I read about it in the books after I found out I was positive about a year

the risk of a baby left behind by a mother's death from AIDS are grounds enough to declare such a pregnancy highly irresponsible, even immoral. The most vociferous do not hesitate to prescribe everlasting abstinence for any HIV+ woman who can become pregnant.

Such views greatly oversimplify the realities that go with being an HIV+ woman. Pregnancies occur even with the responsible use of birth control. Partners lie about their HIV status, their bisexuality, their sexual history. The pre-pregnancy screening test may be negative because the test is administered during the incubation period, before antibodies are present. Or, a woman, newly pregnant, opposed to abortion, is so fearful of HIV stigmatization that she postpones or avoids HIV testing and the specialized prenatal care that terrifically improve the

odds that her baby will never become HIV+.

Lisa's story was an example of what can go wrong. She had established what she believed was a monogamous and committed relationship. She tested HIV negative in her second month of pregnancy. Even if her HIV status had been revealed at this point, her case occurred just before the leap forward in the perinatal use of AZT to greatly reduce the risk of transmission from mother to baby. Her physician did not offer a C-section, which may have prevented infection of Alex. On top of all this, current technology has revealed that Lisa and Alex had high viral loads, making the virus especially aggressive. Perhaps nothing would have helped. Perhaps this information would only have interfered with hope for Lisa and Alex.

later, I made the connection. I had had a tattoo about two days before I went to Greece and for awhile I thought it was the tattoo. But the further I got away from Alex's father, the more I believed it was him that gave it to me. Pieces started falling together and I started remembering things like I'll bet he cheated on me when we had that fight two weeks before I went to Greece. We know now that the viral load that I got was great, a large quantity, because I'm a rapid progressor. I have a large viral count, so it's more likely that I was infected from sex than the tattoo because there's only so much that could be passed through a tattoo. I didn't find out until after Alex was born.

Chris: You came back, got pregnant—

Lisa: Yes, I had a wonderful pregnancy, loved it. Looked good, felt good. I was so excited and happy. Even though his father was a jerk, at that point I still thought we would get married and live together happily ever after. I told myself, I mean I think as a woman you have a responsibility because women get stuck with children. So you have to say to yourself, if this doesn't work out, am I prepared to be a parent and I always said, yes, so even when it didn't work out with Alex's father, I was thrilled.

Chris: Had you always thought that some day you would have children?

Lisa: Yes, about six. I always wanted to have a bunch of kids. I was nineteen when I got pregnant. I had two years of school behind me and I knew I

⁂   ⁂   ⁂   ⁂   ⁂   ⁂   ⁂

Ninety percent of childhood infections are attributed to perinatal transmission (5 percent to transfusions or transplants, 3 percent to hemophilia treatments, 2 percent to unknown causes). How does a pregnant woman pass the HIV infection? Perinatal transmission occurs *in utero*, in delivery through exposure to blood, or through breastfeeding, which alone increases overall risk of transmission by at least 14 percent. Other possible co-factors include mother's viral load, CD-4 cell count, neutralizing antibodies, genetic risk factors, coexisting infections, and vaginal delivery, especially for women whose labor goes on four hours after the water breaks.

Prior to 1994, approximately 30 percent of children born to HIV infected mothers would become HIV+. Often, the family and caregivers had to wait 18 months before knowing for sure the HIV status of the child. However, in 1994, the year of Alex's birth, research trials indicated that AZT could significantly cut the risk to about 8 percent. AZT was to be taken five times a day for 5.5 months of pregnancy, beginning no later than the fourteenth week of gestation, making early prenatal testing extremely important. After birth, AZT was given to the newborn five times a day for six weeks. The AZT pregnancy regimen was quite a breakthrough, although the possible long term effects of AZT on the fetus may not show up for years. Other strategies being explored as possibly reducing transmission included active and passive immunizations to induce antibodies and neutralize the virus, vaginal rising of the birth canal, cervix, and baby's head during la-

didn't want to wait until I got out of college. It turned out to be five times harder than I ever thought it would be because I never anticipated HIV or AIDS or my child getting sick. But even with all that I still feel like I was a really good parent. So I like to think, gosh if that never would have happened, I would really be doing good! So it's hard when you think how different things could have been.

Chris: Was his father around during the pregnancy?

Lisa: His father was in jail, but we kept in close contact. We wrote two times a day and planned on doing better when he came home. But after I found out I was positive, I went to a therapist. I had major migraines, I just couldn't function. I was clumsy for a year, knocking things over, wrecking cars. I was trying to just trudge along, but you could see by my actions that I needed help. I talked about a lot of different things with her, but a lot of what I talked about was my relationship with men and my family. So I started thinking, I don't need to save anyone, and what am I doing with this guy? I'm sorry; he's the father of my son and I'll do what I can to give him the opportunity to be there for him, but it's not my responsibility, I'm not his mother! So I decided to move us back up here and it was a good decision.

Chris: So the pregnancy in terms of your health, at this point you did not know you were HIV+. You went through a healthy, normal pregnancy on

🐚   🐚   🐚   🐚   🐚   🐚   🐚

bor, Vitamin A therapy, and C-sections (*World*, August 1994).

By 1996, the year of Alex's death, there was even greater optimism for healthy outcomes of pregnancy. At the XI International Conference on AIDS, Dr. Yvonne J. Bryson of UCLA's Children's Hospital noted: "Current goals include reduction of HIV transmission to less than 2 percent. Intervention studies are directed at both further reduction of maternal virus load and providing prophylaxis to the newborn, including the use of potent combinations of antiretrovirals, passive antibody, and vaccines given to the mother and/or newborn infant" (*Positively Aware*, September/October, 1996). AZT monotherapy will no longer be the only or best treatment choice.

These treatment possibilities are uplifting, but raise complicated questions, ethical dilemmas, and roadblocks. First, the roadblocks: globally, the majority of HIV+ pregnant women live in poor Third World countries, and AZT and other drugs are undreamed of luxuries in such global contexts. The worsening global picture is indicated by a surveillance survey in Swaziland which shows a 16 percent HIV rate among pregnant women in 1994 (*World*, August 1996). In Uganda, the AIDS rate among pregnant women is 29.5 percent. It is grievously predictable that inaccessibility to education, testing, prenatal care, controlled deliveries, and drugs will mean the births of millions of children who will eventually have AIDS. The mothers of these children are not helpless though. As noted in *Newsweek* (September 25, 1995, p. 52), women spurring change is "turning the continent's cultures upside down" around

the one hand thinking the relationship might continue and on the other hand prepared to be a single parent. Then you decided to move up here after some therapy, to disengage from this guy. So when did you find out you were HIV positive and that your child was at risk as well?

Lisa: Alex was born in June of '93 and I found out two weeks after he was born that I was positive and that we wouldn't know for sure about him until he was thirteen months. But at eight months we knew that he was positive.

Chris: And at that time they didn't have the AZT treatments.

Lisa: Yes, now you take AZT when you're pregnant if you're positive. I didn't know I was positive, but they didn't have the treatments then, anyway.

Chris: What initiated testing?

Lisa: It was weird. I was tested when I was two months pregnant, when I went in for my first prenatal visit. The only person I had been with since the last time I was tested was Alex's father, so I just wanted to make sure everything was OK. He had said he'd been tested and he was not infected, but I just wanted to make sure. And I tested negative. Then I had to change doctors because of some insurance problem and my lab results never got forwarded although I just assumed they did. But in my ninth month, the new doctor did new labs and came back a week before I had Alex and said, normally I don't tell people this because there are a lot of false positives, but I have to tell you because we don't want you to breastfeed until we know for sure. We have to do the Western blot, because the Elisa results are positive. I remember driving home thinking there's no way this could happen. I delivered, I was scared, I didn't breastfeed, I was pumping my milk. I was just sure he was going to call me back and say everything was OK. It was terrible, it took like a week and a half after the baby was born because it took like two and a half weeks to get the results of the Western Blot back. We were calling everyday. We were just sitting there waiting and wondering. My mom is a lawyer and she was trying to get results. Finally they told her that I was positive. You hear about how people don't get counseling with their results

Although no final results can be known until a child's immune system develops, at about eighteen months, there are three methods currently used to diagnose HIV in newborns. Viral culture has been used the longest. Expensive, it takes about 6 weeks to get an answer. At two to four weeks, it is 50 percent accurate. By two to six months, it is more than 90 percent accurate. PCR costs less and takes about 48 hours to get a result. Its accuracy rates are the same as viral culture. p24 Antigen is least expensive. However, at two to four weeks it is 20–50 percent accurate. Even at six months it is still only 20–40 percent accurate.

Risk factors for everyone, pregnant women included, are (1) shared needles since 1977, (2) had unsafe sex since 1977, and (3) had a blood transfusion before 1985, when the HIV test became available (*World,* April 1995).

Maternal risk factors that influence perinatal transmision include (1) sexually transmitted disease, (2) low T-cell count, (3) use of injection drugs, (4) no first trimester healthcare, and (5) low infant birth weight. It is unclear whether caesarean section delivery lowers the risk of infection (*World,* October 1996).

and I didn't. But I was lucky my parents were there. Things had happened so quickly. If it had been at another time, I wonder if I would have told them. You know, a lot of people just don't tell their families. But things worked so that everything was so crazy that I just told them and I'm so glad that I did. My mom was down in Houston and my dad and step mom flew down and were immediately supportive. They were uncomfortable, but they felt like they had to do something.

Chris: Kind of stunned?

Lisa: Yeah, yeah. I think scared. My dad even asked me if I was disposing of my sanitary products in the right way. It just blew me away. They just

such issues as genital mutilation, violence against women, and AIDS related health and welfare issues: "The AIDS crisis is making men listen to women."

In the United States, the situation is somewhat different. Testing and treatment are widely available to pregnant HIV+ women; however, many of this group never gain access because they are uninformed and/or frightened by the stigma they fear will be attached to them and their babies. Often of Hispanic or African American origins, views of family and acceptable risk may differ from mainstream thought.

This raises the controversy around mandatory versus voluntary HIV testing of pregnant women. In 1995, the CDC calls for voluntary AIDS testing as standard prenatal care (The *New York Times,* May 9, 1995). This is the first time the

CDC suggests voluntary testing for an entire group of people. In 1996, the American Medical Association endorses mandatory testing of all pregnant women and newborns, voting 185–181 in favor of it. While this is only a recommendation, it is likely to carry considerable weight. Some states presently test all newborns blindly, telling no one the results. As of January 1, 1996, all California physicians who see pregnant women have to offer HIV testing and counseling.

Proposals for mandatory HIV testing of pregnant women are bound to be lightening rods for dispute and controversy. If testing is made mandatory, is treatment mandatory as well? Why pick this disease over risks taken by other parents? What about future privacy, discrimination by insurance companies, job loss, stigma attached to the family, the right

didn't know what to do. They turned into being wonderfully supportive, but they just didn't know what to do. They were just in shock; I didn't know what to do either.

Chris: So here you were, you'd just delivered an apparently healthy boy, normal delivery.

Lisa: Yes, that's something else. I can't change things, and money wouldn't help me at this point, but my doctor should have made me have a C-section. I try not to think about it too much because it's really aggravating.

Chris: What are your feelings about that?

Lisa: I can't think about it. I can't come close. I remember reading this list about the risk factors that increase or decrease the probability of an HIV+ mom passing it on to her child, and one of them was continuing to have sex with an infected person during the pregnancy, but he was in jail. Another was drug use. I didn't use drugs. I was just at the bottom of the list, except for vaginal delivery which increases the risk.

Chris: It's ironic that your doctor did tell you not to breastfeed. But where did this leave you? You did do the voluntary testing and tested negative, but it was within the three month window period. Then you were tested again but involuntarily, although you probably would have said yes, if you had been asked.

❦   ❦   ❦   ❦   ❦   ❦   ❦

to choice? Is mandatory testing even enforceable, and what would be the consequences for those who resist? Yet a child born to the possibility of AIDS is a small, helpless being who may end up enduring a difficult and premature death from AIDS related complications.

Whatever the outcome on mandatory testing, it is paramount that voluntary testing be accessible, confidential, and as emotionally safe for the mother as possible. Most mothers, regardless of their circumstances, seek the best for their children. Counselors, doctors, nurses, public health officials, rabbis and ministers, family members and friends must appeal to pregnant women to have an HIV test early in pregnancy. And if she tests HIV+, she is more likely to participate in treatment if she is treated with kindness and respect for her ability to care for her child.

She's entitled to the chance to become a good mother, just like any other woman. It is unjust and irrational to assume that HIV+ status is an absolute predictor for a bad outcome, any more than HIV negative status is an absolute predictor for a good outcome.

This brings us to a new dilemma: some women, knowing their HIV+ status, will be choosing to become pregnant, accepting the increasingly better odds that proper care will produce a healthy baby free of HIV infection, and that the new protease inhibitors will prolong their own lives as well. As one highly educated, well-informed woman said to me: "I'm obsessed with having a baby. Coming from a black family, I don't worry about leaving a child with no one to care for it. My family would love to have some part of me go on. *What's so hard is not know-*

Lisa: Yeah.

Chris: And then found out you were positive, I mean the timing of all this. Then once you did have questionable test results, they weren't treated seriously. I mean you should have had a cesarean. I almost find myself wondering if your doctor was afraid of a cesarean. It sounds like such a clear medical misjudgment.

Lisa: Right. And it was. I don't know, gosh maybe I should go back and sue them. But it's almost too painful and like I said, money's not going to help me. Sometimes I think I should just write him a letter and say make sure you don't do the same thing to someone else. But you know—

> There are seven known cases of women contracting HIV through artificial insemination, with 75,000 women seeking such services yearly. Judith Billings, Washington state superintendent of public instruction, announced that she had contracted AIDS while trying to become pregnant in 1986 through artificial insemination with donor sperm and that, rather than retreat, she may run for Congress (*Columbus Dispatch*, January 17, 1995).

ing. AIDS used to be a death sentence in a couple of years. It used to be assumed that women progressed more quickly with the disease. Now you just don't know."

Until 1996, an HIV+ woman who birthed an HIV– child could expect to die while her child was quite young. This likelihood is now replaced with confusion and ambivalence born of the hope that protease inhibitors will finally make HIV infection a manageable chronic condition. With treatment making possible a healthy baby and a healthy mother (or father) for years to come, how will HIV+ women and men dare to see their futures? Will their vision include the dream of having children, and when it does, will their decisions be met with optimism and support, or condemnation and isolation?

Meanwhile, how can we understand and assist the children and mothers who live day-to-day with HIV infection? There are 7296 children infected with HIV living in the United States. Fifty four percent are African American, 24 percent are Hispanic, and 20 percent are white. Of the four million babies born in this country, 7000 have HIV+ mothers (Centers for Disease Control, June 1996). And it is impossible to count the numbers of children whose mothers become HIV+ while the children are growing up. Michaels and Levine (1992) conservatively estimate that there will be 80,000 orphans of AIDS by the year 2000.

The problems and challenges are beyond comprehension to those of us who never face such circumstances: confusing medical information and choices, juggling clinic visits, school appointments, and childcare, facing insensitivity and prejudice from professionals, alienation from

Chris: So where do you come out now in terms of testing for pregnant women?

Lisa: I think women should be tested. It's like diabetes or RH negative. Women should be tested. It should be confidential, but children's lives are at stake and women won't get tested because they're afraid to find out about themselves or whatever and here we're giving a child a chance to go through what my son did?

Chris: Yes, I think seeing what your son went through which we'll talk about in a minute is pretty strong motivation to require testing for pregnant women.

Lisa: Of course he's my child, so it's so much more painful for me, but there's a lot of other kids going through the same thing. He's not the only one, he's not one in a million.

Chris: So tell me about Alex?

Lisa: Well, I mean, you know, the love of my life, the best thing that ever happened to me. He was a great kid and sometimes, you know, I used to think, and people would say that to me sometimes, that there was something angelic about him. He just had this good personality and he was so funny, a charming little kid. Sometimes I say to myself, you know, whoever is in charge, somewhere, something, children who have these life threatening illnesses or chil-

❀   ❀   ❀   ❀   ❀   ❀   ❀

family due to the stigmas associated with AIDS, drug use or homosexuality, coping with the death of one or both parents, financial survival, planning for the children's future care, contagion fears at daycare centers, Sundays schools and birthday parties, feeding a sickly child, administering medicines and other treatments, keeping up with routine tasks like work, laundry, groceries. . . and somehow keeping it all together so that there is something left for savoring the all important moment of right now.

It is possible here to only marginally address a few of these problems. Medical and social work needs for child and mother can be centralized to one site and offered by a team of professionals. FACES, which stands for Family AIDS Clinic and Educational Services, is one such program out of Children's Hospital in Columbus, Ohio. Each child/family in the program receives case-managed care from a team consisting of a physician, nurse and social worker. The team coordinates *all* medical and social work services, including testing, treating, counseling, education, mental health assessment, and assistance with housing, transportation and legal matters when necessary. Clients receive transportation to and from medical appointments, and childcare is provided during clinic visits. The adult family members are cared for at the same site at appointments that coordinate with the child's appointment. As Lisa relates in her story, these professionals are sensitive, highly trained and experienced, and become extended family to their patients.

Psychiatrists Mellins and Ehrhardt of Columbia University (*Positively Aware*, August/September 1996) report the need

dren who are going to die, it's like you pack ninety years of personality into three years and they just blow you away. And he did, I mean he just, you know, I mean, my friends who have kids and my family, I mean there was just something angelic about him. He was the sweetest child. There's nothing you want more than to see your kids grow up, especially when they're so remarkable and smart and wonderful. You think, God, this child could be anything and he should have his turn and he should be able to grow up and he should play and make friends. By the time he started slowing down he was about eighteen months, but he really started slowing down at about twenty months.

Chris: So the first twenty months were normal and you got to enjoy being a mom? What was it like knowing HIV was looming in the background for both of you?

Lisa: Part of that defense mechanism was up to about eight months, I said I'm going to think about it and do everything I can, but I'm not going to worry about what I can't control. When they told me he was positive, I just took a deep breath and said OK, what do I have to do now to make sure that he lives until there's a cure?

Chris: So at the beginning you were motivated?

Lisa: Oh yeah. As soon as they said he was positive, it was a little premature, but I said OK let's do the a drug trial. We started that right away,

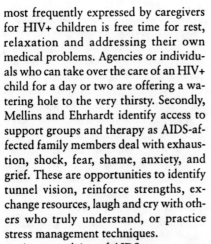

most frequently expressed by caregivers for HIV+ children is free time for rest, relaxation and addressing their own medical problems. Agencies or individuals who can take over the care of an HIV+ child for a day or two are offering a watering hole to the very thirsty. Secondly, Mellins and Ehrhardt identify access to support groups and therapy as AIDS-affected family members deal with exhaustion, shock, fear, shame, anxiety, and grief. These are opportunities to identify tunnel vision, reinforce strengths, exchange resources, laugh and cry with others who truly understand, or practice stress management techniques.

A parent dying of AIDS must emerge from denial and engage in "permanency planning." This is making legal arrangements for the future care of surviving children. For children old enough to understand, it may also be time to get honest. For example, I worked with an African American father who contacted HIV from secret homosexual behavior outside of his long term marriage. He was broken and shameful with guilt. But several weeks before his death he was finally able to tell the truth to his 10 year old son (who had figured it out anyway). The father apologized for hurting the family. The son replied that he did not care whether his father was gay, but that he shouldn't have gone behind their backs. The father was stunned by his son's acceptance of his homosexuality; his own self-hatred seemed to diminish somewhat after this difficult conversation.

Dying parents grieve leaving their children. They grieve that their children will not remember them, or forget their personalities, or feel angry or deserted.

making sure we did everything. You hear about these positive kids that live to be 15 or 16. I thought OK, unlike a lot of parents with HIV+ kids, I'm not sick myself, I don't have a drug problem, I have family support, I have everything going for me. I can take care of this kid, make sure he lives to be 14 and there will be a cure. When I found out I was positive, everybody said there would be a cure in two years.

Chris: So you really felt a strong hope.

Lisa: I was not admitting that he would die at all, no way, or myself, at all. We had everything going for us. At that time, they weren't talking about the different kinds of progressors. They said that the people who lived a long time were the people that did all the right things. At that point they didn't realize that people could do all the right things but just have a really aggressive virus, which is what happened to us.

Chris: And in terms of the care you received, tell me a little about your family's role and what was good and bad about the medical care you received.

Lisa: Moving to Ohio was the best thing we did, about four months after we found out he was positive. Medical care up here is much more organized. The hospital, they just coordinated our lives and everything was all there together, his care and mine. And Medicare pays for almost nothing down there. I had to quit work, quit school, couldn't even get AZT down there on Medicaid.

A wonderful idea to address this is Project Legacy, originated by Susan Taylor-Brown and Lori Wiener (1993). With the help of counselors and professional videographers, a dying parent can make a quality videotape for the children. The parent can chat, tell stories that keep alive memories, show a favorite place, leave important messages and requests, say good-bye and express their love. Such a project is emotionally demanding for all involved, but is a superb use of technology to meet psychological needs.

Lisa had to ask "how do children die?" because for Alex, life was very, very short. But many children survive their HIV infection for many years. And thousands of children are surviving the deaths of one or both parents to AIDS. For all these children, we must ask how do they live?

Have a childhood? Escape prejudice, isolation, have fun, create memories of good times? One answer: camp! Camp Sunburst, the original camp for HIV affected children in northern California, is the model for other camps around the country. In Ohio, Christin Locke is the founder and director of Camp Sunrise, a nonprofit corporation that depends on volunteers to provide a completely subsidized camping experience. The children participate in the typical camp activities, including nature studies, hiking, horseback riding, swimming, mask-making, talent shows, dancing and campfires. They form communities in their cabin groups, and learn to offer peer support when issues do surface related to HIV/AIDS. Most of all, the children learn to believe in themselves. Locke reports that it costs about $550 for a child to attend the camp, a tax-de-

Chris: What about the emotional support at the hospital?

Lisa: They really became our family, plus my parents. They are people who really care, these are people who stick it out and break their heart year after year.

Chris: I don't know how they do it. How do you think they do it?

Lisa: I don't know.

Chris: They knew Alex and loved him?

Lisa: Oh yes, those are other people who would testify about his angelic personality.

Chris: It's so interesting that you have used that word several times and I've heard you use it before. Does it connect with his becoming an angel?

Lisa: He's an angel in my life. I used to call him my angel dear.

See *In the Absence of Angels* by Elizabeth Glaser, who contracted HIV in 1981 and passed it on to her two children at a time when no one knew about the disease. Her daughter died in 1988 at the age of seven. As of 1996, her son is twelve and still asymptomatic. Elizabeth Glaser died of AIDS in 1994. Co-founded by Glaser in 1988, the Pediatric AIDS Foundation conducts pediatric AIDS research worldwide. Its primary objective is to create a future that offers hope through research. The goal is to find therapies to prevent transmission from infected mothers to newborns, to prolong and improve the lives of HIV+ children, and to eliminate HIV in infected children.

---

ductible donation that anyone can feel good about!

Lisa has learned the importance of embracing whatever there is to feel good about. She has not focused on the negative, the unjust. She has not become bitter. Instead, she has relished the time she had with Alex, a beautiful little life that lasted just three years. Lisa has cherished the family support and the loving care from a skilled treatment team. She was a good mother, and she can give credit to herself for this. I have reminded myself that as of this writing, she was only 23 years old. Like her little boy, she has crammed a lot of living, loving, and maturing into a short amount of time. No person, perhaps especially a parent, can know her story and not feel tears, heartache, and inspiration.

Angel's Lullaby (Richard Marx)

I was never alive till the day I was blessed with you.
When I hold you late at night I know what I was put here to do.
I turn off the world and listen to you sigh
And I will sing my angel's lullaby.

From *For Our Children Too!*
Musical collection to benefit the Pediatric AIDS Foundation
Hopeline: (800) 488-5000

Chris: So he started having some deterioration around eighteen months?

Lisa: Yes, that's when his counts really fell. That's when I quit work. Four or five months later, I quit school because he was doing all right. He had gone in for surgery for a feeding tube while he was still pretty healthy and that enabled us to do homecare. Then he was hospitalized for the first time and the next month he had mouth ulcers which was a repeated thing. Then he would be out of the hospital for a few weeks and then something would happen. He was in and out, another surgery, wouldn't gain weight, hard to get a two year old to take meds by mouth.

Chris: And you were providing his care?

Lisa: Yes. He would have bad days, but he would still have good days when we could go to McDonald's and it wouldn't hurt him to move. We did a lot of traveling. When he felt good, nothing got in the way. And when he felt bad, we sat on the couch and did whatever he wanted to do for one day or two days or five days if that's what it took. And still, he was my baby. I loved to sit next to him on the couch. We were still having good days. Then in October of 95 he was having a lot of trouble with his feeding tube, we were in the hospital for two weeks, but again, the people at the hospital did everything they could to make it easy for me. I can't say enough about everybody there. They just loved Alex.

Chris: And you could see they weren't afraid of him because he had HIV?

Lisa: No, no. The only time I had a bad experience was in the ER and some nurse said "You don't play around with this stuff" and showed up in what looked like a space suit. Even Alex noticed. She said she had pink eye and I got so mad, I said, first of all, if you're nervous, that's fine. But tell me you're nervous. Don't stand out by the door and say some crap and then come in here and tell me you have pink eye and you're on antibiotics and that's why you're wearing this shit. But the rest of the staff, I felt like it was my obligation, my debt, what I was in a position to do, was to educate them and let them know what it was like to live with this. They would say, oh you're so nice, you come from such a nice family, and I liked to hear that because the next time they see somebody who's so nice and comes from a nice family, they'll think, well gosh.

Chris: It helps to shoot down the stereotypes that this can happen to anyone. So back to spring of 1996—

Lisa: He had a decent summer last year, good days and bad days. The fall was tough. I could list all the things that went wrong. After he died we found out that his internal organs were as much as five times the size of a normal child's, so that was a lot of discomfort. He hated his meds. It was just one thing after another. He preferred IV meds. We went to DC and tried to get on protease inhibitors, tried to get him on them when they first came out. On our initial trip, they gave him a drug and said come back in a month to see if we can get his white blood count up. By the time we got back he had so much trouble with his feeding tube that we couldn't go anywhere.

Chris: How was his morale?

Lisa: He didn't feel good. There's no question that he knew that he was the boss. Whatever he said went, with my parents too. When he wasn't feeling good, I mean, anything he said, we would do. You just want to make them feel better. But when he felt good, I mean, he had such a pleasant personality. Sometimes he would get up to play and you could tell it hurt him, but he wanted to laugh and joke and hide and scare you, I mean he was a two year old kid.

Chris: Was he ever able to articulate any questions about his illness?

Lisa: I would hear him talking to other kids about the tube in his stomach and his body not working right and this special thing that helps him get his medicine. And he liked to show his IV stuff and I had him be in charge of doing what he could to push the syringe in.

Chris: Looking back, when did things start to turn the corner in a downward direction?

Lisa: We thought he was doing well, we had to keep up with him. But you hear about really sick kids, toward the last, they really rise to the occasion, live fully. The last time he felt good for a week was at Xmas. It was a really special time. I just had a big grin on my face all week.

Chris: So you came back from that trip—

Lisa: Then one hospital trip after another, they kind of run into one another. He probably had fifteen hospital stays in his life. He did OK, but we knew he was winding down. I still wasn't accepting that there wasn't going to be a miracle, although at this point I knew there was a good chance there wasn't going to be. And I had known probably for a year, when his counts dropped and then mine did too. I stopped being so aggressive with his meds. I said this is a child who maybe has six months ahead of him. Is this daily shot I'm supposed to give him going to increase his quality of life? I had to balance everything like that. I worked with his two main doctors, the case nurse and a social worker and we worked together, a family approach. Something would happen and they would say, here are our options. I would ask my questions and the decision was mine.

Chris: It sounds like one of your criteria was quality versus quantity of life.

Lisa: Definitely. I wanted to do the right thing; it would kill me to not do that. I had to think about it but I kind of detached myself in a way. I knew he wasn't going to last too long. I didn't have fifty years to be a mother, I had to condense it.

Chris: So what do you remember about the last month or so?

Lisa: Mmmm. I think he was in and out of the hospital a couple of times. God, you know, I can't even remember, it was just so—we finally had a surgery to get his feeding tube taken care of. That was really exasperating, we finally got it to work. He had a couple of good times, but he had mild vomiting, frequently. He was swollen, so puffed up. We set up a hospice meeting, there wasn't a dry eye in the room. We talked about our options, what we can stop, what we should keep up, whether we should stop all the meds, the IV nutrition. I knew what I was doing; I said we'll do this because it makes him comfortable, but we're not going to do this because it's not helping and it makes him miserable. I listened to everything. I read a lot about every decision I had to make and when I had to make those decisions, I felt I made the right ones. They talked about how most families aren't ready to let go of kids, and the kids suffer. They didn't tell me that until after he died, but I couldn't keep him suffering so much. So I asked, how do kids die? What are the different ways? How long does it take? Will I know?[1]

They gave me some stuff about warning signs. I was just afraid that he had two or three months of suffering ahead of him, because that happens. I even said to my father, if he gets really bad and I think he's going to last two months, I mean, I'll overdose him. My dad said he'd call the doctor and I said what are you talking about, the doctor gave me a refrigerator full of morphine. I mean, once again, you never want your child to die, you never want your child to be sick, but for it to happen, it was the way it should have been. I thought we'd have at least a month before he died. But we had the meeting on Thursday and on Tuesday night I was talking with a friend and Alex was sleeping on the couch. We had played with him that night, he wasn't feeling good but he was talking and playing. Then he fell asleep and we sat there for maybe four hours, my friend just not wanting to leave, talking about him. Then at four in the morning he was having trouble. He'd been on morphine maybe a month or two and a week before that he had started asking for it. About six in the morning he was fidgeting around again and he said he wanted more medicine and I got up to get it. When I looked out the kitchen window the sun had started coming up and light was just coming in. Those few minutes it took me to get that stuff ready, the light came up and I went in and I saw his face. He was sitting there, curled up on the couch, I saw the light on his face, and his skin just looked sallow, like big bags under his eyes, and his color was bad. And just like it was written across my mind, the word Death came and I thought is it going to happen now or is he going to be like this for three days or what? And I stopped dead in my tracks and he was breathing really heavy and I thought should I call the hospital? So I worked towards him thinking I'd just make him comfortable before I did anything. I sat down, I was looking at him and watching and counting his breathing and checking his hands and at that point I thought he was going to die although I still thought it could go on for two days. I thought of people I should call but I picked him up and held him in my arms on the couch and he was breathing so heavy, so labored. And I just said I love you, I love you. And about ten or fifteen breaths and then he just stopped, just stopped and closed his little eyes and I thought oh my God, you know. What if I had gotten up, what if I had gone to call someone.

Chris: It was just so right.

Lisa: He just laid there in my arms. And I just couldn't believe that it would happen so fast. That day I kept seeing him with my aunt that had died over a year ago, like her holding him on her hip. You know, I'm not one of those people that sees angels that much, but I just kept seeing it. Two or three days later, I kept seeing him running. I thought, my god, this child hasn't been able to run in so long. But I kept seeing this and I guess I just gave up on the idea of keeping him around, I mean there's nothing in the world I want more than to have him back with me, but not if he has to suffer. So for him I felt like, god, he's finally at this party. To have a child that's so sick, to have to go through so much pain, I mean it's almost unbearable. So for him, I feel the loss of his personality and the joy he brought to everybody, there was so much more that could have happened, that he could have done, that he could have been, some more times he could have made me laugh or laughed.

Chris: It's been how long since he died?

Lisa: June 5.

Chris: So it's only a little over two months since he passed. What has your time been like since then? How do you get on?

Lisa: I don't think I deal with it very well. I still feel like I can't let go, there's just so much, if I let it out—I laugh about how I can't go eighteen hours without having to talk to my folks, and that's unusual.

Chris: Well, it's like Alex, you've crammed a lot into your experiences with them, too. You've got lots of feedback from people for what a good mother you were, and you seem to have some sense of that.

Lisa: Yeah. I loved doing it so much. There's nothing in the world that made me happier than being a mother. I liked being a mother. That's also sad. I think I'll never do anything as well as I did that.

Chris: And that there's not a chance to do it again?

Lisa: No. Not unless there's a cure. Because even if I thought I could live forever, I'm not going to take a chance of having a child that's positive. But the main thing is I'm not going to have a child if that child's mom is going to die.

Chris: What are your thoughts now about your own health? Have you been able to focus on that?

Lisa: It's hard. I'm trying. I'm going back to school and I'm trying to travel to family I haven't seen for awhile. But like I said, being a mother was my most favorite thing in the world and to completely change that focus—

Chris: It's an identity shift, a loss.

Lisa: Right. Who am I? What am I going to do with myself? I haven't wanted to do anything. I mean I wanted to go to school so I could buy a house for Alex and me. Now, I don't know—

Chris: You did get a puppy.

Lisa: Yeah. But I may have gotten her too soon. I'm not as attached as I should be. I got mad last night at her playing . . .

Chris: She's not a good substitute for your little boy. You also just emotionally, to bond with anything, your loss of that bond can't be repaired or replaced anytime soon. You've been so even headed about it, I just wonder if there isn't some part of you that thinks, damn, this is just so unfair.

Lisa: Yeah. It goes along with everything else on that back burner. It is terribly unfair and if I sit and think about it, I'll get crazy because it's so unfair, it's so not right.

Chris: And for yourself?

Lisa: I have a real hard time just figuring out what I want to do with myself. Right now, I don't think I'll live more than two years. I hate to say that and my family would just fall over if they heard me say that, but I don't think that I will. I mean I saw Alex just—and I got the same virus, the same counts shooting down quickly. I've gone a year since my count went way down, but it will pop out just like Alex.

Chris: What do you want HIV+ moms and extended families to know, not so much in the educational sense, but in a spiritual or emotional sense?

Lisa: There's the obvious things. I mean I can't tell you, there were plenty of men who would have slept with me in a minute and even after Alex died, people still didn't put two and two together that I was HIV positive! They were trying to fix me up with guys. So there are some obvious things, I mean obviously condom use. But the best thing is, I haven't had many bad experiences around this with people. It's like cancer, so stop it, stop not treating HIV people right.

Chris: What about Alex's father and when you go back and think about Alex's father and having been infected by him?

Lisa: I have had dreams that I would murder him with a knife. In some ways, I think he has major defense mechanisms too; I don't think he's in touch with what's going on. I don't think he's told anyone. He doesn't even know Alex has died. I think in some ways, his knowing he's not here and knowing what he did, has to be enough. I know it would be for me. But, in some ways, I think he's not in touch with that, so I'd like to give him a little more to think about. I believe in karma and that people get what's coming to them.

Chris: But your family has stood by you?

Lisa: Yes, everything they could do. I have extended family that just says, we're thinking about you. It's the ones who say, we don't want you coming close to our children, not that there are many, but there are some. I really lucked out in the family department.

Chris: And wasn't there a special song at Alex's funeral?

Lisa: At the church they sang "Amazing Grace," but at the burial they sang "I'll Fly Away." The gals at the hospital said they've been to a lot of funerals, but this was the best one.

Chris: And your father played?

Lisa: Yes, my father, and his brothers. That just blew everyone over the edge. Now I have to pick out a headstone. I wish I was Jewish and I could wait for a year. I gave him a bath after he died. I didn't know until later that was a Jewish thing to do.

Chris: Well I really appreciate you going through all this. I know it's a journey once again.

Lisa: It's healing. Sometimes your friends are afraid to talk to you about it.

Chris: Yes, I think sometimes people think you want to forget, when talking about Alex is probably pleasurable.

Lisa: Oh yes, I brought some pictures. I've thought of putting a book together.

Camps for HIV Affected Children

Birch Summer Project, New York
  (718) 528-5754
Camp Heartland, Wisconsin
  (800) 724-4673
Camp Sunrise, Ohio (614) 297-8974
Double H Hole in the Woods Ranch,
  New York (518) 696-5676
Sunburst National AIDS Project,
  California (707) 769-0169

Note

1. The Families' and Childrens' AIDS Network (FCAN) has information packets on AIDS in Families, Women and Children and Children and AIDS which includes an overview of the disease process and psychosocial issues. FCAN is listed in the Resources.

10

"Love and Prayers, Mom": Linda B

I'm a small town girl from northwestern Ohio. Married at 18, we had two daughters who are now 23 and 21. My first husband and I divorced after nine years. I remarried in 1975, and my husband left me after eleven years. I felt worthless when he left me. I started a relationship with B on my 39th birthday. He was 29. We married in 1988. He died of AIDS in 1990. A few days later, I found out that I was HIV+. I composed this letter in 1990 when I had not yet told my oldest daughter. In 1991, I told her. My hope is that when I die and someone asks my daughters what I died of, they can say, my mother had AIDS and not feel ashamed.

Dear _____,

I need you to help me fight a battle that none of us are ever prepared for. I am fighting for my life. I've waited to tell you this because I wanted you to have a clear mind and calm life as you finished your graduate degree. I am so proud of you.

It's time for you to help your sister with some emotional support. She has been bearing a burden for a long time. I must also ask that you tell not any other soul in the family nor anyone who might know us. I and only I will be the judge as to who knows and when they know.

In April, B died of PCP—a form of pneumonia associated with AIDS. A week after his death, I tested HIV positive. I may or may not become sick with the virus.

I am so sorry that you must deal with this. But, please, hear me out before you panic. First of all, you need to realize that you cannot get this virus from just being around me. You can hug me and give me a kiss. You don't get this virus from casual contact, only by sexual contact and/or the transfer of body fluids, period.

Yes, honey, women can get AIDS. While there is not a whole lot known about what the virus does to women, there are ongoing studies and trials. I have volunteered to be part of those studies.

While I have been diagnosed as HIV positive, I am what they call asymptomatic. I do not have AIDS. I have been exposed to the virus. I am considered healthy, just like you. I may never get AIDS.

I am asking that you not curse the dead. I don't know if B knew he had AIDS. I do know that he was bisexual and that his lifestyle of using drugs contributed to his death. His immune system was in shambles. I'm sure it can be said that he did not practice safe sex. Neither did I for that matter. After all, I loved him so much. I'm like many, many other people. I figured it could never happen to me.

I do have an outlet to deal with this virus. I belong to a group of women who have tested HIV positive. I count on this group as a means of dealing with the virus now and in the days to come. They understand. I count on them for the love and support that is not out there in a world of unfounded hate and prejudice. I am counting on your love and support, too.

My first reaction to the diagnosis was disbelief and anger. I remember feeling like a leper. I wondered what kind of screwed up life this was going to be. I wondered if I had made a mistake in getting the test, but I believe it's better to know so we can fight to stay healthy.

How is my life now? I have a hard time with loneliness. I sometimes wonder if I'll die of a broken heart before I succumb to the virus. Because even if I were ready for some kind of relationship, I would have to tell about the virus. With that, I may be setting myself up for the hurt of rejection.

Of course I'm mad as hell! And some days I'm scared to death. I'm not afraid of death. I'm afraid of the end. It's a hideous way to die.

I must stress that I won't beat myself for being in this position. I didn't do anything wrong to get this. I don't think that God is punishing me. I'm not a lesbian as some people think. I'm not a slut. I am not an IV drug user. Simply stated, I am only guilty of being human and falling in love with someone who unknowingly was sick or got sick. And then he died, leaving me alone.

I've always been the one to help others. Now, I am asking others to help me and all those who have this virus. The isolation hurts most of all. I don't like not being able to talk to just anyone about the virus. Sometimes I hate my body. It is devouring my soul.

Some have no compassion at all. They don't realize that they, too, could come face to face with this virus one day. In 1988, I heard it said that by the year 1990, each and every one of us will have been touched by AIDS. Well, it's 1990, welcome to the real world.

Don't give up on me. I have a lot of fight in me. I am at this time, very optimistic. I believe in God and a positive attitude. I need your support and understanding. I want to spend time with you, doing all the things we always do. I am not an invalid. I am well. I am very much alive. I need lots of hugs. So let's get started.

Love and prayers,
Mom

11

"I'm a Sexy Momma"

Chris: What is the worst part for you now?

Linda B: Being alone.

Patti: Does being alone mean particularly a lover? A romance?

Linda B: No not necessarily. I'm not a part of a pair anymore. At first, I went out with a couple of guys and they say, hey you want to have a drink and I would say, well I don't know; I've got AIDS. Then I learned how to be a little gentler about it. If they call you, you're busy, you're out, because you don't want to tell them, you don't want to go through that, so you don't let it progress any further. You have a good time, go out and then say, see you later. You develop a big wall, a wall that could beat that one in China. There's a guy at work I'd really like to get close to. He's right there, you know, and he flat out asked me one day, he says are you really that cold? You know you don't want to say, well now, if I told you the whole story . . .

Chris: We never discussed sex in my home. When I finally started to date, my mother said, "You know what to do and what not to do, right?" Of course I said "yes," glad to move us off that topic. Attitudes toward sex were different then: girls in my high school were either "good," or "bad," or at least this was the outward perception. Boys, of course, were "just boys." There was no forum in my home or my school for sex education, or even more importantly, discussion of

all the issues and decisions raised by young sexuality.

While I was too early for the era of sex education, I was still very fortunate. I had educated, healthy, and married parents who were prepared to take care of me. They taught me self-respect and to work hard for reachable goals. What I lacked in sexual preparation, I made up for in part with self-esteem and optimism for my future. These characteristics helped me make some good decisions

Lori: I think sometimes you have to take a chance though, get to know him and then decide if it can go anywhere.

Rosemary: You all know how I felt about ___; I'm so glad he's gone. I didn't know that he was a pressure, because I always had to say, no, no, no, we can't do it the regular way, we've got to do it the safe way. I got tired of trying to duck it, to keep from confronting this. On my nights off, I would wait until he went to sleep before I'd creep into bed. This is like having this change, like someone choking you, and now it's like, it's a relief like having this open shirt, that's how I feel inside. It was a stressful thing.

Carol X: When I found out, relationships with men got real weird. The hardest is when they say they can handle it and then they get really crazy with it no matter how much information you give them. I'm longing for someone who will love me wholeheartedly and unconditionally. As far as the relationship I was in with ___, when I found out I had to tell him and of course he went through his crazy period, but I was willing to accept him going crazy because I thought that was the only thing that I was going to get because now I got the virus. He knows and nobody else is gonna want me so I got to accept this shit. Until you get beyond that and start loving yourself for you and say, hell, I can be this miserable by myself. Being with him and him not wanting to touch me anymore, and just wanting a hug, because he

❀   ❀   ❀   ❀   ❀   ❀   ❀

about sex and relationships, along with the bad decisions I made as well.

I was not only fortunate, but lucky. I just missed the age of AIDS with regard to my own sexual behavior. I "settled down" in the late 70's, just as the AIDS virus was silently moving into the United States. I have often reflected that some of my 70's choices in the 1990's could have resulted in HIV infection. And now an aunt to a teenage girl, I want to discuss sexuality with her, but it is embarrassing. I dutifully teach my daughter that she has a vagina, like it is any other body part. Maybe I can do better with her. I joke that when she is a teen, I'll give her a choice between a convent and military school. This is my way of saying that I am simply scared of what lies ahead for her and my capability to prepare her for it. I think AIDS will be controlled by the

time of her adolescence, but there will still be danger, whether it is to her body or her soul.

Patti: One of the ways AIDS has changed my sexual attitudes was made clear when I first heard Madonna's song "Spanky Spanky" in 1990. Upon hearing my feminist rant of "why would she be endorsing such male power trips," some lesbian friends pointed out that Madonna has learned from gay men how AIDS revalues sexual behavior. Now instead of "normal" and "perverted," sexual acts were being divided into "fluid exchanges" and "no fluid exchanges." Patton (1994) notes that, with shifting norms of sexual practice around HIV prevention, the greater visibility of diverse gay practices may make it more possible for heterosexuals to imagine non-penetrative sexual pleasures. This is but one ex-

was still afraid and not there with me. Girl, we had the oddest mechanical sex you ever want to have and then jump up and run to the shower. I just remember sitting there and crying, I didn't want him to touch me, but I did need something, thinking you asshole, I can't continue to put myself through this. If this is the way it has to be, maybe I'm better off without it. It just totally changed, and that scared me, but then I hadn't calculated all the way out that maybe another man would be different, that it didn't have to be like this and it's OK to cut him off. I wanted a relationship badly enough that I was willing to face rejection on a daily basis. As far as having the virus, you come to know that a bad relationship is no good.

Linda B: I'm more alone now than I've probably ever been in my whole life. Some of it is self inflicted; a lot of it is the fear of being rejected. I'm better off being by myself alone and being sad, rejection is the hardest thing a person has to go through. But there's other days when I see some of these other people going through relationships that are absolute stinkeroos, I think, god I'm glad I don't have to put up with that.

Lori: I think it is possible to have relationships. When you're ready, you take a chance on somebody.

Linda B: I've lost a lot of confidence in myself. I don't feel guilty or ashamed, I haven't lost any self esteem. I think it's different in that you have to make

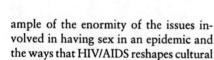

ample of the enormity of the issues involved in having sex in an epidemic and the ways that HIV/AIDS reshapes cultural practices.

"Let's Put an End to It": Iris

When Iris read her words from the original interview, she at first wanted to pull out of the book because she felt she had changed so much due to going through drug and alcohol abuse treatment. Patti went to see her in June of 1995, showed her the above, and, as they talked, it struck both of them that having Iris's words about the changes she had gone through at the bottom of the page might help readers understand how, for some women, AIDS can be used to make changes in a life. What follows, then, is what Iris said as she and Patti read through her words from the original in-

terview with her support group almost three years ago.

Iris: Today I'm real healthy and sober and proud of it. When I talked to you before, I was in so much denial. Alcohol and drugs blur your mind; they make HIV so hard to deal with. I've gone through so much with my girls and we're so bonded now. Until 18 months ago, I often wanted to give up, but today I would never think of taking my life. If I do start getting sick with the virus, I want to go out laughing and smiling. I mean we get sad, but we have so much laughter in our lives I would never think about taking a handful of pills. I want to go to heaven; I'm going to heaven; that's my reward for all this!

I've been sober 18 months; my 12-step program is foremost now. Now that I'm sober, the kids are like my little ducks. If

choices, you have to pick people a lot more closely. I don't put up with BS anymore. Nobody's got problems like we have and sometimes you just feel like I don't want to deal with your bullshit. What I have to complain about is way more important.

Tommie: What makes me sad also is I've been in a relationship since my diagnosis, but now I'm out of that and now that I'm back in the dating world, it's real sad. One guy said "you're walking around like a loaded shotgun; you have something that will kill people," and I said, no, what I have will kill me; I have it, not you.

Iris: And people have this attitude of so what, and you got these macho men who refuse to wear a condom.

Tommie: I think they should apply them at birth.

Iris: I wanted to say something about the men and the condom thing. Since I've found out, I've been real open and honest with men in the bars and I've told them I am HIV+. The first reaction is "you don't look like it." Then I go on to say, how am I supposed to look? Their reaction is, well I still want to fuck ya, but I don't want to wear a rubber.

Melody: That's because they think down there sometimes, instead of up here. I had a man who told me that if I was HIV+ I'd have brown spots on my boobs.

Tommie: I am dating a younger man. I am a recovering alcoholic too but I still frequent the bars and this gentleman recognized my motorcycle. Next

⁂   ⁂   ⁂   ⁂   ⁂   ⁂   ⁂

I'm healthy, they're healthy. They're dealing with my past alcoholism and my AIDS. Until they're 18, my main concern is getting my girls through school and into a career. It's not that I'm not willing to love. I think I've grown so much. I like myself today.

It's so scary to have sex with someone and not tell them about your HIV status. It's real scary; you're taking such a risk. So today, I'm just so cautious. A relationship should be based on togetherness, not just sex.

Guys seem to think, it's my body, I'll take the chance, it won't be your fault if I turn out positive. Yeah, OK, but if you do get it, how do you think that will make me feel? You're the one choosing not to use a condom, you're the one who will end up with the virus, you say you'll deal with it, it'll be your fault. But today I just want to be responsible. I like myself and I have pretty high standards and morals that I'm not going to change for anyone.

As a woman first finding out about HIV you think, oh no, no more sex life. As time evolves it's like sex is just an afterthought of the intimacy and being able to share with someone. Let people know you're not going to lower your standards as far as condoms go. You've got to love yourself. Where I'm with all of this today is, I just want to stop the spread of the disease. Let's put an end to it. I have two beautiful daughters growing up; I want to slow down the progression of the disease. If I pass it on to one more per-

thing we know we were there by ourselves and he said was that you in that article and I said yes it was. He just looked over at me and he said OK, and I said OK? And so all the coolness went right out of my body and I've got another date with him. It's something when you are first diagnosed that you think you will never do again.

Patti: How is dating different?

Tommie: I was always one to wait to have sex anyway, now it is longer.

Melody: I am in one hell of a relationship and it's been a year. I am taking a risk that I never would have taken in the past, especially with a man. I never had that much trust, intimacy with a man to turn my life kinda over

> The development of female controlled barrier methods and topical creams is key for preventing HIV infection in women. A gel or cream protection for women is being worked on that could be vaginally inserted before sexual intercourse to kill the HIV virus. Such "vaginal microbicides" are especially important in terms of giving women more control to protect themselves, although there are worries that irritating vaginal tissues puts the user even more at risk due to creating opportunities for the virus to enter the bloodstream. There is also the female condom. Call 800-274-6601 for a free sample.

son, that person maybe passes it on to one more person. If I can do my little part by stopping it, it's my little minute part and it's better than nothing.

My girls and I, we're so close now that it's hard to put into words. We're each other's rock. I think the girls will grow up stronger because of all the roads we've had to trudge. Maybe I'm prejudiced because they're my daughters, but I perceive a couple of wonderful little women. The world's going to be lucky to have them because they're just really neat kids; they're honest and outgoing. The youngest loves volunteering here at the AIDS drop-in center. They're non-judgmental kids; there's no one they look down their noses at. Everything I do is like a step in teaching them and helping them along in their lives.

Someday the virus might get me. But we're getting them through school and if I'm not so well or strong down the road, the oldest can help with the youngest. I don't want to put it all on her, but we talk about how I'll need their help down the road. The youngest hasn't told her friends, but the oldest has. Her friends think she has a cool mom. God had a plan for me and it wasn't killing myself. I just want to live. Deep down in my core soul, I just want to be happy with my kids. God has carried us so far; he had us all in his arms. You asked me what gave me the courage, but I don't think I made the decision to get my life back. It got made for me by the Almighty. For anyone who's newly diagnosed, don't give up and keep on following any dreams that you have. 🦠

and have a partnership like we have. When I first got diagnosed in 89 I ended up in a relationship with a man, he had a need to fix people. I was at a point because of my diagnosis that I was grasping for people and wondering if I would be loved again. But he wore surgical gloves when we had sex, I mean if we had had a body condom he would have wore it and he'd go wash immediately. The man I have now, we have been through the different phrases: do we practice safe sex or don't we? Can we live with the thought that I might be infecting him with such a thing that could kill him? But he is in a place in his own spirituality, in his own way of thinking, that everything has a reason and if that be so and I get it OK. He's not frightened a bit. He's been through a lot himself; his wife committed suicide while he was in the other room so he's been challenged with death to begin with. So, I am grateful.

Tommie: Can I say one thing about the negative things that happen? I just got out of a year and half relationship. He's still negative, but since I have left him he has given me more grief. He went around for two years telling people, "She tried to give me AIDS." He did this to me in a big public bicker scene and embarrassed me to death. I had to press domestic violence charges against him and he humiliated me in court with it, like here's a woman with HIV,

The standard approach to safer sex: presume all partners are infected; use a latex barrier with each sex act; know which are the riskiest behaviors (unprotected anal intercourse, followed by unprotected vaginal intercourse); use a water based lubricant. Fifteen years into the epidemic, the limits of such an approach are evident in present figures which estimate that one third of urban gay men in the United States will sero-convert in their lifetimes. The original safer sex guidelines were devised on the assumption that the cure was just around the corner. "Second wave safer sex" argues that unfailing condom use as a standard denies the complexities of human behavior. New models of risk management and a focus on staying uninfected, especially among gay men, are developments in some tension with not writing off the needs of the infected. Sustaining safer sex practices over a lifetime includes negotiated safety, risk reduction versus risk elimination, experimentation on differentiating the safer sex message, including greater sensitivity to the needs of people of color, building self esteem, and the concept of "good enough" AIDS prevention. For example, controversy around the dangers of unprotected oral sex is addressed by one gay activist: "Oral sex can transmit HIV, but the risk is comparable to everyday, ordinary risk in modern life, like driving a well-maintained car at moderate speeds on the superhighway with a lap belt and shoulder belt on. Not to acknowledge the low risk is to deny the value of sex between men. . . if erring conservatively means giving instructions that we know will not be followed, is that the best approach to education?" (*The New York Times Magazine*, September 15, 1996)

why would I want to hurt her? Why would I get blood over me? It was like he took everything good and turned it to all bad. So there are things, it was an experience for me to learn. I need to watch for those people, they are out there.

Sarah: I went out with a guy and he's HIV+ also. I got it from him; we weren't living together then. I knew him ten years ago and we were lovers for a brief time and then he moved away. He was in love with other people. I visited him and it was really wonderful. It was a surprise to both of us that we fell in love again and at that point he didn't know that he was HIV+. But his lover had died of it and he had never been tested. So I told him I wanted him tested and then we knew that he had it and we were sorta careful and sorta not. Sometimes we would use rubbers and other times we wouldn't but we always used withdrawal. But I got it anyway and that was a challenge for the relationship. We visited each other for a year and it was in the middle of that year that I got it and before that we decided that we wanted to live together. We had to go through some stuff after that, but it didn't change. I mean I was just certain that I wanted to be with him. I never felt that way in my life and I still feel that way. He is a wonderful person. He's been positive since 1982 and he has a real low T-cell count but he's not sick at all. He moved here. It's a good relationship; I feel real lucky.

Amber: OK, I had a relationship with a guy for four years and we lived together. I thought he gave it to me, but he didn't have it. It has changed our relationship which wasn't very good to start with. We didn't have all that much in common and we had a lot of problems. Having the HIV made me realize that I might not have longer to live, so I thought, I don't want to live like this for the rest of my life and I left him. We still go out and stuff, but I am trying to find out who I am right now.

Sarah: There are ways I have low self esteem.

Chris: Yes, because you had unprotected sex after you knew he was positive,

He took me to summer one winter day
Landed my ass in downtown LA
Yes, he had that virus, that flu
You know the kind you don't live through.
He smoked reefer, loved Budweiser,
Found he shot up too
To top it all off, boy he could screw.
He left me alone to contend with this
Needless to say—Yes, I get pissed!!!
To think I must do another lonely day
I'm sure his spirit's in
downtown LA
I can't sit—boo hoo and cry!
I must stay strong, healthy and spry!
So I can warn all you fools
That this too can happen to you.
Don't let yourself get this flu!
Take care of yourself, spend some money
Check him out good before you call
him honey!

—Linda B, 1-4-95, 3:20 AM

knowing how easy it is for a man to transmit to a woman even though you did practice withdrawal and stuff. Was it like you wanted to get it in a way?
Sarah: No. I wouldn't say I wanted to get it at all, but it was a risk I was willing to take.
Iris: One boyfriend of another woman in the group, he wants to get it. He wants to have it out of empathy so he can be closer to her, walk in her shoes.
Chris: You're saying whatever risk you did take, it wasn't coming from a place of feeling badly about yourself?[1]
Sarah: I'm not sure, it's hard to say. It was a risk I was willing to take because I felt that the relationship was really the right thing for me. I just had a stronger feeling than I've ever had in my life that things would work out, that this was sort of my destiny. I've never felt that way about a relationship. I've never felt so strongly. I didn't want to get it. My sister and mom really

Two of the women in our study who had previously identified as heterosexual found lesbian partners after being diagnosed. The rate of lesbians with HIV is obscured by the earlier mentioned classifying as heterosexual any woman who has had sex with a man since 1978. In the early 1990's, under considerable pressure from clinicians, activists and researchers, the Centers for Disease Control began to investigate transmission in lesbians, a task complicated by the range and diversity of sexualities that do not fit tidy categories of heterosexual, homosexual or bisexual. Patton (1994) writes of how this move is often seen as "a political diversion and waste of researcher's time," attributed to lesbian envy of the attention gay male sexuality has received, all of which leaves lesbians having to guess at what safer sex might mean for them. She goes on to note that lesbians who inject drugs have twice the odds of being HIV infected as lesbians who have sex with men.

The world's first meeting convened by government officials to address woman-to-woman HIV transmission took place on April 20–21, 1995, a result of the tremendous efforts of lesbian and bisexual activists over the past several years. Outcomes of the meeting included a call for more research on woman-to-woman transmission, the development of guidelines for health care providers on how to conduct sexual histories and how to fill out surveillance forms so that lesbians are counted, and the review of CDC guidelines for heterosexist bias (reported in July 1995 *World*).

A 1993 survey of San Franciso women indicated that HIV infection was more than three times higher among lesbian and bisexual women. Ten percent of the sample was current or previous injection drug users, 81 percent had had sex with men (*World* December 1995). A lesbian safer sex video, *Current Flow*, is available from GMHC Videotapes/Publications Distribution, 129 W. 20th St., NY, NY 10011. See, also, "AIDS Videos By, For, and About Women" in *Women, AIDS & Activism* (1990, in Resources). For more on lesbians and HIV, see Hollibaugh, 1995, also in Resources.

talked to me a lot about it when I was with this guy and they were saying, don't do it, just don't be with him, you're gonna end up like him. I said I don't want to end up that way. I don't know if I will or not. I hope I don't, but if I do, I still feel like it's right for me to do this. But then I was real surprised when I got it. It was like, shit. I was very surprised. I was always afraid at different points, but when I went in for the test, I'd done some work on myself and I'd been in therapy for years and years and I am in the field. So I went in with the mind set that everything was OK, and so when I got the test results, and she said boy you're taking this better than anyone I've ever seen. And I said, no, I'm in shock. It's hard for me to believe. I guess because I didn't burst out crying or something.

Danielle: Well, my boyfriend that I have now, I knew about my situation when we were dating, and I thought I just won't let this become anything, you know, there was no way I can tell this guy. And then we starting getting really serious and every day I was stressing out on this, just losing my mind. How am I going to tell him? I was driving my friends crazy. I don't know how I managed to go from my day to day because all I could think about was what a dilemma, I mean what am I going to do, should I just kill myself? How am I going to tell him? This guy is going to put me in jail. And then I put this little charade together and we go down to the health department and I act like I was concerned and like I had just found out. But it was a horrible thing carrying that around with me as long as I did.

Chris: Did you ever tell him about the charade?

Danielle: No because if he knew that I withheld information like that I think that he would be pretty devastated, so as far as he knows, I just found

Women are more vulnerable than men to heterosexually transmitted HIV infection, because women involved in heterosexual intercourse are generally on the receiving (receptive) end. Reception involves at least minimal tissue trauma and this is especially true when force is used during sex or when sex damages vaginal or anal tissues. Oral contraceptive use, the use of intrauterine devices, and vaginal or other reproductive tract infections increase women's susceptibility to HIV, as do the physiological changes that accompany menstruation. Teen-aged girls are particularly vulnerable because their vaginal linings are not as thick as those of mature women and they often have sex with older men who have a greater chance of carrying the virus (Bezemer, 1992).

The larger pool of hemophiliacs, bisexuals and IV drug users also increases women's risk of heterosexual transmission, with the latter two especially pertinent for black women. Black men, for example, are "dramatically over represented" among bisexuals in the US, representing 28 percent (Sobo, 1995, p. 17).

out last summer. Then he did the natural thing, to go get tested and he wasn't positive and then, I don't know, he is just so cool, he is so open. I am not trying to label or pass judgment, but it seems that people who are pretty educated tend to handle the information a little bit better. They are not like, oh my GOD. And he was just really cool about it, very supportive and he said, I love you and I will be with you. Now the question is marriage, we've been together for two and half years. Will I be here long enough for the marriage? I have zero T cells. I always feel like, God, I am probably going to die this year. I am very afraid of that, but at the same time—

Alisha: After my divorce was over, I tried dating different guys. There was one guy I dated for awhile, and when I told him I was HIV+ he said it didn't matter. We dated for about six months and he raped me. He was drunk at the time. So I decided to discontinue the relationship. He apologized and said he would never do it again. I said, one time, that is enough. And that was the end of that. I realized that I was a very strong person at that time. I didn't just go back with him. He cried and begged and begged me, but I've read about women being abused and I didn't want to be like that so I decided that I was going to stand up for myself. As time went on my friend ___, who is a very very good friend of mine, we started developing a very close relationship and because she gave me so much support, we became lovers. I felt so good as things went along. I realized my life has changed a great deal. And she says that the HIV doesn't bother her and she is HIV negative at this time. And that is not an issue for her. And I feel like it is not an issue for me neither as long as we are able to give each other love and support. We are great company; we try to take advantage of the time we have together. As I look at my life that I have had, with her I feel like I finally have someone to talk with about sex, about a wide variety of things. And I really enjoy my life at this point. She has taught me many new things that have made me realize who I am. I was afraid to confront things, but she has taught me to respect myself. She taught me so much about happiness. We share everything.

Chris: Anything else that anyone wants to add? It doesn't have to be connected to anything, just something you'd like us to know.

Iris: But with the sexuality part and HIV, I still feel sexy; I'm a sexy momma.

Amber: I read an article and I got so upset because it says that HIV is equally transmittable. Women are much more at risk of getting it from men. But at the same time we don't want these guys out there thinking that they ain't gonna get nothing because they might have it and be giving it to everybody. They don't give a damn. I want to say something, this is brutally honest, OK. When I walked into the door, the first meeting and stuff, I thought, I'm not like these girls, I'm different. And I talked around to people, well I am going to a weekend at a convent with a bunch of hookers, boy it's gonna be fun. And I just hate to, damn it ever since the beginning of time, women have been at the mercy of men and being called disease spreaders and everything and they always have the articles in the paper about hookers giving it to everybody. Well, if we tell these men that they don't have nothing to worry about, they will refuse to wear a condom and we are all going to be at risk, so we have to go ahead and take the flack from men.

Tommie: Right, we all have to be hookers.

Melody: This is a disease that's not getting the attention that it deserves and all these women out here are at the mercy of men, like we've always been.

Tommie: Now it's deadly.

Note

1. AIDS-risk denial in the hardest hit population of poor, urban black and Latina women is explored in *Choosing Unsafe Sex*, by E.J. Sobo, 1995, in Resources. This book argues that AIDS prevention education must be culturally appropriate, gender sensitive and encourage risk personalization if it is to effect behavioral changes. A more structural analysis is offered in *Women, Poverty, and AIDS: Sex, Drugs, and Structural Violence*, edited by Paul Farmer et al. (Common Courage Press, 1996).

As Patton (1994) argues, heterosexuality has always been dangerous for women, given the numbers on rape, domestic violence, and sexually transmitted diseases. But the new danger of AIDS raises the issue of the responsibility of culturally dominant males in the face of their willful refusal to wear condoms, as safer sex educational efforts shift from risk groups to risk behaviors. Research from the International Center for Research on Women, using participatory research designs to educate both males and females, especially recommends educating women in condom use, de stigmatizing condoms and weakening their association with illicit sex, and supporting biomedical research aimed at producing a technology that can be used independently by women to prevent HIV transmission in the face of non-consensual sex and patterns of gender power dynamics. Research summaries are available through ICRW, Publications Department, 1717 Massachusetts Avenue, NW, Suite 302, Washington, DC 20036.

INTERTEXT 2

The Angel of History: AIDS as a Global Crisis

Every two steps Death danced him backward, [he] took one forward. Death was the better dancer, and who could tell when our once-around-the-floor was next, when the terrible angel might extend a raven wing and say, "Shall we?" And then I was angry at myself for thinking that, for elevating this thing with a metaphor. . . . Oh, for a guardian angel, oh for the palm of its hand.

—Allen Barnett[1]

Thus . . . there is an infinite amount of hope, but not for us.

—Walter Benjamin to Gershom Scholem, 1938[2]

Why the upsurge of interest in angels in late twentieth century American culture, especially in writing and thinking about AIDS? While a respect for the spiritual in a time of plague and danger is by no means new, some possibilities quite contrary to the more common Hallmark angels are suggested by Walter Benjamin's Angel of History. Based on twenty years of contemplating Paul Klee's small watercolor, entitled *Angelus Novus*, Benjamin's Angel of History marked his experience of a Europe that had erupted into the war that would cause him to take his own life in 1940, fleeing from the Nazis.[3] In his "Theses on the Philosophy of History" (1940), Benjamin writes of the Angel of History:

A Klee painting "Angelus Novus" shows an angel looking as though to move away from something he is fixedly contemplating. His eyes are staring, his mouth is open, his wings are spread. This is how one pictures the angel of history. His face is turned toward the past. Where we perceive a chain of events, he sees one single catastrophe which keeps piling wreckage upon wreckage and hurls it in front of his feet. The angel would like to stay, awaken the dead, and make whole what has been smashed. But a storm is blowing from Para-

113

dise; it has got caught in his wings with such violence that the angel can no longer close them. This storm irresistibly propels him into the future to which his back is turned, while the pile of debris before him grows skyward. This storm is what we call progress.

No longer singing, melancholy if not desperate given the debris of history, the Angel of History is both witness and guide to the wreckage of human history where the millennium has come too soon and the air seems thick with danger. Also called New Angel, the angel is a guide into fresh paths of thought that do justice to the demands of the present by using the ruins of the past to create moments when the future announces itself. This is about using the past to make strange our familiar habits of mind as we move into and through the shocks of our time in a way that yields some promise of a space in which a different history can become possible.

History is full of scandal and unacceptable worlds, a situation Benjamin terms history as "a permanent emergency." In this emergency of AIDS, where is hope? How are we to think about the future? Will the disease become a manageable chronic condition? What relations is it structuring across multiple differences and cultural practices, locally and globally?

AIDS first received attention in the United States in what was termed a "gay plague" in the early 1980's. More recently, "at risk" categories have been changed from types of people to types of behavior, particularly unprotected anal and vaginal sex and sharing needles. In spite of earlier hopes, no cure or vaccine seems imminent and future global predictions of illness and death underscore how race and class and sexual politics are acted out in the trajectory of the plague. An epidemic among sex workers in Bangkok, the decimation of African villages and gay male communities in the United States, the steady increases among heterosexuals in the United States largely via IV drug users, particularly hard-hitting for people of color, the scourge of hemophiliacs world-wide: across our differences, we face a disease that defies our belief in the endless capacities of modern science to save us. Prevention effectiveness has become central, given the capacity of the virus to mutate, making treatment difficult.

But while education was successful among gay men

In the United States, fifty percent of the twenty thousand people with bleeding disorders were exposed to HIV+ contaminated blood products prior to the development of the HIV blood test in 1985. See Patton, 1994. For women in families with hemophilia, see Greenblat, 1995. The first ever Women with Bleeding Disorders Conference was held in Dallas in August of 1994, attended by twenty-five women, some HIV+, some not (*World* October 1994). National Hemophilia Foundation: 800-42-HANDI.

> The total number of AIDS cases among US women increased from 15,495 in 1990 to 27,485 in 1992 to 78,654 in 1996, with Hispanic (22 percent) and African-American (53 percent) women making up 75 percent of AIDS cases. And globally, the World Health Organization estimates that by the year 2000, up to forty million people worldwide will have been infected with HIV, with more than 70 percent of HIV infections occurring through heterosexual transmission. More than half of newly infected adults worldwide will be women. Of the twenty-two million affected by HIV worldwide, over 60 percent are African (*World* fact sheet on women and AIDS in the US).
>
> In the US, while there is some fluctuation in cases reported annually, the estimated incidence has increased by 5 percent overall, with the largest increases among heterosexual men and women who acquired HIV through injection drug use or through heterosexual contact with injection drug users, with minorities assuming an increasingly large percentage of this increase (June 1996 *HIV/AIDS Surveillance Report*).

and their reduction in cases in the late 1980's, the number of cases among young gay men is on the rise again. In what is called the "second wave" of AIDS, minorities and women are at particular risk. Concepts of blame and otherness stymie effective AIDS education. To shift from blaming individuals requires taking into account the national and international order that has contributed to the transmission and spread of the pandemic.

In the newest phase of the global AIDS epidemic which has killed three million worldwide since the late 1970's, South and Southeast Asia will soon be the epicenter. In Thailand, for example, an estimated four million people will be infected by the year 2000. This is due largely to Thailand becoming the red-light district to much of the world. In a country of 56 million, relief agencies estimate that there are two million prostitutes, up to 800,000 of them children. The Thai sex industry, expanded to serve US air bases and soldiers on leave from the Vietnam War, now draws male tourists from all over the world, although 80 percent of the customers are Thai men. Thousands of girls are kidnapped each year across Burma, Laos, Vietnam and China to serve the sex industry. More than 40,000 are believed to have been lured from Burma alone. Relief agencies estimate that 40 percent of Thai prostitutes are HIV positive, many of them girls who customers believe are less likely than more sexually experienced women to carry the virus. With the epidemic reaching well into the middle classes, undermining Thailand's regional economic position, the government has teamed with the World Health Organization to develop AIDS awareness programs, particularly through human resource operations systems in business. But sex tourism is a growing problem in the Philippines, Brazil, the Dominican Republic, eastern Europe and, most recently, Cuba. With the onset of AIDS, the global abuse of women is receiving new attention, but many relief workers are skeptical of the will of governments to fight the sex industry which brings wealth to developing countries.[4]

India now has more HIV carriers than any other nation; currently .02 percent of India's population has HIV or AIDS. By 2000, the World Health Organization predicts one million will have AIDS and five million will be HIV positive. If trends continue, by 2010, thirty million will have HIV, about twice today's worldwide total. More people will contract HIV in South and Southeast Asia than even Africa where in the worst-hit countries, almost twenty percent of adults are infected, primarily through heterosexual contact, creating millions of orphans and overwhelming government health facilities and social services. And since it takes about ten years for HIV to turn into AIDS, the effects of the disease are still largely hidden, making it difficult for politicians to justify large scale spending when other killer diseases such as malaria, typhoid and hepatitis are more visibly rampant.[5]

In the United States, talk about "the democratization of AIDS" and "the changing face of AIDS" attempts to make AIDS the concern of Middle America. Opinions differ as to which populations are at risk and some fear a backlash. One doctor say, "I fear the reason is we live in a racist society where the health problems of whites are considered to be more important. So we have to package this disease as a threat to the white middle class to get funding for it, to get attention, to get support." The message of middle-class risk flies in the face of those most afflicted—homosexual men and needle drug users, with 51 percent of cumulative cases reported being the former, 25 percent the latter, and 7 percent men who have sex with men and inject drugs. Eight percent were heterosexually transmitted cases (CDC *Surveillance Report*, June 1996).

A 1994 study by a conservative group, the National Academy of Science takes issue with how widespread the epidemic will become. The disease will have only a limited impact on much of the United States, they argue, because it is concentrated in "socially marginalized" groups. "Instead of spreading out to the broad American population, as once feared, HIV is concentrating in pools of persons who are also caught in the synergism of plagues: poverty, poor health and lack of health care, inadequate education, joblessness, hopelessness and social disintegration." This while by 1996, for people aged 25–44, AIDS was the leading cause of death for men and the third leading cause among women, with the largest increase in AIDS cases among teenagers and young adults, most of that from heterosexual transmission, a transmission rate that increased from 1992–1993 by 130 percent.[6]

Some hope on the African front is news from Uganda that the disease has slowed down in its spread among young adults in the last five years. With an infection rate as high as thirty percent in some villages, the epidemic may have peaked. With millions of dollars spent on prevention programs in this country which was the first to explode with what was called the "slim disease," there appears to be a sea change in rituals of love and sex as young people try to avoid the disease. Have they, like gay men, been scared into abstinence, monogamy or condom use after seeing so many die? In a country where almost 200,000 die of AIDS yearly, confidential tests are widely available and courtship rituals increasingly include testing prior to sexual intimacy. Radio, television and billboards are saturated with messages about AIDS aimed at young people, as well as education programs at schools and churches (*New York Times*, April 7, 1996).

How are we to think our way into such a global situation? As both witness and guide, the Angel of History is about learning to find our way into a future that is always in the making, bereft of the fictions of certain knowledge that supported past generations as they wrestled with the scandals of their own historical time. In Bill Haver's book on our sense of history in the time of AIDS, he argues that serious engagement with the questions of AIDS leads to a "shock" of recognition that we will not be saved by any of the familiar ways of making sense of crisis: god, heroic science, the dialectic of history, education.[7] Our task, Haver argues, is to use AIDS to think what it is impossible to think, by refusing the consolations and easy evasions of habituated knowing in order to think the ruins of our ways of making sense as the condition of possibility for movement toward a different kind of future. It is the capacity of AIDS to shock us into a different relation with the future that is of interest here. As Haver notes, in our present historical moment of struggle where we all live and die "in AIDS," as earlier generations lived and died "in religion," regardless of personal belief, we have to live "somehow." What help can do us any good?

In Benjamin's secular reinterpretation of Jewish theory of apocalypse and messianic future, hope is turned backward via catastrophic upheaval toward a future state which has never existed. Here, the only power in which hope still resides is in a leap into the past through which the present becomes filled with now-time, standing still, shocked into connecting discontinuous realms, releasing an otherwise unavailable meaning, creating a constellation of meaning between past and present historical events, a defiant affirmation that expands the meaning of events. Outside traditional theological or secular victory, the Angel of History moves toward some way of being that is both and neither secular and holy, irony and hope, out of the ruins of the secular which distresses the angel who has been salvaged from the ruins of the sacred. Encompassing horror, blessing, melancholy, and hope, the angel's tidings are unclear and its power is limited as the angel connects the fragments in its field of vision, caught between catastrophe and hope, past and future, in a now-time pregnant with tensions.

In sum, the Angel of History is about interrupting how we come to think about the global crisis of AIDS, a crisis that troubles ideas about the progress of human history, belief in science and/or divine intercession, the weight of social inequities in the shaping of the crisis, and the onus on human governments, social organizations and individuals to wake up in a time that is both too early and too late.

Notes

1. Allen Barnett (1990). *The Body and Its Dangers and Other Stories*. New York: St. Martin's Press.

2. Letter to Gershom Scholem, June 12, 1938. *The Correspondence of Walter Benjamin 1910–1940*, edited by Gershom Scholem and Theodor Adorno, trans. by M. Jacobson and E. Jacobson. Chicago: University of Chicago Press, 1994.

3. Gershom Scholem (1988, originally 1972). Walter Benjamin and His Angel. In *On Walter Benjamin: Critical Essays and Recollections*, edited by Gary Smith. Cambridge MA: MIT Press, 51–89.

4. *Columbus Dispatch*, April 11, 1993 and *The Australian*, December 3, 1993.

5. *Columbus Dispatch*, August 20, 1995.

6. Figures from the Centers for Disease Control and Prevention, reported in the *Los Angeles Times*, June 16, 1995.

7. Bill Haver (1996). *The Body of This Death: Historicity and Sociality in the Time of AIDS*. Stanford University Press.

Paul Klee, *Angelus Novus*, 1920, watercolor on transferred drawing. Used by permission of The Israel Museum, Jerusalem.

Making Meaning

12

"I Don't Know How to File It Away That This Has Happened to Us"

Chris: How do you make sense of your experience with HIV?

Louisa: Well, I think of it in two different ways. I think of it negative and like wanting to give up. Then I think of it spiritually. I say to myself the Lord has a purpose, the Lord's gonna rescue me from all this pain.

Lori: I was always a very religious person, but I've kind of turned against religion with this. **I don't know how to file it away that this has happened to us.** I know a lot of people who are a lot more deserving of having this illness than any of us in the room, if there really is justice up there in the sky. I'm not trying to question what God is doing. I'm Jewish and I went for my annual holiday last weekend and I sat there in temple and I was saying the words about God makes the decision about who's going to live and who's going to die. And I thought, "How did I end up on this side of the fence?" What did any of the people in the Holocaust really do? It's making me really question why, why me, why you, why any of us?

Patti: What shapes our lives, fate, accident?

CR: I think about if I had fallen down and broken my leg, I would have had to go to the hospital, I think of all kinds of things that could have happened, I could have grown a wart on my nose, but it was to be. It might sound crazy, but I've grown stronger since I have the virus. Before I would let little things upset me, but now I think I have a purpose here. I enjoy people and relationships that don't have to revolve around sex or looks or money—the close circle of people who know about me having AIDS, I feel good about that.

Chris: So how do you make sense of HIV in your life?

CR: After I joined this support group a reporter asked me how did I feel being Afro-American and having the virus. And it's just another stumbling block, that's what I told her. I know the disease can progress and you can die. But I've struggled being a black woman and a single parent and I'm scared of the virus and I'm scared of what it's doing to my body, but it's like I've always been struggling and I've always been afraid whether it was to pay the rent or buy food or whatever. So it's not like I've been on some island and nothing bad ever happened to me. It's like, I was thinking, I probably was born to be prepared for whatever—for racial discrimination, lack of education, the virus, whatever.

Chris: Are you saying that this fits the script that you've been living all along—it's not really a big surprise?

CR: It's a surprise when you sit and someone says your test is positive, you do have the AIDS virus. And at that time you don't know that you can somehow manage it and live with it. But it's just like I don't have time to get scared. I don't really have time to sit and cry, or go on the pity pot and say, "Oh, poor me." It's just something else that I got to deal with and keep going.

Lori: My life has not been a struggle. I think my life has been wonderful. I have had the best relationships, I have had opportunities that a lot of other people haven't had. I got to travel, I've had great careers, there is nothing I

Patti: All sorts of people deal with terminal illnesses. As I listen to the women in this study, I am struck by how similar the experience of making meaning of HIV is to that of women with breast cancer. In a January 1994 issue of *The Women's Review of Books,* three books on breast cancer are reviewed that outline how women see the disease as a way to recreate themselves. The initial panic at diagnosis is often quelled via gathering medical information. Some develop an activist stance. Support groups often extend lives. Diagnosis seems to fuel a kind of existential journey, often buoyed by feeling singled out to learn something profound. There is a great deal of unevenness in terms of plumbing despair and doubt, but many find the typical pieties hollow.

What structures our capacity to "name" ourselves, to "speak" ourselves, to make a "self" in the midst of the collision of shifting identities and movement across different contexts? What inherited meanings do we draw on? And how do we make sense when inherited meanings break down? How do we come to know ourselves? How do we make ourselves knowable to others? What is revealed and what remains hidden, perhaps even to ourselves?

As I read the transcripts, I hear bits and pieces of memory of events that are in excess of our frames of reference. For example, there is both the frequent use of ready-made cultural discourses and some sense of the inadequacies of available language. Inherited languages include religion, 12-step programs, psychotherapy, New Age, self-esteem, feminist, civil rights, African-American empowerment, medical. The support groups be-

would do differently, even knowing in the end that I might die of AIDS. I would rather have lived the life I've lived and die a young death than to be like everybody else and live the mundane suburban life. I just can't be ordinary and I think this is one of the things that makes me not ordinary. Sometimes in my mind, it's like of course you have this, it's just another adventure to you. I feel really lucky and then maybe the luck ran out.

Linda B: After my diagnosis, I changed in a way. I tried to get spiritual and tried to understand. At first it was anger. After all the shit God's put me through, now you're going to put this on me, too? Thanks a lot, Bud. Come on, give me a break. I was spiritual when I was younger, then it was the complete opposite, so now I'm wanting to get back to it. If I'm gonna die and go to hell, it's like is there a God? All of this stuff—I'm just starting to take baby steps, to try the water. It was like I was in a sleep for a lot of years. Now I'm kinda starting to wake up and smell the coffee.

Patti: How about you, Geneva? How do you make sense?

Geneva: Oh, God, I can't, I can't make any sense of it. That is what is frustrating about it. There are people out there, I shouldn't say this, who almost deserve it—not deserve it, but I feel like I could have been a really productive person, I know that I am a good mother. All of these things, why would God do this to me? I am a good person.

---

come the lived experience of multiple social meanings. My particular interest is in how the women negotiate the clash of voices, which ones they invest authority in, which ones they find internally persuasive, where they find breakdowns in available discourses.

People make sense of their lives via story lines or narratives that are available at particular cultural moments. No life fits neatly into any one "plot" line and narratives are multiple, contradictory, changing, and differently available, depending on the social forces that shape our lives. Some cultural stories are easily available to us, some not. Some help us tell our lives well; some break down in the face of the complications of our lives and times. Some we are conscious of "choosing"; others more or less tell us in ways outside of our conscious awareness.

Sometimes we seek out stories that transgress familiar and easily available narratives. In sum, the "self" gets constructed and reconstructed across various times and places, sometimes simultaneously, in complex ways that are more or less open, more or less chosen, more or less stable.

This research provides a particularly fertile site for exploring questions of making a "self" in the midst of the overburden of inherited and authoritative meanings. Contemporary theories of meaning-making and subject formation focus on how subjects construct themselves in relation to the categories laid on them, demanded of them. Such theories assume subjects both shaped by and resistant to dominant discourses. As women living with HIV/AIDS, what is the lived experience of conflicting social meanings? What are the internally persuasive discourses

Patti: Does conversation with God help you make any sense of this?

Geneva: No, at first it did, but now, I don't think God had anything to do with it. Now I think it's more just fate. Oh, of course, this has to be me. Here I sleep with this guy one night and I am infected. Oh, it's just my luck. To be honest, I always had the intuition since I was real young that I was going to die young, I really did. And it was funny because when I told this to my family, everyone said "no, you're not." And now everyone is like, "oh, you are right, you are right." But to make sense—it takes a lot of emotional work to come full circle.

Chris: How have you gotten that work done?

Geneva: In a lot of ways—spiritually, support groups, letting things out, talking about past things that I never would have talked about with someone without this happening. So a lot of therapeutic work, doing different readings and just time, I think in a way, time kind of takes care of . . .

Rosemary: I used to think it was a punishment. Now I think it's in the plan for me, a roll of the dice. I think this is just what it is supposed to be for me.

Chris: Just the plan.

Rosemary: Now if I could only get my mother to see that. You know, there's been some things that I've done that weren't quite right, in my younger days. And things that I've asked forgiveness for. And I thought when this came, because everything goes through your mind for the reasons, and a lot of these things came back up front in my mind. And I thought maybe this is the

"that speak to deep convictions, investments and desires as they struggle to make meaning of their experience" (Britzman, 1992)? How are available discourses inadequate, burdensome, "empowering"? These are poststructural sorts of questions with their emphasis on language, power and meaning (Henriques 1987; Smith 1988; hooks 1990).

There are many ways that "researchers" could make sense of the ways these women make sense of living with HIV/ AIDS. The preceding has used some academic "high theory" to sketch such an effort, but it raises questions about the ethics of reducing the fear, pain, joy, and urgency of people's lives to analytic categories. George Marcus, a poststructural anthropologist, has wrestled with such issues in his own research. He writes of the move away from such theoretical analysis and toward evocative portraits, a type of data reporting that "emphasizes a direct exposure to other 'voices' . . . unassimilated to given concepts, theories, and analytic frames" (1993). "We are," he says, in a moment "when the need to chronicle the world seem[s] to outstrip the capacity to theorize it. . . What we're saying. . . is kind of old fashioned: that is it possible to present the voices of others in a more or less unmediated way."

This raises issues of what is called the crisis of representation in academic "high theory." This study of women living with HIV/AIDS provides a laboratory in which

reason why—that I met this person at this particular time and this is the way it's supposed to be. And I felt guilty about that for awhile and then I just came to grips with myself.

CR: I re-live that time when I got the virus and I think if I had done this or that, I wouldn't have met him. If he hadn't of said this, I wouldn't have been attracted to him. If I hadn't been celibate for six years and a time bomb, I would have told him to go jerk off. I was celibate because I didn't want to have a flim flam relationship and I did not want the same thing to happen to my young daughters that happened to me. My body was at such a peak. I was lonesome, a little conversation. I was like a watermelon ready to pick. All that I had tried to protect myself and my daughters from for those six years, in one week it just went out the window.

Rita: You know, when I was first diagnosed, one of the first things that came to my mind was "Yeah, Dad, I've finally lived down to your expectation." It took coming to this group to realize that I didn't do anything wrong. This happened. I didn't ask for this, you know. It wasn't like I set out to do this. My behavior was no different than it had ever been or any different than anybody else's behavior who didn't get this.

Linda B: That's want I want everyone to know. It could be you. It could be anybody.

Sarah: You know, one stage that I've noticed is the question mark stage where you've just got a million questions about everything. And it just sort

🐚   🐚   🐚   🐚   🐚   🐚   🐚

to explore the textual possibilities for telling stories that situate Chris and myself not so much as experts "saying what things mean" in terms of "data," but rather as witnesses giving testimony to what is happening to these women. Methodologically grounded in qualitative/ethnographic and feminist poststructural research in the human sciences, this project enacts an interest in what it means to tell the lives of others. Both within and against conventional notions of social science research, the goal is not so much to represent the researched better as to explore how researchers can "be accountable to people's struggles for self-representation and self-determination" (Visweswaran, 1988).

Hence this research is situated in efforts toward generative research methodologies that register a possibility and mark a provisional space in which a different science might take form. This project is also about science as a contested site and the contributions of feminist research to practices of seeking our answers to a different science in inquiry as it is lived. Finally, this study is about being "invited in" as a feminist qualitative researcher in order to chronicle the stories of these women and get them into broad circulation. Positioned as somewhat of a "hired hand," a primary interest of mine is to be of use to those who brought me into the project to do a very specific job. 🐚

of throws everything upside down. And "why me?" is one of those questions. And it's more than that. And I still wonder, what does this mean? Where's it going to go, how is it going to develop? I like to have things set, a plan, and know exactly where I'm going and how it's going to turn out. And this doesn't exactly fit in with the way I feel comfortable.

Lori: Why not someone else? I'm not at all angry, and I'm not upset, but I'm trying to figure out how does it all fit into my spiritual belief that I always had: you live a good life, you'll get back. And it didn't happen.

Patti: If you say why me . . .

Sandy: I question that. In the beginning, if there was a God, then why would he have invented something this cruel? And I really didn't deserve it. Now I feel like, if it was him that invented it, then I am here for a purpose and maybe someone else will learn something. I mean it is unbelievable how much my mother has learned from me. She subscribes to every AIDS magazine there is and mails it to me with outlined things for exactly what I should read. So I am here for a purpose; someone else is going to get something from me being positive.

Chris: Any sense what that is?

Sandy: I would want other women who are infected to know that if you want to go to school, there is absolutely no reason on earth why you can't go back to school. Even if you don't make it through and finish, at least you did something that you. . .I feel, and these are just my opinions, OK, that there is just something inside of you that it is not just because you are HIV positive—that I don't believe. We could still do everything that we want to do and probably more. I keep telling myself, with my luck, I will be here when we find a cure.

Patti: So you are kind of at two opposite ends with the luck stuff?

Sandy: See, but I've always been lucky. When I was using, I should have been dead a long time ago anyways. So someone has always been watching over me.

Chris: You have taken bigger risks with more serious consequences than HIV?

Sandy: I've messed up on a drug deal and had a gun to my head and they actually pulled the trigger and, God knows why, I mean I don't know if he had bullets in there. Shit, I mean, that was scarier than being diagnosed with HIV.

Alisha: I thought that I would always be healthy. When I found out it was so frustrating for me. It just smacked me in the face. It was completely conflicting with what I always believed.

Maria: My life has just been, some people might say horrible. And for this to happen to me. I understood that if it was going to happen to anyone, well it was going to happen to me.

Chris: Kind of an inevitability to it?

Maria: That's how I took it and that's how I accepted it. I've never really accepted it.

Sarah: For me, it intensified a spiritual search. I was on that path anyway, but it really intensified it for me. The issue of trust calls into question trusting myself and my body and that if life is divine, that things happen for a reason, as part of your soul's growth. It's not all coincidence, though maybe some of it is. But things are meant for your growth, not to hurt you.

Melody: I think that God didn't make this happen to me; I think he allowed it to happen to me because I'm a very special person. I'm here for a reason and I think one of those reasons is to help the other girls. And he thinks that I am worthy of this task.

Tommie: And you are, you definitely are.

Melody: I didn't really have purpose. I was looking for purpose. I was looking in the bottle; I was looking in people; I was looking in the world, work, school, my child, my dog, where's my purpose? But now it's like I do have a purpose because this is killing people. It's hurting people. It's OK though, I'm not alone. There are other people. To me this disease is going to show the world their capacity for love and caring one way or the other. It's like a godsend in a way to me, because humanity has come to that point where there is hardly any humanity or compassion and this disease will make people look.

Chris: You sure as hell strike me as a woman with a purpose. What are our tears about as she speaks?

Sarah: My tears are about becoming so close to myself and the energy of the universe and the conception that there is something greater than ourselves, that we're just a piece of the puzzle, and together we can conquer, we can overcome anything and have peace. And that's what this disease has brought about for me.

Amber: I'm not there. I wish I was there. For me, it seems inevitable. My life has always been like, if bad luck could happen, it happened to me. I just don't think really there would have been any way to avoid this.

Chris: You were on the path?

Amber: I was on the path. As far as tears, I think, maybe, a lot of this, for all of us, has to do with what happened in our childhood. And maybe HIV isn't a disease; maybe it's a symptom of low self-esteem. Low self-esteem is the big disease here, not feeling worthy of love. When we were in high school in our health class, we had to write epitaphs. Mine, I've always remembered, it was real simple. It was just, Of Amber, who hugged many, who was loved by many, but who never thought she was loved enough (tears). Sorry. I still feel that, and I don't think I'm ever gonna get it.

Chris: I saw some of you nodding when she said this is a disease of low self esteem.

Tommie: Yeah, it's like looking for love in all the wrong places.

Chris: So you think the roots of low self-esteem are feeling unworthy of love?

Tommie: She hit it right on the nose. I believe that too. HIV is a symptom of low self-esteem. That's all it is. If we can remember that: it's just a symptom.

Robyn: I think my lack of self-esteem is what got me to this place. If you have sex with guys, maybe they'll like you. I never had many friends in school, a couple people were close, but not like let's get together after school and like that. I mean, I don't know, I don't know if I have changed any. I never really liked myself.

Chris: Have you got better friends now than you did?

Robyn: I still don't except for the friends I have here, but outside of that. . . I've got a couple of people I used to work with.

Patti: So your life is not that much different?

Robyn: Yeah, not really. The friends I used to work with, but it's like I have to call them and it's like who needs that? I'll just sit here and watch TV.

Chris: Those of you who are Hispanic, are there any cultural factors that particularly affected your experiences or the fact that you became HIV?

Sandy: At this point in my life, I can not even relate to Spanish men or the older generation. At family gatherings, I run in the opposite direction. In Puerto Rico, I didn't fit into their ways of thinking. They are so narrow minded and ignorant as far as I am concerned. I don't know that it could be any different being an American family, because I wasn't raised in an American family, but I certainly noticed how backward Puerto Rican thinking was, especially with relation to sex. I wasn't allowed to date at all which led to promiscuity and the drugs.

Chris: Do you connect being Hispanic in any particular way with what has happened in your life?

Geneva: I think a little bit as it relates back to self-esteem. I think it is always that inferior kind of feeling, that you don't fit in so that you are more eager to please men or whoever, so I think that as it relates to self esteem, yes.

Iris: When I first found out, it was "why me?" Everything happens to me. When I was a teenager I had a venereal disease, then I found out I was HIV+, and I was like, "oh yeah, bring it on." After the "why me" set in and all the denial stuff, it was like I feel like I am chosen. And I know, when Iris has her shit together, she's gonna help somebody. That's what I want to do, I want to help other women, other people, somebody with this disease that needs the help. I feel like I am strong and somebody up there maybe knows that. I always heard, and I believe this, that God doesn't put anything on you that you can't handle. There's been times when I didn't think I could handle it, but I kept plugging away and I am still sitting here to tell it. I'd like to think that I was strong before I found out, but I think I am a lot stronger because of it. It's opened my eyes to life and the way I should be living it and not wasting it. I've wasted it in the past two years, but I don't want to give up.

Tracy: For me, everything happened to me. Like I got the disease, it was MY father that died, and I figure out of all my friends and relatives, I will end up being the one who ends up getting something. Even though the girls in here are stronger than I am, I feel that in some kind of way it happened to me so I can help all of my friends, and give them all of these articles, so some reason, some kind of good can come out of it. I don't know what stage I'm in, maybe denial. I'm having a really hard time, but I had this feeling that I had it and I had it for a reason. Maybe I'm not the strongest, but I'm somewhere able to help other people, so here I am.

Patti: Nancy you started to say something when we were talking about how you make sense of this.

Nancy: I don't remember.

Chris: How do you make sense of this?

Nancy: I can't. I never thought I would be, I mean I've never been sick. I jogged every day and went to the health spa and now I can't do that anymore.

Chris: So do you feel like you don't know who you are anymore or is that shifting for you or are you just angry that you can't do the things you used to do?

Nancy: I'm angry. I cry a lot. I try not to but it does seem to help. I feel bad, I mean physically. I have to lie on the couch all day.

Chris: Are there any other explanations for understanding the AIDS virus?

Tracy: I keep wondering if this is some government conspiracy, because where are the heterosexual men? Why does it seem to be affecting certain populations? Population overgrowth is a major concern of the world. How are we going to take care of everybody? And it just seems that after twelve years that they haven't advanced at all. It just makes you wonder, what is going on, what is going on? It is very fishy. It concerns me quite a bit.

Joanna: I have always felt that too. I am kind of cynical about the government anyway. When my husband was first diagnosed, he was in the hospital, and he was reading a particular book. He would do his own research, talk to doctors and stuff. But he read that book and he would only tell me so much of it, even though we always shared when we read a book. So finally, last month, I decided it was time to read that book, and it just confirmed what I already thought. They really don't put the time and effort into it. Native Americans are an important population, just as much as anybody else. But twelve Native Americans died and they poured thousands of dollars into it in just a couple of weeks. And it took two years to get that same amount of money into research for AIDS. Where is the balance here? And the Legionnaire's Disease, they poured a million into that. It was the rich white heterosexual males who were the veterans of the war.

Tracy: Yeah. It just makes me very angry. Sometimes I hear people talking and I will say well, why? Because you think we are the dregs of society or something? Just let us die and then everything will be OK? Well, guess what?!

Linda B: When J died, she decided she'd had enough and when she suddenly and simply left like she did, it strengthened my belief that this is just a journey, this is one of many journeys. I'll be back. I've always felt that I'm here now to learn patience and I'll be here for awhile.

Lori: I believe that my life is a collection of experiences and for whatever reason, this is the path I was put on and this is just another series of experiences. I got married, which I never thought I'd do, and lived a normal suburban life, then I lost my husband, now I'm facing whatever will happen in the future. It's all like a collection of experiences.

Linda B: This is not just happening to me, as far as myself. It's also happening to my family, it's happening to my friends. We aren't all here to learn a lesson ourselves. We are to collectively learn a lesson.

Sarah: So it's strange for me, it's strange for me to make sense of it. I don't know exactly what it means in my life.

Patti: Do different kinds of stories come through in terms of making sense of it?

Sarah: Yes, there's something I read in some book that I thought, boy, that strikes me as really true. It had something to do with people who were in plague sorts of situations. They were on the cutting edge of transforming that society. They bought about a change, a social change. With their life and with their death they sort of moved and propelled consciousness forward in a leap. And I sort of believe that. I mean, I sort of do.

Chris: You want to be one of the chosen ones?

Sarah: Yeah, in a way. I still have a lot of questions about HIV. It just comes down that you sort of have to trust. I don't know, it's just something that happened to you, it'll change your life. When I went to a therapist, she said disease is a transformation, it's a metaphor for transformation, and you are about to embark on some amazing transformations in your life. Things will change and they will change in incredible ways. And I'm still sort of saying, huh? But I sort of believe that. I don't know.

Patti: It's also really interesting to me that the story of feeling like a chosen one at some level and the story of feeling like it's low self-esteem can be together, and you can believe both of them at the same time.

Melody: I think, it makes you face your fears and as a society it makes us face our fears. It's one of those things that does sort of polarize people, and either they are going to be more compassionate and loving or else they are going to shut down. It has a tremendous impact.

Carol X: Sometimes I even think that having this can be a blessing to bring people together, to touch other people's lives, to be an education, to be that spark in somebody's eye. And, then again . . .

Linda B: There has to be a reason for it.

Patti: And where do you look for that reason?

Linda B: What do you mean, where do I look for that reason? You don't look for it. That's probably what gives it meaning. There is a reason, but you don't know what it is. You're going on faith or trust, whatever, assumptions that there is a reason, that this is not without meaning.

I'm not done here yet, there are too many things left to do,
Just because of AIDS, does not mean my life is through.
My time may be limited, so they say,
Regardless, I will struggle each and every day.
Yes, my life has taken on a drastic change,
Due to the fact of taking an honest look, knowing I had to rearrange.
Rearrange the priorities to attain a different goal.
So that when it's time to leave here, I would be whole.
This disease called AIDS has given me a second chance,
To see what was inside my very being, never before giving it a glance.
My time may be limited, so they say,
But I can seek, search and mold, like a soft piece of clay.
Bringing out the goodness that I've learned was always there,
Covered by hardness, my exterior was, from years of wear and tear,
That now I look back upon and am thankful are no longer there.
No, I'm not done yet, my work here has just started,
Trying to make a difference in this world that has become so parted.
We must stand together and walk hand in hand,
AIDS not only affects us personally, but throughout the land.
My time may be limited, so they say,
But working and striving as one, we will *all* see another day.

—Holley, 15 May 1994

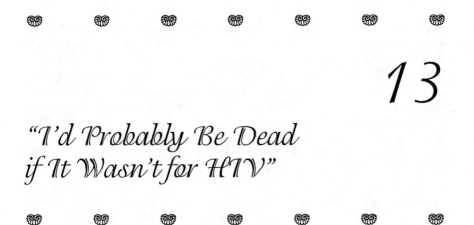

13

"I'd Probably Be Dead if It Wasn't for HIV"

Chris: How has being HIV+ changed your life?

Rita: Well, I liked something that Lori said. This is a gift for me to take a second look at life, at what the value of life really is. I'd probably be dead now if I didn't have HIV. At first, I used it as an excuse; I'm dying anyway. Then my family invited me back home; it was a shock and a relief. I got on methadone and off of the heavy coke and heroin I was on. I sold drugs to support it and the other things you have to do to support your habit. Here was a chance to wipe the slate clean and start over. I just went for it completely. It was just such a relief to go back to being the person I wanted to be twenty years ago. It was a slice out of my life and then I got to come back and be the person I was when I left here. So, **I'd probably be dead if it wasn't for HIV,** as crazy as that sounds.

Chris: What would your life be like if you didn't have the virus?

Patti: Early in our reading of the literature about living with HIV/AIDS, we were at first disappointed when we saw that our findings from this research study were "nothing new." For example, in a movie called *Living Proof: HIV and the Pursuit of Happiness*, a woman who had been a drug addict says, "If I hadn't found out I was HIV positive I'd probably be dead." This repeats a quote that is used for the title of one of the story chapters in this book, a repetition that initially dismayed us. Then we decided that this repetition of themes is a kind of validity—if our findings were being repeated across various sources on dealing with AIDS as well as other terminal illnesses, then we must be on the right track. Another example of this is John Clum's essay on how HIV+ people tell their stories, "'And Once I Had It All': AIDS Narratives and Memories of an American Dream." In *Writing AIDS: Gay Literature, Language, and Analysis*, edited by Timothy Murphy and

CR: When I think of the rocky marriage, the rocky childhood, and then going into adult life, I've always given. I became a mother at twelve and I never had time to be young. If I hadn't contracted the virus, I'd still probably be in some shit relationship and taking care of kids. Now I have time for myself. About three months ago these religious women that live next door to me asked me if I'd like to come live with them, because people aren't coming to live in the convent anymore. And I said no, this is the first year of my independence and I ain't sharing a toilet with nobody [much giggling]. And when I don't want to make up the bed, I don't make up the bed, if I don't want to sleep in the bed, I sleep on the floor, I sleep on the couch, I mean, it's fun. If I hadn't had the virus, I mean, I'm two steps from eating pork and beans out of the can just to say I can do it. I'd have been worried about whether some man is gonna call, did I say something to make him mad, I mean all that shit. Before the virus I didn't think I could live without a man.

Chris: I have heard some people who have the AIDS virus say that it has been a gift, an opportunity to change and grow. What do you think about this?

Melody: You have to believe in yourself. You have to get to know yourself through this disease. I've had to look at me and where I'm at and get a perspective on where I want to be and yet actually be where I am at. It's hard to explain, but this disease makes me look consciously and subconsciously

Suzanne Poirier (Columbia University Press, 1993). This is similar to Louisa's story at the end of Story Series 4, "We Had a Real Nice Life."

Another example of how our research findings cut across other contexts is the work of Bill T. Jones who conducted survival workshops for those, including children, with life-threatening illnesses in the construction of his dance performance, *Still/Here*. Jones, an African-American, HIV+, gay choreographer, emphasizes that this work is "not about AIDS" as he focuses on the issues involved in living with deadly diseases: the loss of easy belief, the fear of losing one's ability to care for oneself, the facing of death. "Through these workshops, I'm learning to talk about hope in a hope-less world," Jones says (*Columbus Alive,* December 5 1993). The nationwide workshops allowed participants to create theatrical and movement vocabularies about hope, will and survival in the face of mortality. The video-documentary of these sessions were combined with newsreels, talk show tapes, and still photographs into a full-length work which is followed by a post-performance symposium entitled *Managing Mortality.* "A victim is someone who has been diminished," said Jones after the Wexner Center performance. "My experience in the survival workshops is that the circumstance of the participants has given them an opportunity to become more whole" (*Ohio State Quest,* Spring, 1995).

every moment because I don't take the moments for granted. I don't procrastinate and just let them slip away. I just want to seize everything. It's brought back the child in me and the wonderment when everything is like doing it for the first time, because it's a different moment. It might be the same people and the same type of situation, but yet it's a different moment. And that's what makes me grateful for being diagnosed with AIDS. Because I wouldn't have done that; I would have procrastinated until the day I died.

Lori: I think it would be surprising to people to hear that infected women's self esteem has risen.

Patti: That is a surprising statement; how do you explain that?

Lori: Well, look at Rita and how she abused her body and womanhood for so many years and this one little sentence changes her life and now she's on a campaign to make herself wonderful. My life hasn't really significantly changed and I don't think my self esteem has changed but I think we all now, we are very self absorbed. I think, looking in the mirror, you wouldn't look at stuff like we do and you have to take people and things that are said in two ways. How do I respond to that, do I process that as a positive woman or just as a woman? There's a lot of different ways that you have to process information but this adds one more that makes you very protective of yourself, not getting hurt, not getting physically ill. Like Robyn talked about this woman at work coughing, well I have never noticed people coughing like I do now. You're just more aware of this kinda of stuff.

⚜   ⚜   ⚜   ⚜   ⚜   ⚜   ⚜

What does this mean in terms of understanding how the women in our study make sense of their HIV experiences? The most important thing I've learned is the doubled need for hope when the languages of hope that we have are no longer broadly persuasive. Especially for those outside of traditional religious thinking about death, the lack of philosophical options, of secular resources to think about death is a situation of at once too little and too much knowledge.

Largely struck dumb by the data, in spite of the preceding efforts to make some interpretive sense of it, wanting to hold back analytically, I am left feeling that no one has the right to take away hope, whether it be through participation in experimental drug trials or the succor of traditional religion or investments like my own in social justice struggles. The task is to proceed in a way that works against what *Angels in America* playwright, Tony Kushner has termed the "stupidly optimistic" (de Vries, 1992). By focusing on the ruins of history and the fragmentation of agreed upon meaning, we move against a victory narrative couched in the very conquering optimism that has lost its credibility, and toward some sense of what it means to use the now-time of a crisis of otherness to struggle toward a more just society. The following update from Rita speaks to the complications of thinking about hope and the possibilities for change and community across our differences in the midst of epidemic.

Linda B: Right! You want to get your Lysol out!

Chris: Rita, Lori used you as a reference for self-esteem.

Rita: I probably would have kept going and going until I overdosed and then this. When I found this out, I don't know why that was the point that made me stay with treatment. At first I thought why should I quit now, I'm dying anyway. I had a friend who has it that decided that, but I kind of think like maybe God gave this to me to help someone, maybe myself. I sure wasn't worth a damn. I didn't even know what the word self-esteem was. The methadone lady started a group for women and she asked me if I wanted to join that group down there and I said no, I got this other group I go to. No offense, but I don't want to get to know any of your people. And she said well there are people here who don't do drugs, but I have no interest in cultivating any relationships with those people.

Chris: You made some real strong decisions.

Rita: Yeah, finally, finally, I've started making those kind of decisions. I have no desire whatsoever to even look where the drugs are in this city.

Chris: You're doing well and you mentioned earlier that you don't care to have romantic relationships.

Rita: That's the biggest thing, not looking for dates. I had no friendships with women, because it was a competition. I didn't look at women as friends. Now, with guys, I feel I would have to tell him about HIV. Some of the people I told, I found out afterwards, would say things like, she came in my bathroom, she gave me a hug, she talked to my kids. It's like people were so ignorant about it. And then I thought that's too much to even invest. I'm not inter-

❀   ❀   ❀   ❀   ❀   ❀   ❀

"Relapse Is a Constant Battle": Rita

October 1996 Phone Call

The interview started when I was 38. I'm now 42. Reading what I said I'm wondering who that phony hypocrite was or was trying to pretend to be. One of my biggest struggles is substance abuse and depression. I've been waiting to die since the day I was born. It's hard for me to remember a time ever when I was happy or able to form, keep or even want any relationship. After finding my status out, I was involved with the court system. After a six week drug related hospitalization, my family arranged for

me to come home. For the twenty years I was gone, they only heard from me when I was broke, sick, locked up or in the hospital. I wanted to be the daughter they always wanted but never knew how. For two years after coming back, I did. I was perfect and set myself up because I wanted to believe it. Finally, no more suicide tries or putting myself in situations where I could die or being a prostitute or a thief or anything else I had to do to support a man who taught me the ropes for his benefit. Twelve years ago, I felt like I deserved getting beat up, raped, traded, put in jail, but by God's grace, not in prison. I don't

ested in investing that much emotional energy. I like being by myself. I'm very selective. I've got a lot of acquaintances, but only a couple of friends. People in this group, I've learned more about them than I've known people in my life.

Chris: So what's it like having this group?

Rita: Learning how to be a friend to a woman. I like it; it's something I've never done before. And it's not for anything other than wanting to.

Chris: Is that related to self esteem?

Rita: Yeah, 100 percent. Now I'm finding out that I've got something to say that's worth listening to.

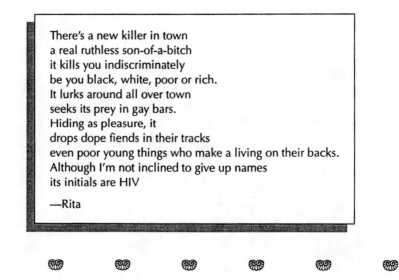

> There's a new killer in town
> a real ruthless son-of-a-bitch
> it kills you indiscriminately
> be you black, white, poor or rich.
> It lurks around all over town
> seeks its prey in gay bars.
> Hiding as pleasure, it
> drops dope fiends in their tracks
> even poor young things who make a living on their backs.
> Although I'm not inclined to give up names
> its initials are HIV
>
> —Rita

want to revert and go to jail here and hurt my family. I'd rather die. **Relapse is a constant battle.** I'm so sorry there is no HIV and substance abuse program here, because it would really be more helpful for me to be in such a group. In the other support group, I never felt like I fit. There's such a stigma attached to how you get AIDS and I always felt kind of odd man out because of how I got it. I felt at the bottom, which is where I've always felt I belonged. I've tried going to AA and NA [Narcotics Anonymous], but they never deal with HIV issues. Sometimes it's just easier to pretend the HIV is not there.

It's taken me a lot to build up to be able to say this to you, but it helps and I think I'll show it to my doctor so he can understand me better. I'm in a clinical trial for the protease inhibitors which would cost me $30,000 a year if I had to pay for it myself. My doctor made it clear that I'm usually not very consistent, but that if I'm going to receive these drugs, I have to do it right. Otherwise, there are plenty of people who will take my place. I might not be so motivated if it was just for me, but I am motivated to think my being in the clinical trial might help other people.

INTERTEXT 3

Angelology:
A History of Truths

> But angels are supposed to be immortal, so even if the plague did claim them as victims they couldn't actually have died. So if they emptied the old mansions of Heaven where did they go? And where are they now?

> —Malcolm Godwin, *Angels,* 1990

Over the centuries, interest in angels has waxed and waned. Until the reign of science, they were considered to be the overseers of the cosmos, guiding everything from time and space to the particulars of each human life. The scholarship of the Middle Ages was full of controversy regarding whether angels had wings or not, what their number and essence was, and the nature of their link with humans. The erosion of faith in angels, both their ability to serve as intermediaries between humans and a higher power and their very existence, began with the bubonic plague of the fourteenth century and was exacerbated by the Age of Reason ushered in by the scientific revolution of the sixteenth century.

Jewish angelology, Islamic and Christian angels of the Lord, Hellenistic, Buddhist, Hindu, Gnostic, Native American: the concept of angels is multiply-coded and carries with it a certain emotional residue. A survey of the history of the concept shows 4,000 years of Judeo-Christian angelology. A major sphere of inquiry and dispute, angels were an important part of the theology of the Middle Ages. Thomas Aquinas, for example, in 1265 AD wrote *Summa Theologica* with a Treatise on Angels. With the progressive demonization of the Western world, the Inquisition and the sixth century rise of saints, martyrs and the cult of Mary as intermediaries between humans and the unknowable, angels were largely displaced in canonical discourse.[1] Post-Reformation speculation on angels included John Locke and Francis Bacon, and the seventeenth century had its share of the angel-haunted like Milton, Blake and Swedenborg, a tradition carried on in the twentieth century by poets, artists, and seers like Paul Klee, Rainer Maria Rilke and H.D. In terms of the Catholic Church, Pius XI reaffirmed angels in 1950 and Pius XII in 1968, and theological conferences were held in France and Germany in the 1950's and 60's on angels.[2]

While angels have suffered some displacement over time, they have reentered the popular imagination in the United States, particularly via New Age interest in angels as mediators between worlds. As Mortimer Adler points out,[3] for centuries angels were all we knew of superhuman intelligence. Now we have cyborgs and UFO's as part of the grammar of available possibilities. *Angels and Aliens* by Keith Thompson[4] posits a link between all of this. Primarily about UFO's, the book surveys various myths and mystical beliefs from shamanism to angels to undergird his arguments.

In a section entitled "What is an angel," Thompson probes the connection between angelic and alien encounters. Surveying the history of thought about angels from early Sumerians to Hebrews, Greeks and Christians, Thompson traces the construction of angels and demons across time and culture as neither static nor consistent. When sixteenth century science displaced the earth from the center of the universe, many theologians were only too glad to get rid of both angels and demons. Martin Luther, while keeping Satan, threw out angels and Catholic leaders remain split on the reality of both angels and demons. The Renaissance painters have imprinted a particular concept of angels in our mind, but the concept of intermediary beings between God and humanity both precede Christianity and carry into the present, including over forty years of alien sightings. Thompson notes parallels between the ways angels and aliens have come to be known. Both are "heretical" in being mostly discussed outside "approved" channels, be they theology or official science; both can be seen as messengers. Both are surrounded by debate on their type of embodiment and their interest in human sexuality. Early legends, for example, posited a race of giants issuing from angels coupling with the daughters of men, and contemporary alien tales are full of abduction stories, some pleasant, some horrible, that often include a sexual/reproductive dimension. Whatever the conjunction of angels and aliens means in Thompson's book, he urges that we see beyond Hallmark notions of angels as "females in nighties tripping through the sky" toward beings of might and terror who alert us to how nothing is fixed and move us beyond our conceptions of our capacities to change.

To overview the way angels have been studied over the centuries, across cultures, from pagan myths, Jewish, Christian and Islamic early writings, canonical texts of the Middle Ages, up through contemporary efforts to link angels with space aliens and the New Age revival, is to raise questions about how we come to know what we think we know. Comparing this with the way AIDS has been studied over the last fifteen years suggests how our practices of knowing are deeply shaped by culture and history and power interests. As the bubonic plague rewrote the Europe of the Middle Ages, AIDS is rewriting much of contemporary culture, for example, right to die issues and the bringing together of long-warring mainstream and marginal medical cultures, now termed "complementary therapies."

To look at the construction of the epidemic is to look at the techniques by which the media has packaged information for the American public. What one sees is less an objective, epidemiological phenomenon than a social construction. ACT UP (AIDS Coalition to Unleash Power), for example, has been active in interjecting counter meanings and interrupting mainstream media presentations. One instance of this is the sexual morality issues that surround a person with AIDS. Particularly at issue are themes of blame and "otherness" in the way AIDS gets presented. Stigma and finger-pointing lead to misinformation and discrimination when AIDS is seen as a disease of homosexuals, Haitians, intravenous drug users and hemophiliacs, with all but the last considered to be "deserving" victims. In the case of Haiti, Randy Farmer (1992) tracks how economics, politics and the disease intersect within the context of North American imperialism to shape how Haiti was blamed for being the origin of the disease in the Western hemisphere. Apathy from

---

An example of AIDS rewriting culture is the move to legalize marijuana for medicinal use, particularly glaucoma, relief from the nausea and pain of chemotherapy and other drugs, including AIDS drugs, and appetite improvement. Proposition 215, on the 1996 California ballot, was approved. Proposition 215 doesn't limit the amount of marijuana an individual can grow or smoke and requires only oral permission from a doctor to obtain the narcotic. The June 1995 issue of the *Journal of the American Medical Association* includes a plea to physicians to encourage open and legal exploration of the therapeutic potential of marijuana. Forty "compassionate use" marijuana buying clubs have been started by AIDS patients. The Federal Drug Administration was so deluged with applications on behalf of AIDS patients that in 1992 it canceled the very limited medicinal use allowed through the US Public Health Service. Thirty-six states have enacted legislation that approves of medicinal use, although federal laws bar possession, distribution or cultivation (*Columbus Dispatch*, March 25, 1996).

Patti: While on a speaking tour of Australia in the fall of 1993, I encountered a Maori woman from New Zealand who told me about Tohunga who are viewed as either angels or witch doctors, depending on which tribe one is from. 🐚

the Reagan and Bush admin-
istrations, obstructed by federal bureaucracy and drug industry greed, scientific infighting as documented by Randy
Shilts in *And the Band Played
On* (1991): all have helped
construct how we come to
"know" the epidemic. Cindy
Patton (1994) tracks the ways
this knowledge about AIDS
has been shaped by attitudes

In a 1990 survey of 1000 black church
members from around the country, one-
third believed that AIDS was produced by
the US government as germ warfare; another one-third was unsure. The continued heritage of the Tuskegee experiments
leads to less likelihood of blacks getting
tested, wearing condoms, and participat-
ing in clinical trials (*Columbus Dispatch*,
November 2, 1995).

toward women, race and sexuality. She is particularly interested in the media
construction of the "ordinary woman" who is increasingly finding herself
infected, in contrast with the moralistic stereotype of the female sex worker
as vector of the disease, bringing it into the mainstream.

Like angels, how something such as AIDS is thought about over time and
what this might mean socially and politically raises interesting points about
how ideas are produced, framed and sustained. For example, to look at the
intersection of AIDS, Africa and race moves AIDS to "AIDS," where "AIDS"
becomes a creation of the audience/media interaction. This is not to deny that
AIDS kills people. It is, however, to focus on how living with the burden of
signification is a cultural event that has a profound shaping influence on how
the disease gets lived. Whether angels or "AIDS," phenomena are always socially defined. Whether from churches or doctors, knowledge systems of religion or science, filtered through information media from books to television,
we construct the world we live in by how we make meaning of it.

One example is to look at theories of the origin of AIDS. For many black
Americans, AIDS is a white plot, fed by the historical memory of the Tuskegee
experiments.

On quite the other hand, Robert Root-Bernstein argues that many people
with HIV remain healthy while others without HIV die of AIDS-like illnesses, and that HIV is difficult to sexually transmit.[5] While Root-Bernstein
is particularly worried about the distorting effects of social liberalism on
AIDS research agendas, his theories exemplify that theories of the origins of
AIDS are many and diverse.

The March 19, 1992 issue of *Rolling Stone* carried "a startling new theory"
on the origin of AIDS as caused by modern science itself in either injecting
humans with monkey blood in experiments intended to fight malaria in Africa from 1922 to 1955 or as an unintended byproduct of a live-polio vaccine in experiments with at least 325,000 people in equatorial Africa from
1957 to 1960. The September 1992 issue of *Natural History* traced why
most scientists believe that AIDS arose in central or East Africa because of

One explanation for why some with HIV remain healthy while others die is new research that suggests that genetic resistance to HIV infection is relatively common in Caucasians, but not in those of African descent. Based on a study of 1900 American men and women who have been in AIDS related studies more than a decade, the study subjects have been exposed to the HIV virus repeatedly without becoming infected or are HIV positive but after years of infection have not developed AIDS. It is theorized that these differences are due to partial genetic protection that slows the course of the illness. Caucasians who have this gene are far less likely to rapidly develop AIDS after infection, and they live AIDS-free an average of two years longer than infected people who do not carry the gene. Perhaps 1 in 1000 whites are genetically resistant (*Columbus Dispatch*, September 17, 1996). These findings may explain, in part, why people of color are the epicenter of the growth of the disease in the US and make culturally appropriate AIDS prevention education even more important.

the early appearance of the disease and the natural occurrence of the related simian virus. Benign in monkeys, deadly in humans since at least 1959, the most interesting question is, since Africans have been handling monkeys for millions of years, why is AIDS so recent?

Three types of explanations are surveyed in the *Natural History* article: chance, changing conditions of easy spread of infection, and technology for easy transfer of simian virus to humans. Hence views on racial and cultural differences and the uses and abuses of and by technology and science all shape the search for understanding the origins of AIDS. In sum, not only is there no surety of a cure in the future, we aren't even close to understanding the past of AIDS or how it works in the present.

In terms of the future of AIDS, as slippery as the virus is, the chances of a vaccine are not hopeful. In June of 1994, the National Institute of Health decided to hold off on large clinical trials of vaccine testing, given the inability of a vaccine to combat the many strains of HIV at large in the population (*Newsweek*, June 27, 1994). The delay of large-scale vaccine trials in the United States may encourage testing in other countries where the risk/benefit ratios and the dynamics of the epidemic are different, for example, Thailand where HIV is rampant in groups such as soldiers and prostitutes, with all of the ethical and political dangers involved (*Chronicle of Higher Education*, June 29, 1994).

Is AIDS but the first of many viruses we will see rise up, decimate populations, and be outside the limits of science to control? Will some people develop genetic resistance as a form of survival of the fittest over eons? Will educational programs about safer sex and clean needles take effect? Will governments develop the will to deal with the crisis in a timely fashion? How will the answer to these questions be shaped by the very ways knowledge about HIV/AIDS is constructed?

Notes

1. Theodora Ward (1969). *Men and Angels*. New York: The Viking Press.

2. Georges Huber (1983). *My Angel Will Go Before You*. Westminster MD: Christian Classics.

3. Mortimer Adler (1982). *The Angels and Us*. New York: Macmillan.

4. Keith Thompson (1991). *Angels and Aliens*. New York: Fawcett Columbine.

5. Robert Root-Bernstein (1993). *Rethinking AIDS: The Tragic Cost of Premature Consensus*. New York: The Free Press.

See Laurie Garrett, *The Coming Plague* (Farrar Straus Giroux, 1994) about the bureaucratic infighting, drug-company indifference, environmental degradation and population explosion upon which she posits a world health crisis that includes but goes beyond AIDS. HIV, AIDS and other previously unknown diseases such as Ebola fever, which is more than 97 percent fatal, baffle medical science. There is no cure. Killer viruses and bacteria, unfazed by antiseptic conditions, adapt faster than they can be documented, classified, and studied, let alone stopped.

Will Shively, *AIDS Angel I*, 1994, photograph. Used by permission of the artist.

STORY SERIES FOUR

Living/Dying
with AIDS

14

"We Are the Teachers"

Linda B: When they told J she had PCP, she said "count me out." She was so tired. The intestinal diarrhea had absolutely destroyed her strength. When they told her she had PCP, she refused treatment. She's tell doctors exactly what they could do. I mean, she'd get up in their face. One night at 3 AM I was talking to her on the phone. They came in to draw blood, and she looked at this doctor and she said, Motherfucker, I can't believe you're in here at 3 o'clock in the morning poking me with a needle, now you get your fucking ass out of here, I'm on the phone. Now that's exactly the way J was, but then she got to the point where that didn't work. She was just tired. She told me, I'm going to leave. And she just left.

Chris: What did that do to you in terms of living your own life?

Linda B: Oh man, it's been really hard. I miss her. I miss her really really bad. Because no matter how bad it got, we would laugh. She was this magical little outlet for me and I was the same thing for her. But then after awhile

From Patti's research journal, May 16, 1994

Chris invited me to go with her tonight to visit Debbie, whom I don't know beyond an introduction at the 1993 retreat. I am thankful for the opportunity to once again confront my too comfortable distance in all of this. Chris is out there daily, on the front lines. I sit in my office, writing away, immersed in the data and the storytelling. It's too easy to forget the human cost and

how arbitrary are the made versus the lost stories. Debbie's story, for example, is largely absent in this book due to her intermittent involvement in the support group. Also lost is any elaboration of Diane's choosing this moment to come out to her family as HIV+, as Debbie lies dying at home, caught up in PML, a galloping virus in the brain that plunges this 32-year-old from relative health to death's door in a matter of weeks. [Debbie died at home on May 30, 1994.]

the magic was gone. She was too tired. When J went that way, it strengthened my belief that this is a journey, a series of experiences. I will be back. Life is a collection of experiences and there has to be a reason for it.

Patti: What is that reason?

Linda B: It is NOT punishment. It is NOT an individual lesson, but a collective lesson. **We are the teachers.**

Sandy: I for some reason did not realize I was going to die before I got infected, and now I think about it—I was going to die before I got HIV. I mean, you know; for some reason it reassures me, knowing that you're gonna die, and you're gonna die. Sometimes you feel like you are the only one and that everyone else goes on and is gonna have this wonderful life forever. But life isn't really so wonderful, even if you're not positive, you know what I mean. I don't remember my life being wonderful before, you know. But when you first find out you're HIV positive, it seems like everything was wonderful before that. It did to me, anyway. When I read the things you go through with death, I went through the bargaining, the grieving, the anger, the isolation, the loneliness, all those things. I must have bargained with God for months and months and then I was angry with him. I think I am finally at a full circle.

Chris: What would you name that stage?

🐚   🐚   🐚   🐚   🐚   🐚   🐚

In the car on the way to visit Debbie in her hospital bed at home, Diane tells her story of coming out as HIV+ to her mom and aunt. Carefully choosing the scene so that the aunt would be there to buffer the mother, Diane tells us of how her mom and aunt wanted to know why she didn't tell them sooner. Fearing her imminent death, they have to learn to live with this as Diane has over the last two and one-half years. Wanting to know who she got it from, filling in holes in what they know of illnesses of Diane's friends, now identified as AIDS, they decide to go ahead with telling the rest of the family and parcel out the doing. Making clear how she wanted to be dealt with at the end, "if it comes to that," Diane does not want to be in their homes; she wants a nursing home or hospice. Chris says, "Get it written down." We listen to Reba McEntire sing a song about women and AIDS, "She Thinks His Name Was John," and talk about blame and shame.

As we walk into the house, Debbie is sleeping in a hospital bed in her son's room, now transformed into a sick room. Three children, a husband and a mother-in-law, taking care of her. Walking into the room, it is hard to tell her from a corpse at first, the stillness, the drawn face, the pallor. She wakes; she attends some, but mostly there are her eyes—intense, a Rorschach test for those in the room. Is she pissed? scared? zoned out? She speaks but once, to joke with her youngest daughter about the daughter's hair. She blinks when Chris says, if you want us to come back to see you again, blink once. She throws her bedclothes off twice to pull the catheter out. I witness this with the horror of my not knowing her, witnessing something so pri-

Sandy: Maybe content, being content. I am at peace with it. I am not happy with it, but I have genuinely accepted it. Even before I was diagnosed, death was never a scary thing for me. I wasn't brought up to be scared of people dying. I've always believed that if I died tomorrow, there is still something better where I am going. I mean it has to be better than here.

Patti: Is this a religious belief?

Sandy: Right. So death isn't scary for me and I still actually believe that everybody else is going to die before me. I mean I want to die before my mother, that's the only person I want to die before. But everybody else—it doesn't sound nice, but I don't feel all that bad.

Patti: What is this thing with your mother?

Sandy: Oh, because I would freak there.

Chris: You mean because you can't handle her death or you want her there for yours?

Sandy: Both. I think that she is the only one who will actually pull through with what I want done. If she were to die tomorrow it would be left up to my sister and she wouldn't do what I want. I believe in God; I am not scared of death.

Maria: I am not worried about dying, I just don't want to die from AIDS. If I could die from cancer—I don't want to die from AIDS.

---

vate. Like my in-coma brother's nakedness in the hospital bed when I unexpectedly came outside of visiting hours, but there I was family. Here I am a stranger, riding Chris' coattails as she lets the family know that she is there if they need her, listening to the mother-in-law speak of the last few weeks. Chris tells them how she touted them at a conference on families and HIV that she just attended where they were the counter story to people being deserted by their families: a family rallying from the beginning, coming to the support group en masse, children speaking up and out as children of an HIV mom, now bringing her home to care for as she dies, attending as she wanders in and out of consciousness, a chatty-Cathy now silent, in the words of her friend, Diane. Only the eyes, the restlessness and the pulling out of the catheter.

I think of James Agee's words: "What is it, profound behind the outward windows of each one of you, beneath touch even of your own suspecting . . . so that the eyes shine of their own angry glory, but the eyes of a trapped animal, or of a furious angel nailed to the ground by his wings, or however else one may faintly designate the human 'soul,' . . . how, looking thus into your eyes and seeing thus, how each of you is a creature which has never in all time existed before and which shall never in all time exist again and which is not quite like any other and which has the grand stature and natural warmth of every other and whose existence is all measured upon a still mad and incurable time; how am I to speak of you as . . . 'representatives' of your 'class,' as social integers in a criminal economy, or as individuals, . . . wives, . . . daughters,

Chris: Can you explain?

Maria: I have a stigma of it. I can't—there are people discussing their illnesses at work and what medications they take—not that I am looking for that. I can't say, hey by the way, I am dying from AIDS.

Chris: Other women describe it as a double life. Does that fit for you?

Maria: Very much so. I have to go to work, deal with the public. I get asked out by people who say, you want to go out, I know you don't have AIDS. I have people joking about it in my face. I absorb it and I think that I am not going to let it bother me. And it might not bother me for two-three days and then I will just fall apart and I won't be able to go to work. My boss, he goes what is wrong with you, god damn it, you are intolerable. If I could just tell him. This is why—I get to work somehow, I don't know, but I have to deal with it in public. I actually work at a sales counter, talk to people, I get asked out.

Chris: Danielle, you said you think you might die this year?

Danielle: I feel that way because the media says that if you have no T4 cells, you are probably gonna die. So, it still impacts the way I think about the disease. I mean, obviously I am still doing alright but everyone thinks if you have no more T4's, you don't have anything to fight anything, you are gonna be dead.

  ❧   ❧   ❧   ❧   ❧   ❧   ❧

and as my friends and as I 'know' you?" (*Let Us Now Praise Famous Men*, 1941, 99–100)

From Patti's research journal, December 1992

I think of myself frozen like a deer in Louisa's glare in the hospital room where Chris and I had gone to arrange the interview this very ill woman wanted to contribute in spite of not being able to attend her support group with whom we had just met. The weight of the indignity of being studied, the violence of objectification required by the academic pursuit of the possession of another's life which is turned into information for academic trade: this almost paralyzed me as I entered the room. What was this research project in the face of her story of eight months without eating, a baby dead of AIDS two years ago, hair fallen out from chemotherapy, surrounded by the women in a family she felt she had to protect from her despair and anger? What was her twitching that I carried with me for days afterward, a restlessness, as Chris and I finally named it, to be much about our lives? Was it some horror at turning the tragedy of this 24 year old Puerto Rican woman's life into part of the spectacle of the research? Was it an effort to speak in the research not only *of* and *to*, but *as*, in some recognition of the inevitable instrumentalism attendant upon the research task which I must both practice and trouble at the same time? What did this twitching have to do with what Chris and I had identified during the car trip that morning as our avoidance of anything other than the superficial in terms of death and dying issues in the interview-

Chris: How do you prepare for that?

Danielle: I don't know.

Tracy: I think this disease has made us sort of obsessed with living and we just think that our success is if you make it. A friend of mine died about four weeks ago, and my friend did fight. I saw a TV show with cancer women and some of them did die, but they died empowered, you know. And I think right now some of us are trying to find some strength, something about finding death or maybe some people are more religious, some are looking for the spirituality to fit in that gap. We want to fight this possibility that we won't live that long, but death should not be regarded as a failure. People are talking about living fourteen years, but there are some people who live three years. Look at Louisa, she died in May and the woman fought like a little dragon. She never gave up, she was always trying to empower other people during the retreats. I don't think Louisa failed. I guess, maybe, for women, or for all of us, we need people who can help us with that ultimate side. Instead of just physical healing we need to hear how to heal ourselves. I think there are not enough resources. Danielle and I were talking about it the other day and she was telling me that her parents had never gone to church. She doesn't have that religious belief, whether there is God. I don't believe in Christianity per se, I believe in God, but where are those resources?

ing we had done thus far? What did it have to do with worries about sensationalizing these women's stories, creating work that could feed the kind of voyeurism that often occurs when people are willing to put their tragedies on public display, a kind of Oprah effect?

What is going on here? How can Benjamin and his Angel of History help me to understand what seems to be in excess of available explanations? Situated, partial, perplexed, I seek some "underground of language," that breaks through the limits of its own conscious understanding to speak beyond its means. Positioning AIDS as the shock of an event so excessive that it exceeds our sense of historical intelligibility, witnessing the scandal of a plague, my task is to work against making of plague a spectacle that fails to respect the people involved. Thus the writing debt is

not so much a debt of words as it is a debt of silence, a moving softly and obliquely, a not knowing too quickly.

In her study of teaching about the Holocaust, Shoshona Felman (1992) writes of the inevitable failure and betrayal of the witness in her encounter with looking at history from hell. In the face of testimony about living in history as hell, many positions are created for a listener, from paralysis to awe and fear where we endow the teller of the tale with a kind of saintliness that both pays our tribute to her and keeps her at a distance, to avoid the intimacy entailed in knowing. This, it seems, is part of my logic of invoking angels into the space of this project. It was cooling comfort to engage in the hunt for Klee's paintings, Rilke and Valéry's poetry, Benjamin and Kushner's angels, even the canonical discourse on

Patti: Have you found anything to help in that search?

Tracy: Yes, I joined this interesting church. To other people it might seem like a cult, but the only thing we believe in is God and people in this church are comfortable with death. They believe they are going to come back, reincarnation. That keeps them going. Tomorrow I am going to the library to do some readings like my friend who researched lots and lots of religions until he found what gave him groundings. So when he died he was not miserable although he was in pain.

Patti: Is this part of what you mean when you say empowered?

Tracy: Yeah. Like for me now, I am starting to think about death more, I'm trying to find something

---

Memories of that week

Your strength, courage
Your pain
The clearness of your beautiful blue-gray eyes
Your hand held in mine—
You hold me so tight
I know that you will
never give up, never let me go
For me
For you
Love so real
And when it is all over. . .
I see us holding hands
With all the life in
this world
We are running with all the
Strength of life
Through a beautiful field of flowers
Laughter, Health, Life.

—Barb's journal entry, after her husband died of AIDS, 10-8-93

---

angelology. Additionally, to be beguiled by an angel like Benjamin's that is rigorously unsentimental, unpretentious, and situated so as to make its fiction a contemplation of its own perplexing meanings is to raise questions about the limits and the possibilities of knowing.

AIDS is overburdened with representations. Here's yet another. What is its work? I think of the women I have interviewed, women often treated like lepers. I think of the way Kushner, instead, positioned his character, Prior, in *Angels in America:* in the redeeming shadow of death, living with/dying of AIDS, teacher to the angels who came to him in their

despair over God's desertion of the world. I think of words from the French novel by Herve Guibert, *To the Friend Who Did Not Save My Life* (1991): "Jules once said to me that AIDS was a marvelous disease. And it's true that I was discovering something sleek and dazzling in its hideousness, for though it was certainly an inexorable disease, it wasn't immediately catastrophic, it was an illness in stages, a very long flight of steps that led assuredly to death, but whose every step represented a unique apprenticeship. It was a disease that gave death time to live and its victims time to die, time to discover time, and in the end to discover life."

to be comfortable with. I want it to be a positive experience, because a lot of people who have had those near death experiences and come back have said it is really wonderful and there is no fear involved. So I want to try to set myself up thinking maybe it won't be so bad and not thinking that I am just going to go in the ground and then nothing. I need to feel that there is going to be something positive there so I am gonna research, find that out and empower myself. I want to be passing away, like gone, and say I lived a good life. You know, that kind of feeling, not miserable.

Patti: The death itself is not a failure?

Tracy: What else can I do?

Diane: We all die.

Tracy: I don't mean to make it sound like teasing. At times I am scared to go to bed because I hate to black out; I hate anesthesia; I hate to go to bed. This is not easy. This is my ideal. This is what I am working toward.

Joanna: I think I am fortunate in my family because we are grounded in our faith and I can see other people who don't have a belief system or faith. It scares me for them. People in my family are all older, so I have always been around death and dying.

Chris: Do you think about it, Diane?

Diane: Spirituality matters, yeah. Not so much about death. I mean I am not afraid about dying, I believe, like they do, that there is another life waiting for me. It doesn't scare me, I am ready. But I am looking more for the spiritual. I started going to church again. And then I stopped going in December after I had a chat with my minister and I told him about my HIV+ status. And he asked me if I was promiscuous. So I think I went back maybe one time and then I stopped going to church and I even stopped reading my

In November of 1987 the United States Catholic Conference approved *The Many Faces of AIDS: A Gospel Response,* which urged Catholics to treat those with AIDS with love and understanding and to take part in educational programs discussing how the spread of the disease can be stopped. But the *St. Cloud Visitor* (Catholic newspaper of the Diocese of St. Cloud, MN), December 3, 1992, interviews HIV+ people who tell stories of not finding the support they need within organized churches, "especially the Catholic Church. They see the church's emphasis on the sexual morality issues surrounding the person with AIDS as getting in the way of other Christian ideals like love and acceptance." The paper also carries a story about an ecumenical prayer service commemorating World AIDS Day (December 1). "As people infected with AIDS and the HIV virus struggle to find a sense of acceptance within Protestant and Catholic churches, the words were a poignant reminder that many with the disease have not turned their backs on God or their spiritual life."

bible. I am getting to the point now where I am ready to find another church. I don't feel comfortable going back to that church.

Joanna: I think I attend church for some of the same reasons. The church I was going to, I loved it because of the music. But whenever I tried to get the subject broached with our new pastor, he would try to brush it off and so I just got the feeling that this wasn't going to work. So I went to the church with our former pastor, and one of the guys in the congregation said, I saw you on TV not long ago on the access channel. I was doing a program on AIDS, and the people there had no problem with it. I don't think the church is taking an active enough role in HIV and AIDS education or support.

Patti: What are the taboos in all of this? And there are layers of taboos, there's taboos with your family, with this group, and taboos that we've constructed even in this research.

Lori: The biggest thing that hasn't been brought up is our prognosis for our future. It's not one of those things that you have a constant vision of, it's one of those things where you say one day, I'm not going to die from this, no way, some miracle will happen, I'm untouchable. And then I get into my Sarah Bernhardt, very dramatic period of what you all are going to do when I'm gone. I can't focus in on anything, it's very gray. It's almost a spiritual thing that whatever the person who has control of the strings has in store for me is going to happen. But I don't worry about it, I don't dwell on it, I'm not afraid of it. Which surprises me because I'm a little wimp. I think more about me dying or being gone in terms of how it's going to affect other people than about me, because I know if I start to get sick, I'm going to do some sort of self-deliverance. I'm not going to be a martyr and wait until the very end for some nasty, disgusting death. If you're going to go, you're going to go. It's been a great ride and when it's ready to be over it'll be over. Do the rest of you talk about it with anyone? My family never brings it up, it's like taboo.

Rita: When I wrote for the book from the Hemlock Society, I just wanted it there. Am I the only one who is thinking about suicide? [Several no's.] That makes me feel better. My dad got really upset about my living will. I thought he would understand, but from somewhere this attitude came up.

Linda B: I think there's going to come a time when these conversations have to happen, but none of us are at that stage.

Chris: What about the tension between these death and dying conversations and having a positive attitude?

Lori: I don't know what to say. I don't know how I'll feel about it until I am facing what J faced or my husband. I'm not worried; I kind of know it happens, but I don't really understand how it happened. I still speed, still eat too much. If I was really worried about dying, I would do a lot of things different, like taking my DDI. It's way out there, probably like it is for you guys, which makes it really a weird situation. You know you have this fatal disease, but it's something that you can't really put your hands on right now. It's like a dream. How is this really going to end? So why even worry about it, because until you've got something to deal with, why worry about it?

Linda B: It's weird, when I was younger I always thought I wanted to die young.

Robyn: Me too. I thought I'd die in a car wreck.

Linda B: I guess I thought I was probably gonna be by myself and I didn't want to grow old alone.

Lori: Now I think about the Hemlock Society. What do you guys think about it? I'm not real good at pain and I am real good at medicating myself.

Patti: Is self-deliverance a taboo?

Rita: It's kind of like an inevitability. It's like I'm not good at suffering and pain. It's like all of this stuff I've done with my life since I came back, and I think if I go back and do what I ran away from, it's like the other day they made me take pain pills at the clinic. I didn't want to take them. She said you take methadone, what's the difference? But it's like too close to dope.

Chris: What else has not been talked about?

CR: I'd like to say that I've seen both sides of the disease. I see us here with rosy cheeks and laughing, but I've also seen people who have lost all control of their body functions. Toward the end, they're not really there, their mind is gone. And I have made up my mind that I don't want to get to that stage. A man that died a few weeks ago, he weighed 360, you wouldn't think that he had AIDS; he would have been 36. He got up, dressed, went to see his mother and father, ate a big lunch at Red Lobster and had a coronary in the bathroom. That's the way I'd like to go. He knew he was going. I'm allergic to shellfish, so if I call you up and say bring two lobsters. The disease seems like it doesn't let the person go, the person has to let their body go. One man there at the hospice where I worked, his mother came every day and fed him. When his mother would come into the room, the look on his face was like, get her away from me. The nurse said, ___ is very angry because they won't leave him alone. He wanted to go and his mother wouldn't let him go. I've learned that from working there, at the very end, if a person is ready to go, let them go.

Lori: I think we have that choice, that power. I'm going to do that [assisted suicide], when the time comes. One of the weirdest things for me, when J decided to die and my husband did the same thing, that is something that has shaken me for two and a half years now. We have that power in us. That's something I am still struggling with. When my husband died they had to do an autopsy and they still haven't found out what killed him; he just decided he didn't want to go through this and put himself in a coma and checked out. It's something that I am having a really tough time understanding, that and the fact that J was making this decision and maybe she was vocal, but I lived with my husband and I had no idea he was going through this. In a way it was a blessing to know that I have that choice. It's not suicide in the terms that we know suicide as. It just amazes me that humans have that ability. They're putting that Dr. Kevorkian on trial but those women can probably do this without him. That part really freaks me out and it's something that I'm filing away in the front of my mind in a very special place, so whenever I'm ready, I can, hopefully, get to that point. All this talk about mercy killing, why does it work for some people but not others? Are they just really not ready, and maybe J and my husband were ready? It's something that has really shaken me.

Rita: I just did my living will and stuff and I thought my family was all together about it and my dad and I were sitting talking and all of a sudden out of the blue he said that it wasn't fair of me to do that. And it was like wait a minute, we've already done it and why are you changing your mind? He said it's like I put a lot of pressure on them, and I never did. I thought it was something that they understood that I wanted. So now I had to go back and change it all and go to the doctor and ask him how we could do it now. And he was so cool. He just said well, you don't think you're leaving right now, do you? I just told you your T-cell count is up, you don't have to come back for three months and you lay this on me. He was so understanding about it. He just said that as long as he had my request in my file he would do my wishes. As long as it is in black and white and the social worker at the hospital helped me get the papers. I mean the hospital is so cool about that. They understand; they didn't give me no lectures, no nothing, and it's just like what I wanted. But I felt bad in that I thought my dad understood.

Patti: What about this concept of the unsayable? What parts of this are there just not words for?

Lori: Why? Why any of us? Why not a clean disease, a pretty disease? Why won't they give us money for this? Why have some gone and we haven't? There are so many whys.

15

"A Greater Risk of Hope": CR and Linda B

CR: I sure have come a long way from when you first talked to us four years ago.[1] I had a pie in the sky attitude. Now I have a completely different attitude since I know people who have died. Before, I was thinking "the cure is gonna come," but we keep losing friends and this shows me the real depth and the death of AIDS. I used to do panels two to three times a week, but no longer feel I have anything positive to say. With Lori's death on top of so many others, I had to go on Prozac. I just couldn't take anymore. Now we know it's gonna get us. I've had two opportunistic infections; I know it's gonna get me. Prozac helps me to not feel so bleak, to not just sit all day in front of the television. It got so bad, I see a therapist every week. I still feel sad, but I can get up and get on. I did agree to do a panel in two weeks for a group of psychologists. Mostly I do minority women, especially in shelters and jails. But I don't think I can face those women and say "You can make it." I try to give hope but now I'd probably scare them to death. I wouldn't want to scare them into not getting tested. As you grow old in the disease, you have to deal with what comes. But the things we say about taking care of yourself, now we know no matter what you eat, death happens. I just shut down around Lori's death. I went around in a dark fog thinking it could be me. It feels so heavy in my body. I need to cry, but I can't.

Patti: One of the hardest things for Chris and me has been how to present hope without it being false hope; we call it our search for "non-stupid hope."

CR: There's a greater risk of hope for the newly diagnosed, with the new drugs and treatments, but how long can you take such toxic drugs over time? I'm on a three drug cocktail now, but I've been infected so long, ten years. I don't know what my viral load is and I don't want to. *General Hospital* is running hopeful stories about how HIV+ people can have relationships and

161

all, with the new hopes for treatment so that AIDS is becoming a chronic rather than a fatal disease.

Patti: What do you mean by "a greater risk of hope?" That is such an interesting phrase.

CR: Maybe I meant "chance of hope."

Patti: But let's play with this "risk of hope" idea. Maybe it can help us with this false hope/non-stupid hope thing.

CR: False hope gets you through each day. You think, "it won't get me." You do have to live; ignorance IS bliss. If you knew all the hard things to come, you'd jump out a window. This disease is just so bad, not knowing is a gift.

Patti: One reaction Chris had to Lori's impending death was to think we should not say in the book that any particular woman had died, that we could give the number of how many had died, but that the book would take away hope if the reader saw individual women struggling to live and then knew who had died and when.

CR: Maybe she was angry, like the days I get angry that the new treatments came too late for me. I hope I don't get so angry that no one wants to be around me when I'm late in the disease. You don't want to give up, but you know you're dying. You do go through bodily changes and deterioration and people treat you differently and that makes you mad. I'm just making myself a little better for a little time, but you know what's coming.

Patti: Does the support group help with this?

CR: The group still helps. We scattered after Barb's husband died, but after Lori's death we went to the wake as a group. The group has grown through this. The first meeting after Lori died was hard. I never saw so much crying. Lori was part of this from the beginning. Now there's only Linda B and me, and Barb who came a little later.

"Hope Is Starting to Be a Four Letter Word"

Linda B: In terms of Lori's death, is death ever "expected" or "welcomed"?[2] Well, in this case it is both. I felt so sorry for Lori. It's still a blow to the group. You always hold out for a miracle. We had all been together about six weeks before Lori started to really go "downhill" rather quickly. Personally, I want to remember Lori as she was then. I didn't see her after she came to group that night and was resolved to the fact that her time was coming. She was fragile looking. Her hair, which was always combed, was a little disheveled. She seemed to be very alert and with it.

I miss Lori. She was so "put together." If I needed help in some way with a problem I was trying to think through I could go to Lori. She was a ray of sunshine on many a rainy day.

You know, Patti, she talked very honestly and openly with the group when she was in the hospital. She was ultra pissed off when she woke up in the hospital because she wanted to be on the other side. She really was ready to die. The funeral was very hard for me. Lori had a very full and happy life, but the funeral was so solemn. Suits, suits, and more suits. No music, no poetry, no prayer cards. Just a eulogy by the rabbi. It was tougher at the cemetery. I had never seen a person's casket lowered into the ground. The finality of it. Her tiny little body being lowered into that BIG DEEP hole. CR's knees buckled. My heart sunk. It was so hard to watch.

This is a chapter in our support group's story that is inevitable. It isn't the first. It's not going to be the last. I feel like we're trying to stop a freight train. Who will be next? Can we somehow prevent it from ever happening again? Well, no, but you just keep hoping for that miracle.

About Lori's death and its effect on the group, yes, over time the group's identity shifts. This group consists of several smaller groups. In other words, some of us "hang" together outside of the group. It has to do with class placement, I think. The two I am closest to, we came from the same lifestyle. Our parents struggled to raise us. We were hard heads growing up. We are from the working class so to speak. We've gotten our hands dirty to make a buck. But even though Lori was in the other group, the group is minus another charter member. Suddenly we aren't that healthy support group, we are vulnerable, and it hurts.

Hope is starting to be a four letter word. Here lately I think more about "my time left." Whenever a thought like that comes to mind, I catch myself and try to erase. But as time goes by, it takes longer to go away.

CR and I talked about this the other day. I try to boost her up when she talks about how we are being strung along.

I've been at this now for seven long years. And, yes, it is getting old. I'm starting to REALLY compare it to the Vietnam War. As long as people are infected there's money to be made. Then I think of what all it takes to research a new drug. I go back and forth.

When my doctor asked me a few weeks ago if I would consider coming out of the study that is the three drug cocktail, I felt like I had just flunked the most important test of my lifetime. I almost cried. I didn't want people to see that, but the book of HOPE had blank pages for me.

The bottom line for me is: I have days that I feel like there is no hope. But, for every day I get to live, it's one more day to hope.

Newly diagnosed women DO NEED to know the harsh reality of this disease. They need to know that you REALLY need to take care of yourself. Don't give them false hope and paint a picture of a disease that's not going to "get" you. Because it just might get you sooner than you think. To cover their deaths is to dishonor who they were and how they left. Lori left with dignity. She fought the battle. She got tired of it and left. Women need to know that, that that option is available. That it doesn't take Dr. Kevorkian to get out of this place.

I agree with CR's theory of "the risk of hope." Do we allow ourselves to think more than three months ahead? Do you believe what the news tells you tonight about something you knew a year ago was in the basic research stage? Or are they just "teasing" you into watching what is old news?

I think I'm getting hard because of this disease. Harder than I ever was. I don't like that. I don't want to be mean to other people, to trivialize their problems in comparison to mine.

And, yes, ignorance is bliss. CR and I have said more than once we wonder what our lives would be like if we had never gotten that test. If we hadn't then hope would be about winning the lottery instead of what it is now.

On the other hand, without this disease, I never would have known someone like Lori. I never went to the ballet until the local AIDS foundation gave me a ticket. I would not have seen any live theater. I wouldn't know what it is to meditate. I wouldn't have ever listened to New Age music. I would not have done ANY public speaking other than standing on a barroom table and singing "Delta Dawn" back when I was about 25. I would not appreciate life. I would still be afraid of death. I would still be living with some miserable asshole. I would still be driving by the forest instead of stopping and admiring the trees, one at a time. Think about it, Patti. I would be taking today for granted. I would put things off. Forget to be kind, be in such a rush. Each day is such a blessing.

Notes

1. Phone interview, September 6, 1996.
2. From e-mail correspondence, July–September 1996.

16

"We Had a Real Nice Life": Louisa

Chris: When were you first diagnosed with HIV?[1]

Louisa: The real, real first time was in November of 1988. But I kept it a secret until July of 1989.

Chris: Did you really? From everyone?

Louisa: From . . .

Chris: Are you OK?

Louisa: I have a heating pad on . . .

Chris: Anyway . . . why did you keep it a secret?

Louisa: Because I didn't want somebody to start feeling sorry for me and doing things for me.

Chris: It's kind of like you knew things would change once they knew?

Louisa: Yeah, I never worried about whether they were going to accept it.

Chris: As I begin this section, I am living in a hotel room in Asunción, Paraguay, in the process of becoming a mother to my newly adopted infant daughter, Elena Marie. I am captivated by this small bundle of wonder, already finding unimaginable the thought of any kind of separation.

Several days after receiving Elena, age 3.5 months, I take her to a pediatrician. The baby seems healthy and happy to me, but I soon learn that "health" can be in the eyes of the beholder. Doctor Frutos is quite concerned; Elena's skin lacks tone, and she has poor head control. Most significantly, she is gaining too little weight since her birth. He wants me to take her across the street to the lab for several tests. All I hear is "HIV test." I panic, tears come to my eyes, and I can hardly breathe as I consider the possibility that she just might be HIV+. What would I do? Could I still adopt her? Probably not, because people with HIV infection are not per-

Chris: But just that it would be like a burden for them? And who did you tell first?

Louisa: Frannie, she was born in 1987, so I knew she would be at risk. She died when she was four and a half.

Chris: I remember you talking about her at the retreat, that whole weekend. I bet you miss her a lot.

Louisa: Oh god yes.

Chris: You know, when we talked one other time, you said getting to see her soon is one of the positive things about dying. Are you still anticipating that?

Louisa: Oh, yeah. She would be turning six this March.

Chris: What are you going to say when you see her?

Louisa: I don't know. I don't know if she will recognize me. I don't know how it is. I can't explain it.

Chris: When we talked a couple of months ago, you said geez, you thought this might be over soon and that you would be dying before long. Do you think that is still going to happen soon?

Louisa: I had one doctor ask me that, you know, he said how long do you think you will be around? I said the beginning of next year.

mitted to immigrate to the United States. How would I take care of her? And anger—after so much effort to adopt, what if my child is sick, perhaps even terminally ill?

After three months in Paraguay, Elena and I are home in Columbus, Ohio. She is happy and very healthy. As I prepare to write tonight, I carry her cozy, sleepy little being from her crib, to the cradle by my work table. I must have her nearby. For the moment, I can protect her. But she has been born into the age of AIDS. As she grows and develops, and eventually makes choices regarding drugs and sex, will AIDS still be a deadly threat?

Yes, I must have her near me, as I begin the painful work of recalling Louisa, her young daughter Frannie, and the many others I have seen taken by AIDS.

I first meet Louisa in 1991, at a retreat I organized for HIV+ women. Thirty women gather in a circle, in a large but cozy room at a convent. We pass the "talking doll." When the small, brightly beaded doll is in your hands, it is your turn to speak, without interruption, of whatever you hold in your heart and mind. Everyone else simply listens, often punctuating a woman's story with nods or tears or smiles. Louisa, 21 years old, thin, Hispanic, speaks of her daughter's HIV infection, then AIDS, and then a final wish trip to Disneyland. Louisa's words bring alive every detail of that special time. Frannie, four years old, had delighted in the experience, unaware that her childhood would be condensed to several days in the land of Goofy and Mickey. For little Frannie, Disney is the gateway to heaven.

Chris: Well, I sure hope so, at least that long. So you are feeling more optimistic right now?

Louisa: Well, my family says they are ready, so . . . they always say that.

Chris: What's been hardest about this for you?

Louisa: Besides losing Frannie? Taking so many medications, going to the clinic so often. I had some chemo and all my hair fell out. And I haven't been able to eat for quite a long time.

Chris: How old are you now?

Louisa: 24.

Chris: It sounds like it's a way of life for you.

Louisa: Right, Frannie's father, he helps a lot. When the baby was here, he did everything. His mother is across the hall. . .

Chris: Well, you know when I visited you in the hospital, I certainly got the impression that there is a lot of close family.

Louisa: Yeah. Whenever I get sick, forget it. The phone doesn't stop ringing.

Chris: You've gotten a lot of attention and a lot of support, it sounds like.

Louisa: Yeah. I feel sorry for some of the girls in the support group that claim they don't have anybody. You know, they can have some of mine.

Frannie waits for the presence of her parents by her bedside before she dies. Two years later, Patti and I visit Louisa, in the hospital again. There's the I.V., feeding a woman who eats nothing by mouth for months. Louisa is surrounded by the women from her family. Eventually we meet Louisa's mother, who now watches *her* little one, only 24 years old, wither and die from AIDS.

Louisa acknowledges the unconditional loyalty of her family. But she also feels obliged to protect them, especially her mother. It is only when alone that Louisa will cry. Protecting loved ones is a common thread among those who are sick and dying. Occasionally, it is my task to clear the room for awhile, to allow the person to be alone. Or, I may gently invite her to talk, reassuring that she does not need to protect me from her real feelings. We may speak very openly of her impending death. I encourage her to reminisce. There are many memories to revisit, a process that may be too painful for family members.

It is most remarkable how many women find purpose and meaning in their own deaths. Louisa anticipates a reunion with her daughter. Julia chooses to die sooner rather than later, so her sons can get on with their lives with new parents. Anne has such a profound faith and spirituality that she knows she is going to God. Caroline, formerly a nun, infected by her one and only sexual partner, dies quickly, probably so she can protect her farm family from the prolonged embarrassment of AIDS.

And many people with HIV/AIDS create meaning in *living* with the infection. It is often the "accidental victims" who

Chris: You have an overflow. Nobody should have to do this alone. You know you are so young. I just think back to when I was 24 and how much I still had to do and how much I took for granted and it just seems so very young to have gone through what you have gone through. Do you get angry about it, like why in the hell did this happen to me?

Louisa: Yeah. There's times when I get angry at him [her daughter's father from whom she contracted the virus]. But I've already forgiven him and I know he didn't do it intentionally. But there's times he'll make a joke about it and I don't think it's funny. He stopped doing that. He's all right; he works and everything.

Chris: It sounds like you and Frannie's father, your relationship, boy you've been through a lot, but it has survived. Do you love each other a lot.

Louisa: Yeah. That's why everybody was like "you taking him back?" My dad, especially; he don't want nothing to do with him.

Chris: I know when I visited your support group, there were several women in the group who have really no one to help them or love them as they go through this. Geneva is going to take care of them all, I am afraid. Did you know Geneva before you all got HIV?

Louisa: No. We met at your retreat.

become famous. Ryan White, remarkable with his youthful wisdom and courage, inspires people throughout the entire country to re-think their prejudice and hostility. Elisabeth Glaser crusades for children with HIV/AIDS. And even Kimberly Bergalis, angry and bitter that she was infected by a healthcare professional, speaks out for what she believes. Greg Louganis, already famous, tells an honest story about living in secrecy, denial and fear. Such stories may help others stay safe or care more lovingly for someone with AIDS.

Most of the women with whom I work do not become famous, except perhaps in their local communities. But most of them find a way to make meaningful their experience with HIV. Lori is the keynote speaker at a public AIDS event; CR joins the local Public Board of Health; Diane

instructs medical students; and Holley, who may lose her voice to AIDS cancer, is now a poet. Melody starts a women's support group and an AIDS center. Dawn sues her employer for AIDS discrimination, and even though she loses the case, she speaks out, setting an example for her young daughter, also HIV+. Linda B, an IRS employee, "comes out" as HIV+ and keeps her job. And Carol X is preparing to attend medical school.

Louisa is too sick to participate in the group interview for this research, but asks us to her hospital room. Too crowded with family for her to really talk, she emphatically states, "*Call me.*" It is awkward for me to do this interview over the phone. Patti describes what I feel: that our research process is objectifying, intrusive. However, most women with AIDS participate in research, whether in a qualita-

Chris: Oh, is that where you met? She is such a gem. Oh that is wonderful. I didn't realize you had just met there. Is she coming by and seeing you and stuff?

Louisa: No. In fact, I don't even think she has called. Maybe I'll go to group tomorrow. I don't know if people think about going. I don't know. The group fell apart.

Chris: That's too bad. Our group in Columbus is going through some of that, too. It's hard. So what's something that you want people out there to know about this whole experience that you have had?

Louisa: Well, if they have already been exposed, to accept it and don't be negative like a lot of people want to be. And if they are not infected to be careful, you know, the usual. So really, it would be a lot of safety tips.

Chris: The practical. Did you ever think about committing suicide or doing anything like that?

Louisa: No. I got to the point of real deep depression. But still—I would think about it, and then I would think about my mom. You have to think about those you leave behind.

Chris: So when your attitude has felt real negative or you've felt real down, what do you do to get yourself back up again?

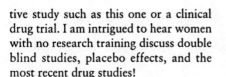

tive study such as this one or a clinical drug trial. I am intrigued to hear women with no research training discuss double blind studies, placebo effects, and the most recent drug studies!

Participation in research is activism, a contribution. Quite recently, one of our participants, eager to see this project come to fruition, laid it on the line: "When are you guys going to publish? Some of us are on deadline, you know."

On deadline. We are all on deadline. One HIV+ woman told me that she divides people in two groups: HIV+ and dying, and HIV–. She feels such envy and resentment toward HIV– people that she can not be around them, until she remembers that they (we), too, *are dying*.

The *process* of dying frightens me more than being dead. I hope to die quickly in an accident, or from a stroke, when I am very old, of course. With my rather controlling nature, this is the antithesis of how I live daily life. But now I vacillate, because I witness the profound personal transformation, relationship enrichment, and spiritual growth that come from clearly foreseeing one's own death. Guiltily, I acknowledge that my life is enriched even by the dying of those I know and love, but nothing protects me from the pain, the anger, the helplessness. I cry, usually after the funeral, usually by myself. I use an imagery as a ritual for saying good-bye.

I am especially close to eight women who are living with HIV for six or more years. Many have AIDS and are getting sick. Now that I live in another city, I see them less often, but perhaps I am also "pulling back," trying to protect myself from the pain of losing them. We have such

Louisa: Pray. I do a lot of that. Cry. I do a lot of that when I am by myself. I don't feel like doing it in front of my mom. But sometimes when they leave me alone, and that's when I love it, because that's when I can let it all out.

Chris: Yeah, it sounds like you are so sensitive to how other people around you are feeling. Do you think about dying much?

Louisa: No. The last time I was in the hospital, they kept asking me, you know, how long I felt I was gonna last and all these questions that it did worry me. The other doctor said that he had done everything that he could for me. In other words, if you get another infection, we can't do anything.

Chris: Is that hard to hear?

Louisa: You pretend like it is no big deal at the moment. But then you burst out when you are by yourself.

Chris: Were you with Frannie when she died?

Louisa: Yeah. She was at the hospital. Me and her dad had gone out to get something to eat and we were in there all morning and we went ahead to get something to eat and the doctor told my mom it's a matter of minutes. And me and her dad weren't even there. So when we walked in the doctor was waiting for us and he was like hurry up, hurry up. So when we got up there, the machine was like pumping real slow and when we got there, she felt us. It was like, mom, dad. Because her machine started going real fast, you know, like I am not going nowhere until my parents . . .

Chris: Did you cry then?

Louisa: Oh God. Her dad did all the crying for me. Now him, I believe, is suicidal.

Chris: Does he have some support or is he in a support group or anything? Does he talk to you about being HIV+?

Louisa: Sometimes. It's not a subject that he would pass out fliers on.

Chris: Do you worry about him too?

Louisa: I can't. I can't worry about him.

Chris: Good, you have to set some limits. What's it like seeing your body change so much?

marvelous times together, laughing, playing, eating, traveling, talking. At times, I feel that if these women die, my AIDS work is finished. They say I help them, but they are my anchors, my "AIDS roots."

These women, their partners, friends, and children have a "welcome Elena" picnic. I want to freeze frame my joy as I watch my 8 month old daughter lovingly passed from person to person. Elena is not afraid; she makes no judgments, and she models the wisdom of living in the moment.

That Elena is in my life is a testimony to the big lesson of the gift of this work: go after your dream and make it happen.

Louisa: Well, it feels the same. But when I look in the mirror, I am like, who is that? No hair. I am darker. I feel like Louisa, but I don't look like Louisa.

Chris: Are you staying in bed?

Louisa: I hop from the bed to the couch. That's all I do.

Chris: Are you bored?

Louisa: I heard a lot of people [she is readjusting herself], I've heard people say I'd rather commit suicide than live with that or even that they will give it to other people, which I think is very wrong. Oh, my feet. I don't know why they are so swollen. They said it's not from the chemo. I thought it was. And then I was bleeding. Yesterday I called the doctor in GYN and I told him nothing is healthy. I am in pain and I need something better. So he said OK, I am going to prescribe something else.

Chris: Good. It sounds like you are still in charge. Well, I don't want to wear you out. Is there anything we haven't talked about that you would like to talk about right now? What would you have liked to have been different in your life?

Louisa: Let me see. If you ever get diagnosed with HIV, a lot of people go out and go crazy. I don't regret no part of my life. I just wish things would have been different. I would have everything the same, except the virus which came along and ruined everything. **We had a real nice life.**

Note

1. From a January 1993 phone interview.

Death Makes Angels of Us All

> Death makes angels of us all
> & gives us wings
> where we had shoulders
> smooth as raven's
> claws
>
> —Jim Morrison[1]

The German poet Rilke wrote about the hard to grasp parts of life, what he termed the Too Big, especially how to live in a world marked by death. He tried to bring such knowings to words in a way that created a widened space that was about the oneness of life and death. What Rilke called the "work of the heart" posits angels as about living without certain belief and truth. In essence, Rilke's "assenting Angels" are about the paradox of affirming from negation, about overcoming the lack of hope that comes when life is "teaching its most desperate lessons." For Rilke, the test of living was an alchemy that used pain and suffering in order to earn hope in a hard world. His are *terrible angels*, annihilators of images we have built up "fondly and lazily," in our delusions of some higher order. Shatterers, great undeceivers, this is "the angelic terror" where we have to learn to live without redemption, no longer sheltered by the ruins of Christianity. Here the angels are about saying yes to life in the face of disaster, sickness, murder, cruelty and senseless death.

Sixty some years after Rilke's terrible angels is Benjamin Jones' papier mache AIDS Angel. Names cover the angel's body in a roll-call of accountability for governmental neglect and ignorance. "Fuck George Bush" screams across the angel's belly. Slash marks and names track the dead. Dollar and cent signs on the angel's feet underscore the fiscal bottom line. Reminding one of a piñata, each whack would be like the women at the Women and AIDS retreat whacking a softball and shouting out objects of their anger, from the government to "bisexual men who lie." This is the angel as an exorcism of rage. Part of an art show in Cleveland the spring of 1994, "Creating in Crisis: Making Art in the Age of AIDS," the AIDS Angel addresses the emptiness of words, trying to overcome that few are listening, trying to say something more, to find a new way of getting the same old message across, trying to inspire the strength to keep on fighting, working under and through the shadow of the virus, trying to address death which makes no distinctions between sexes, races, or classes, the great leveler, the ultimate common denominator.

Not knowing how to act, being caught unaware, inadequate, without resources, is almost a mark of facing the Too Big. In an economy so marked by loss as the place of AIDS, is the angel what the poet Wallace Stevens terms "necessary angels"?[2] Necessary angels are about our need to create and believe in what we can hardly avoid suspecting are fictions. In this move to "trouble" angels, no longer so smitten with them, the "necessary" move locates the angel as a ruin/rune, shot through with inadequacies, a perverted and deflated angel, witness to the human capacity to carry on and even sing in the midst of anguish, an audience of astonished angels, come down to earth to learn about living in an historical time of permanent emergency.

Notes

1. Quoted in Queen Mu, Orpheus in the Maelstrom, *Mondo 2000*, #4, p. 134.

Benjamin Jones, *AIDS Angel,* 1992, papier mache, housepaint. From "Creating in Crisis: Making Art in the Age of AIDS," Spaces Gallery, Cleveland, Ohio, May 27–July 1, 1994. Photo by John Seyfried. Used by permission of the artist.

Support Groups

17

"It's Taken Me Years to Get Here"

Linda B: I remember the first support group meeting that CR came to.

Lori: Oh, I do, too. She was shaking and crying.

CR: I came to the group meeting about a month after I found out I was HIV+. I was real scared, but once I saw everyone, they gave me hope that I could live with it. The first time I got the flu or a bad cold, the group did me more good than anything, cause I was just sure I was going to die. Me and Linda B used to talk to each other on the phone and she'd say, "You still alive? How much is your temperature?" I said "I am going fast, honey."

Linda B: But you know, we worked through that and we got over that cold. Then we were so happy, we were still alive, we made it. Then we went to Famous Recipe and had some chicken and mashed potatoes.

Lori: All of us have a pretty strong sense of survival or we wouldn't be in this group. I'd never think of not moving ahead. People always say "How do

Chris: "It has taken me years to get here." This poignant statement reflects the personal odyssey of any HIV+ woman who eventually joins a support group. The journey to the group includes her entire life experience, with its victories and disappointments. Her identity is much more than just HIV or AIDS.

Significant practical and psychological obstacles exist that delay or hinder the process of attending a support group. Perhaps the woman is without transportation or childcare, or perhaps she is fearful of who or what she may find at a meeting, or perhaps she simply acquiesces to the needs of another person. Anne, a middle class African American woman, lives secretly with HIV for five years before finally coming to group. Her husband, shameful that he infected his wife, can not bear the thought that anyone will hear her story.

The purpose of this chapter is twofold. First, I urge HIV+ women to join a

you deal with this?" Well, you don't have any choice. You just deal with it, it becomes part of your life. I have a lot of hope, a lot of hope.

Alisha: When I first found out that I was HIV+ in 1991, I did not have any support. It was really hard on me and I was in shock. I was incredibly hurt and I kept asking "why?" When I got home, after I got tested, I cried forever. And then I was wondering whether my ex-husband knew he had it. I was very angry. For eight years of marriage, why did he keep that a secret? It is something that I am very resentful about, that I can not accept. I had sort of an emotional breakdown and finally someone took me to a counselor, and then my counselor couldn't handle all the emotions that I was feeling, so she kinda stuck me here. Seeing all the women in the support group and seeing how positive everyone was and seeing that I was the same as other people, then I didn't feel as alone. I realized that there are people who are going through what I am going through and that I had to get out all these emotions that were tumbling through me. I just had to get them out.

Lori: Two women friends said things over the past years that make me think that they're looking at my time as being limited. I hear constantly "Well, you don't need this aggravation." I had a fight with one of my friends, it was no big deal, she was so stressed out and she felt so bad, and I know if I wasn't HIV+ she would have just been pissed off. I wish this virus would

❀   ❀   ❀   ❀   ❀   ❀   ❀

women's support group. Hopefully, the stories of women who belong to a support group will help someone take this important step toward sisterhood, empowerment, and survival. Second, I hope our experiences will inspire and assist with the formation of new support groups, especially in non-urban areas. All you really need to start a support group is good communication skills, a safe place, and a willing heart; however, there are numerous issues, challenges, and unexpected twists that occur in the life of an HIV support group. The ups and downs are discussed, keeping in mind that every group, and every facilitator, has distinctive character and style.

In 1988, a colleague asked whether I would facilitate a support group for women living with HIV/AIDS. *Living with?* My professional training included perfunctory attention to the then new problem of AIDS. Assuming that there must be literature, I searched the bookstore for an AIDS title that suggested that "women" might be included in the text. No luck. When I asked the clerk for *AIDS: The Ultimate Challenge,* by Elisabeth Kubler-Ross (Macmillan, 1987), a female customer standing within earshot bolted for the front of the store. She must have assumed that I was HIV+. This was a significant introduction to HIV/AIDS.

To the best of my knowledge, I knew no one, male or female, with HIV/AIDS. I had absorbed media images and tales of sickly, wasting, desperate young men. My assumptions, erroneous as they were, included: IF any women came to the group, they would be sick, depressed, uneducated, with little meaning or pur-

bring me closer to people, but it really hasn't. Things really haven't changed with my sister and brother in law, and the same with my parents. We never talk about the virus. It's like business as usual, but there's this big wall. The interesting part has been the women in this group. It's one of the best things that has happened to me. I've always been the outsider, always different by choice, and I don't think that people are naturally drawn to me, but in this group—

Carol X: One of the first things I asked my doctors was, "Are there any other women, is there anything we can do?" It was a godsend that this group was here. I met all these beautiful people who bring such diversity to it. It was just a sisterhood. Sometimes I can't even explain the feeling I get here. We were talking and trying to define that special "bond" but I don't think any word can describe the love that you get here. And it's unconditional.

Chris: What about you, Robyn? What role does the group play?

Robyn: At first I didn't think I needed anyone, and I expected sick people in wheelchairs, like death warmed over.

CR: I remember the first time I saw you, Robyn. I was sitting in the lobby and your strawberry hair was what brought you to my attention. And when I got to our meeting, you were in the room. I told Linda, "It gets everybody."

pose in life, especially because death loomed on the horizon. My purpose would be to offer comfort, safety, and help in preparing for death. Soon I would discover how misguided I was in my assumptions and mission.

I was nervous before the first group meeting. Would anyone come? Would I be comfortable? What would they want from me and each other? Would they talk? I knew you couldn't get the virus from casual touching. Did I really believe this? Mostly . . .

The first meeting, attended by two HIV+ women, was a success. Both women were physically healthy but isolated. Conversation flew; we shared tears and laughter, as well as hugs. As I drove home that evening, I experienced that rare and wonderful sensation that something momentous had just occurred in my life, and that it was, indeed, forever changed.

Why are support groups for *women* necessary? In most cities, the gay community establishes services, including support groups, that usually welcome women. HIV+ women and gay men develop bonds that are loving and mutually supportive. However, some women find it impossible to attend a predominantly gay group, and others report feelings of discomfort and alienation.

Are these uncomfortable feelings simply homophobia? Not always. Some women find the jokes, flirtations, and discussions simply boring or unrelated to their own experience. HIV/AIDS does not neutralize gender and lifestyle differences. And then there are HIV+ women who do disdain gays, who fully internalize social and religious prejudice against gays and

Just to look at her I thought she was going off to the medical library or came to meet her boyfriend or something.

Robyn: It's been great. Barb and I have lunch together. I don't have many friends outside of this group that I talk to.

Chris: And we've learned a lot about baseball from you!

CR: The only thing I had seen about AIDS or HIV was these emaciated gay men and I was saying, "oh Jesus." But when I first came here and walked into the room and saw healthy looking women, I said "When are the sick people coming?" And they were here. But that's been my one saving grace, this group. I can't relate to AIDS with a gay man or a heterosexual man but I can relate to it with my fellow sisters here.

Tommie: My women friends are so important. I feel kind of shunned by the gay male population. I just don't feel well liked and I don't need the rejection or the meanness. I am not saying all of them because there are some I see at the dinners who are very nice. One of them was actually talking to me and then his lover came up and was basically real rude to me. I just walked away. I just wanted to be friends. At the time I was just grasping at anybody to talk to me. That hurt my feelings.

Maria: Right before I found out, my life was turning around. Finally, or so I thought, things were starting to look good. I had come from a severely

lesbians. Clearly, the presence of a homophobic woman in a predominantly gay support group is productive neither for her or the gay men. She should not have to overcome homophobia as a prerequisite for receiving support and services. A women's support group can be the watering hole; often, the homophobic attitude shifts as the woman openly discusses her fears and stereotypes of gays, and when other group members model acceptance and affirmation of gays and lesbians.

Gender/lifestyle differences and homophobia only partially explain why some HIV+ women cannot attend a gay men's support group. Imagine you are married, and you believe your marriage is monogamous. Probably you have children. And then you discover that your husband has sexual relationships with

men on his out-of-town business trips. Naively perhaps, you never suspected. Now, you must deal not only with the marital betrayal, but with two cases of HIV: his and yours.

The anger of a woman in this situation may well spill onto gays for being the unfortunate conduit of HIV/AIDS into the United States. A women's support group can provide a safe place for the expression of this anger; women are traditionally socialized to refrain from the expression of anger, but this is stressful and may cause physical and emotional illnesses. As the group facilitator, I help her move from angry "gay bashing" to a more realistic, more personal, and probably, more painful understanding of her anger. Other group members who have confronted similar situations are invaluable resources.

abusive family. I was involved with drugs and drinking and I had quit that and I had bought a house—and two months later I found out I was HIV and I have been devastated ever since. I have shut down emotionally. I am not willing even to look people in the eye half the time. I've isolated myself from everyone. I come out from time to time.

Chris: Have you been to group recently?

Maria: Today is my first time. It's taken me years to get here. I was really reluctant to even stay [when I saw that researchers were here]. I have a really suspicious nature about me anyway, and the HIV has just magnified that. I have ceased to make goals. I am just living from day to day, from hour to hour. I've tried to commit suicide several times. I go back and forth. I've been dealing with this for a long time and I've had some real positive turn-arounds. I had someone very close to me pass away and it's just taken a long time to rebound from that. I think—it's gotten to the point—as long as I can go to work, so I can feed myself, I guess that's all that matters, even though I would have chosen to lead a better existence. With the HIV—it's always there. In terms of going back to school, that is what I've always wanted to do. I haven't really met anybody, so I've been staying by myself. You know, some of the things that I have yearned to do, but I figured because I was HIV—that's really led me to feel defeated and

Finally, support groups for women with HIV or AIDS are necessary simply because women's psychological and practical needs are often different than those of men. Women with HIV are a diverse group, but in general, they are more likely to be low income parents and as women, less aware of services for the HIV+. For HIV+ gay men, at least in urban areas, there is a community of support available to them. As the AIDS virus spreads rapidly to heterosexual women, a parallel community for HIV+ women is developing; women's support groups are an ideal strategy for building this community.

Like the feminist consciousness-raising groups of the 1970's, HIV support groups often grow AIDS activists. Tommie notes in her story that it is possible to come out of the HIV closet because she feels so supported by her group.

She organizes biker fund-raisers known as BRA, Bikers Resist AIDS. Other women join AIDS speaker bureaus or volunteer with a service agency, or march in demonstrations or appear on TV on behalf of people with AIDS. Often, the security and support of the group is the catalyst for the leap from fear and stigma to activism and pride. Of course, not all group members become activists; privacy and individual differences must always be respected.

To get to a support group, an HIV+ woman has to hear about a group. The most productive referrals come from nurses and doctors who work in the AIDS treatment centers, from counselors at anonymous test sites, AIDS service agencies, newspaper articles, and word-of-mouth. The referral system requires constant attention: personnel changes, dis-

broken. This isn't worth it. If I could find an easier way to kill myself, I would do it.

Chris: What's hardest for you?

Maria: I wanted something better for my life. I feel real cheated. I haven't been able to change the way I feel about this challenge so that I could make the best out of my life.

Chris: What made you decide to come today?

Maria: Not having anyone to talk to. At work I feel more alone then when I am by myself. There are people all around me and they don't know. I was given a buddy at the health issues task force. And I used to call him and talk with him a lot. He had mentioned that he was going to try to find a women's group because I had been going to a homosexual male group, you know, just to go, but really not being able to address some of the issues that I really needed to talk about. With women, not gays, although I still go to them, because they need me, after work.

Tracy: There are days now that I don't even think about HIV. And then there are those days that I can't forget it and I am just "why me," why not that prostitute on the street, why doesn't she have it? Why are all these people testing negative? Why am I the only one? I am not a bad person. And so it is. I have mixed feelings all the time. And how do I deal with it?

🐚   🐚   🐚   🐚   🐚   🐚   🐚

putes, gossip, and image of the support group in the community all affect the referral base. For example, one well-established support group in Ohio is currently perceived as "cliquish" and referrals are dropping off. The group members are attempting to address the problem. In another city, the facilitator has a dispute with a person in power at the treatment center who refuses to make referrals.

How can the support group be as accessible as possible? Considerations include a convenient location near public transportation, a safe area, especially if the group meets at night, and a pleasant, private space. Some mothers will require childcare, ideally provided on site, perhaps by an AIDS service agency volunteer. Will this person always show up? Can he or she provide quality childcare? Does the childcare provider know how to provide special care for HIV+ children? Anyone who organizes childcare knows this can be a daunting task, and compromises and accommodations will be necessary. The presence of children during a meeting is sometimes acceptable, but children are a distraction, and some women need a child free evening. This, and other decisions, such as whether the meeting place be made public, are best decided by the group members in consultation with the facilitator. If the meeting place is public, HIV+ women can just "drop in," but so can anyone else, threatening the privacy of the group.

What is appropriate screening of new members? Sometimes I simply talk with each prospective member on the phone or meet for coffee. We get to know each other before the first meeting. Occasionally, a woman does not want to meet with

Support groups. I hate being dependent on people, but I think this disease has made me very dependent on people. If they don't like it, too bad, they can let me know. I really do care about people and when I attend a women's retreat or support group, every hug that I give somebody, I do it with a lot of feeling. I can really empathize. Would I have been like that before HIV? So I guess in that sense, it has brought out the good in me. I am not so selfish.

Diane: I feel like I have had a very naive attitude. Everybody knows that I just started reading. I think about the negative, but I don't dwell on it.

Tracy: When I felt good, I never thought about it too much either. As soon as you start feeling like shit, it's "Oh, my God."

Diane: It crosses my mind but now it's a been year and a half and I still feel like I always had. I've started doing some positive things for myself to delay whatever is out there. But it is nothing I dwell on.

Tracy: You keep it that way! We are jealous! We are going to talk about the side that you don't know.

Diane: Yes, but I have you to thank for that. I was just blindly going my way not thinking about it one way or another. You got me thinking about my vitamins. I didn't want to think about that stuff and now I am.

Chris: Diane, you feel you have changed?

me, but she gives permission for me to mail a simple newsletter. For Debbie, the newsletter is a reminder of the group, and when she is ready months later, she comes to a meeting and has "her best night in months."

One support group develops a rather elaborate "greeter" system. A woman calls the agency that houses the group, the referral is relayed to a group member, who, in her function as greeter, meets with the new member before the next group meeting. This system has several purposes. It provides immediate support for the newcomer; she does not have to wait until the next meeting. And the greeter may help her get to her first meeting. Practically, she may provide a ride, and psychologically, she offers encouragement to try the support group despite fears and reservations.

The greeter also serves as an informal "gatekeeper," designed to protect the group's privacy. This particular group has experienced several disturbing threats to confidentiality. For example, one member is a social worker who suddenly finds herself face-to-face with an alcoholic client who could not be trusted to maintain confidentiality. Even with a "warning system," this risk is so omnipresent for the social worker that she no longer feels it is safe to attend group. On two other occasions, women who are not HIV+ join the group. These situations will be discussed later, but suffice it to say that this group is now at a difficult junction: how to make the group welcoming and accessible, yet safe and confidential? Perhaps the fundamental issue here is that "safety" for an HIV+ woman is illusory; there's "safer," but no real safety. When a

Diane: Yeah. In the beginning I was afraid to call Tracy, because I was afraid I was going to bug her. I call her now, and I call Debbie.

Chris: You reach out?

Diane: Yeah, with them I do. I know that Tracy is going to take the time to talk with me. If I am feeling blue she usually gets me laughing. I call Alisha, too.

Joanna: That's why I think it is good that people are in a group like this. Because when one goes to the hospital there is all the rest of the people who either call or drop in. The person in the hospital doesn't feel like she has been shut off to surviving in a no man's land somewhere. And there has usually been someone in the group who has gone through some of this before and that helps. That's why I like a group like this, with a full spectrum, because it is very likely that someone is a little further on the path than what you are and they can say, "It's OK, you will make it."

CR: Another scary part is when you first go to the doctor you're taking one pill and they say you're doing fine. But then as the years go on, oh we got to take you off this medicine and we have to put you on this. And you have to take this for this symptom and I mean I'm scared now because it isn't like it was two years ago when I just took one pill. I'd come here and almost

woman joins a support group, no matter what the rules or procedures, she is stepping out, and putting her privacy at some degree of risk.

   Despite some close calls or yet hypothetical concerns, confidentiality does seem to hold up extremely well in these groups. The facilitator and group members must keep this a strong group norm. When a new woman is present, I always begin the group with reiterating the importance of confidentiality. We discuss specific situations, such as encountering a group member at a party, or dealing with a friend or colleague they may know in common.

   Major psychological hurdles to attending a group are: (1) fear of exposure, (2) fear of seeing sick people, and (3) a weakening of denial as in, "If I attend a group for the HIV+, I must really be HIV+."

CR recollects her fear of seeing "sick people," and wonders when they were coming because everyone seemed so healthy. Witnessing this health lends reassurance that there is life after diagnosis. However, there may also be women present who are not healthy, who even represent the worst AIDS nightmare. The dilemma as well as the advantages posed by a full spectrum group are discussed later. And the loss of denial can be reframed as a choice for survivorship; as Lori states so eloquently, "All of us have a pretty strong sense of survival or we wouldn't be in this group. I'd never think of not moving ahead."

   When recalling their first meeting, women recount their fear and uneasiness (CR was "shaking and crying"), but also how quickly these feelings are replaced by hope and relief. I reassure a newcomer

think we were having a slumber party, we'd talk and laugh. But we've lost one member since I've been here and it's hitting home.

Chris: If you get sick, what do you want?

CR: Just see where I am. If I want to laugh, or if I don't want to talk about it, or if I want to just act normal, whatever normal is. But if I can't get out of bed and I call you and I ask you could you come to my house—

Chris: We'll be there, you know that. It's just a matter of what we will bring to eat!

Linda B: There's been sad times in the group and then there's been happy times. It's almost been like another family.

Nancy: I don't have anybody. These people are more family than anybody I have.

Chris: How long have you been coming to group?

Nancy: Since June [five months]. I just sit here and listen.

Tommie: She doesn't share with us, but she knows we are here. She gets feedback.

Chris: What is it like when someone gets sick and dies?

Linda B: To be truthful, when we saw J get really sick, we started bickering with each other, like any other family. Instead of addressing what is going

that she does not have to talk if she is not ready; group members make their introductions first. The introduction is usually a brief version of the teller's HIV story.

While a few newcomers are slow starters, most are overflowing with feelings, and questions abound about doctors and treatments, especially with a recent diagnosis. Information sharing is important, but I try to focus more on emotional needs. Inevitably, what starts as serious and scary becomes bearable, at least momentarily, as women in the group share their humor and insights.

Like any ongoing group, support groups develop certain norms and character that change over time. In one city, a group of HIV Hispanic women meet during the day because their husbands expect them home in the evenings. Another support group struggles through leadership changes, lack of focus, and apathy. Members ask for more activities and less repetitive storytelling. They are healthy and busy with their lives, so meeting once instead of twice a month feels adequate. Another support group, originally small, meets weekly, and functions as a therapy group; as the membership grows, it becomes more of a social and emotional network that functions outside of group as well as during the now biweekly meetings. Then the group becomes so social that members are concerned that the tough issues are being avoided, especially as some long term survivors become ill.

A four year veteran of this group wonders whether she should stay home because she might be a downer now that she has lost weight and most of her hair. Here is an example of the selflessness that some women retain even when facing the

wrong, like "J's going, what are we going to do?" we just went all the other way.

Amber: I'm not sick yet and I feel like I'm apologizing for that all the time to people who are sick in the group. Hey, I'm sorry, I'm not sick yet. I wish I could go out and be more public, but I just can't do that. But I appreciate the fact that they are doing that.

Tommie: No problem babe, we got you covered. I couldn't have gone public without having all this support. I knew that if people rejected me, I still had so much support and I'd be OK. I am a waitress, and as you can tell, I am very bubbly and lots of people know me. I always cry during this part

⁂   ⁂   ⁂   ⁂   ⁂   ⁂   ⁂

loss of health, and possibly, life. However, there are tremendous advantages to having membership that spans the HIV spectrum, i.e., HIV+ women who are healthy, mixed with women with AIDS, who are fighting virus-related illnesses. The illnesses may be a clarion call to the healthy to improve health habits or reduce job or family stress; the healthy provide assistance to those who are ill. And so often the ill model courage for the yet healthy.

Meeting topics might include medical concerns, when to tell family members, how to reduce stress, techniques for strengthening the immune system, dating, children, death and dying, nutrition, loss, depression, and decision making. Activities can include guided imagery or meditation, yoga, singing, rituals (e.g., lighting memory candles), crafts such as mask making or decorating t-shirts, games, and snacks.

The relationships formed in a group are perhaps more important than any of the issues. The bonds are described as loving and unconditional. For women who typically view other women as competitors, this is a remarkable experience. Groups self-describe as a "family." Linda B recalls that her group began bickering

"like any other family" to avoid focus on a member's impending death. Despite my training, I collude with this avoidance, because of my own grief, and because I imagine that it must be unbearable for HIV+ women to witness the deathly outcome of HIV disease. When a member dies, it is crucial that group members share their loss and their memories. This honors the woman who is gone, reassures group members that dying does not mean forgetting, and proves that the group *can* endure the loss of one of its own.

The group deals also with the deaths of husbands, boyfriends, children, and friends in the HIV community. In no way can these multiple losses be understood or ever fully healed, but open discussions are often a catalyst for self-reflection, spiritual growth, deepening sisterhood, and a renewed resolve to make one's own life meaningful.

Death and dying are not omnipresent themes for support groups. Much more pressing are issues related to the challenges of daily living: maintaining relationships, paying bills, keeping a job, falling in love, obtaining medical care, caring for family, reducing stress, growing spiritually, having fun, getting to the grocery store. In fact, the demands and pace

because it is so sad. People would move away from my station or move to the bar or go to the kitchen and get their own food. A religious man referred to me as a "den of rattlesnakes," and all that really hurts. I had one guy at the motorcycle store who just really hates to take my money, so I always lick it before I go in!

Chris: You always have to give a performance?

Tommie: I can't show no fear in public. If I show fear then they get afraid. I have to be very bold, hold myself very sturdy until I can get into the bathroom and breath. I don't want to be a preacher. If somebody wants to come to me learn, then fine. But all that's real sad and I know

❧   ❧   ❧   ❧   ❧   ❧   ❧

of daily life can be so consuming that a healthy women may wonder why does she need this group now? I suggest that she's making an investment in her future: if she becomes physically ill or emotionally drained in the future, she will have ready-to-use connections with the group. Even so, a member sometimes takes a break from group, perhaps because for awhile she needs less focus on HIV. We check on her, encouraging her to come back when she is ready, asking whether there is any way we can better meet her needs. Always the emphasis is on supporting her in taking care of herself.

I prefer to work with a co-facilitator. This is invaluable for support and sharing the work, especially during crises, and allows group members to see two women working together. The facilitators must take care of themselves. When I show up to a meeting tired or stressed, everyone figures it out and tries to take care of me. I try to model good self-care; this is self-preservation, not selfishness. Generally, I can be available for a phone call or a lunch between meetings, but occasionally I say "not today" if I simply do not have the time or energy. My ability to set limits and take care of myself reassures that when I say "yes," I am genuinely glad to

share my time. When someone is ill or hospitalized, I alter my schedule to spend considerable time with her and her family. My family, friends, and my clients are prepared ahead of time for these situations.

Rightly or wrongly, I do not maintain the same kind of boundaries in my HIV work as in my other clinical work. HIV clients become friends with whom I share meals, birthdays, picnics, hospital stays, anniversaries, and funerals. I meet their children, parents, siblings, and pets. This work is a long term commitment with many peaks and some valleys. A reward is what I can learn from people living with a life threatening, stigmatized disease. I can "take" from the experience only when the connection is mutual; otherwise, I am simply voyeuristic. And it is hypocritical to encourage relational sustenance among HIV+ women and not fully participate in the relationships. So, I graciously respond when my birthday is remembered or someone asks to see a photo of my daughter.

I do not discuss personal problems or rely on the support group to meet my own needs. And I do strictly adhere to certain ethics. I maintain confidentiality, often protecting group members from the press

the other girls go through it, too. I am sure they still hear the little AIDS jokes.

Iris: Yeah, people just talking. Always asking "how did you get it?"

Tommie: That's one of the reasons I went public, because there are girls with HIV. I am just bound and determined to make it easier for the next one, for other women in this group especially, because I love this group.

Linda B: If it hadn't been for the group I would have probably already left. Because I have gained a lot of strength (crying). My whole world has changed for the better. I told my mom the last time I saw her that if they cured this tomorrow I would not change a thing as it stands now. I wouldn't, not a thing. It's just that we could all be buddies longer. It has been a godsend.

or a parent who wants to know who infected their child. I also do not participate in acts of self-deliverance (assisted suicide). Clients protect me from direct involvement in these latter situations, knowing that I could lose my professional license.

It is helpful to have some professional training to facilitate a support group. But anyone can befriend a support group. Many support groups develop a circle of people who care about women with HIV/AIDS. These friends help with activities, attend some meetings, and provide another layer of emotional support and resources. As more and more women are infected with HIV, we can predict that they will need the support, love, knowledge, and safety that come with sharing time with other women who live with HIV/AIDS.

Besides finding inspiration, making friends and opening doors to opportunities such as writing this book, facilitating support groups is heaven for a story lover like me. One particular story shot down my stereotypes and leaves me with a sweet memory of Nadine the Mormon lady. She

attended my very first group. At 55, nicely dressed, and Mormon, I thought for sure she was in the wrong place. Or maybe she was the other woman's mother? But she was HIV+, infected by a transfusion in the early days after an auto accident. She modeled a strong religious faith and we saw how it worked well in her life, but Nadine never placed herself above or different than the other women. This was forever confirmed when a transvestite who wanted to be a transsexual came to the group. I was worried about how Nadine was going to handle this. After group, she gave me a ride home, and I asked how she felt about the evening? She said she was completely confused, "was that a man who wants to be a woman, or a woman who wants to be a man?" She needed some clarification; never had she encountered such a person with such issues. She simply said she would pray that he/she would receive the hoped for sex-change surgery. Nadine's loving, non-judgmental spirit is carried on, even as the support group struggles across the many differences of the women who come to it. ✸

Chris, an Earthly Angel

It was not so very long ago
my heart was broke, my head hung low
I felt I had nowhere to go
I prayed to my father please,
send someone my pain to ease
So he sent Chris Smithies.
She's got diet coke and birkenstocks,
wears them with or without socks (laughter).
She knows her ropes, maintains our hopes,
gives us hugs and lots of love
Yes she was sent from above.
She helps us heal our child within,
gives us strength to stay to win
A beautiful world she's visualized
with her heart and not her eyes
A world that loves us no matter what
and overlooks what we've got.
Words cannot express how we all feel so blessed
to be a part of what she sees
to tell her we are also pleased.

—Linda B, 7-14-93

18

"We're Supposed to Be a Support Group"

Support Group Meeting, February 1994

Kathryn (facilitator): We need to begin with what happened last week and people's feelings about it, especially the way we reacted to Lorene's charge that we're here with HIV because of our lifestyles. This violated the one rule of this group: we don't blame one another for being HIV+.

Lori: I was upset at my own reaction, that I would get that angry at what a stranger had said. Later, Kathryn said she had a good suspicion that Lorene was suicidal. I was absolutely horrified; if that had happened I would have had a real hard time living with that. And it's the same old story with this group; it happens with anyone who hasn't been part of our original little group. You might find this distasteful, but we don't ask a new woman where she comes from, no one knows, no one seems to give a shit. And I felt so

Chris: The support group in this chapter is wrestling with a new member's angry vendetta that HIV+ women can only blame themselves for being HIV+. Lori, Jewish and middle class, reacts angrily to Lorene's charge, but subsequently confronts her own behavior and courageously pushes this group to deal with its exclusionary attitudes and behaviors.

AIDS is a rainbow disease, affecting women from all walks of life. Some are poor and some live in the suburbs. Others use drugs, and still others have professional jobs. Some HIV+ women are mothers, some are single, some are married. And some of these women like themselves, and some have rarely, if ever, entertained a positive thought about self.

HIV is a catalyst for women from very different backgrounds to come together: Mormon cares for Appalachian, white embraces African American, and drug addict visits executive in the hospital. So often, HIV does dilute otherwise divisive

193

guilty that Lorene was so desperate. The only two times I've ever seen her, all she talked about was how she had no friends, no support, no one to turn to. **And we're supposed to be a support group.** But we spend our time in these meetings talking about what we did last weekend, and not what people really need. So I decided I'm done.

Chris: What do you mean?

Lori: I'm not going to be a party to it anymore. I've talked to someone very involved in the AIDS community and found out that there's a perception that this group is a little clique, that the door is closed, that there are too many restrictions on who can come. So the caseworkers aren't referring people here anymore. We either need to fix it or just disband it and start over. That's why I asked for this subject to be brought up tonight. If we can't handle and absorb the people that need us the most, then we don't have any right to exist. There are too many people who desperately need this support group, and here we sit, the same four people that have been here for two years. This isn't just about Lorene. It's about Sabrina and Rita and all the other women who stopped coming here.

Kathryn: There's a couple of things we're talking about: one is people's response to what happened last week. People seemed pretty stunned by it. And what Lori has brought up is critically important to the group. What is it

🦁   🦁   🦁   🦁   🦁   🦁   🦁

differences, and this book contains evidence of this wonderful phenomenon. There is opportunity for love and growth as those infected and those who care about them are brought together in hospital waiting rooms, support groups, healing weekends, churches, rallies, and community organizations.

But it is only fair to show that sometimes the process of being together is not so smooth. A support group, like any other group, develops norms and character. Group members may grow impatient or even intolerant when a woman is expressing behaviors or attitudes that challenge the established norms. And regardless of HIV status, we are all positioned in this society by race, class, age, sexual preference, and disability.

CR, African American, a survivor of rape, youthful pregnancy, single mother-

hood, poverty, and now AIDS, can relate to Lorene. She moves beyond the condemning content of Lorene's words to the underlying emotion: *anger*. And then Lori filters out what Lorene really needs: *connection*, expressed by Lorene as a plea to join her at the bottom of the barrel of shame. These insights are achieved too late to benefit Lorene. She never returns to the support group. Perhaps Lorene's gift to this support group is the reminder that racism and classism and other forms of prejudice can divide, even among those sensitized by HIV infection.

As noted in the text, this support group has struggled before with these issues. Barb recalled Wendy: poor, drug addicted, pregnant, and openly anticipating making money off her baby. Wendy's choices, and her poor hygiene, made it difficult to like her. After Wendy had her

that you want this group to be? And why are there a lot of women out there who are not getting referred here? It really worries me.

CR: I'd like to speak somewhat in defense of Lorene. I've seen her outside of the group more than I think anyone else and I've talked to her on the phone. She has to go two blocks to use the phone. She visited me once and Kathryn and I visited her once. A lot of her pain and anger come from her husband. Everyday he tells her "Bitch, you've got it, you're gonna die and I'm gonna bury you." And with that kind of feelings being said to her, I thought about it after the episode in the last group, and realized she came here and she lashed out at us. She *couldn't* lash out at *him*. I don't know if he ever hit her or beat her. I just had the feeling she was saying to us what he says to her, that she can't say back to him.

Chris: She felt it was safe to get angry here.

CR: I knew what Lorene was going through at home. I didn't express it to anyone else, but I felt she was crying out for help. It was anger that came out, and frustration and fear. But I have a sense that's not what she meant. Because I knew how her husband had been treating her, I wasn't angry. What she said was disturbing and later me and Linda B jokingly said, "Oh, it's our lifestyle," but it's just a kidding between us. I felt I knew where she was coming from. We get positive strokes during the day. We can pick up the

🐚   🐚   🐚   🐚   🐚   🐚   🐚

baby, she disappeared. In another situation that I would never have anticipated, we met Lorita, who admitted she used drugs. But there was something puzzling about Lorita. The mystery was solved when Lorita told us that she was a transvestite, specifically, a male who had lived as a female for several years. Lorita had saved money, anticipating the operation that would finally make her body match her female identity. But no surgeon would now risk exposure to HIV for such an "unnecessary" surgery. Initially, the group tried to accept Lorita, but expressed reservations about Lorita's presence for a weekend group retreat. This dilemma "went away" because Lorita continued to seriously abuse drugs and alcohol. We could hardly blame her for choosing this escape, yet we wondered whether we failed this "woman." Was she a woman?

Should we have tried harder to make him/ her part of us?

Some differences have caused anger, alienation, exhaustion, distrust. Winona lied about her HIV status, and for years, gobbled up resources from me, the support group, and the AIDS community. When I made this discovery, what was my responsibility? To confront, to break confidentiality, to leave the outcome to group members, who suspected that Winona was not really sick? I have since learned that HIV impostors have popped up in most communities, especially those that offer services, support, and love to those with HIV infection.

In this country we prefer to believe that hard work and personal integrity assure security, success, and "the pursuit of happiness." We can affirm these beliefs with numerous examples, perhaps including

phone and call someone, or go to a movie, but she is in that house, and that's where she is.

Chris: I have the impression Lorene has had a rough past. Very little has been positive or reinforcing so it's very easy for her to absorb this idea that she's to blame for being HIV+.

Lori: I got the feeling that she was trying to gather us like we're all scum together. She didn't want to be scum alone. After I got over my initial anger, I thought that she really wanted to come here and have a group because she sits in that hellhole alone.

Kathryn: It concerned me that I didn't see anyone respond to Lorene. I understood that it felt real aggressive what she had to say, but I was concerned that no one said what you're saying now.

CR: I was embarrassed. I felt awful.

Lori: It still makes me sick, I mean I'm not a psychologist, but it was such an obvious cry for help and, again, we just shoved it aside.

Chris: Lori, give yourself a bit of a break. It makes sense that your buttons got pushed. You're all in this group as members and you have needs and your buttons are going to get pushed sometimes. If that happens so much that people are feeling excluded from the group, then I guess that's what we're here to talk about. But many people I've worked with are Lorenes,

our own. But HIV/AIDS underscores that this country continues to be one in which opportunity is frequently defined by one's class, race, sexual preference, age, disability, or in Lorita's case, a simple "biological error."

As I review my comments from this group meeting to face these issues of difference, I note my attempt to mitigate guilt or "instruct," when group members are quite ready and able to hit the nail on the head. I thank them for recognizing that all differences must be acknowledged and not just those that are intriguing or easily bridged.

It is easy to rationalize "I have AIDS so I don't have to take this on." But these women recognize that you can't have it both ways. Their support group is enriched again and again by their differences. When they (we) draw a line in the

sand, they (we) jeopardize the very essence of what makes the group viable and interesting. Furthermore, there is the wise realization that *any* act of exclusion can preface exclusion based on HIV status, or *whatever* the zeitgeist identifies as dangerous at a given moment in history.

Patti: In my concluding remarks in the subtext of this book, I address what it has been like to make a book out of all that Chris and I have heard and seen and felt. The first conclusion speaks out of my own desire for meaning, activism and community. The second conclusion interrupts the first, refusing to contain AIDS in familiar frameworks, putting at risk readers and writers presumed to know about worlds presumed to be knowable. Through the fragments and traces of what is impossible to think whole and clear, the "truth" of AIDS is approached

whether they're victims of sexual abuse or battering or AIDS or whatever. In our society, it's typical for women to blame ourselves. It's a tribute to all of you that self-blame is not the norm in this group. That's one of the wonderful things that this group has to offer: over time, you all rub off.

Lori: I don't think we do, Chris. Look at all the women who haven't come back.

Chris: So why isn't that happening? And what's so painful for you all going through that period of time before that person can catch up or change? Or maybe, in some cases, not change.

Kathryn: Can we accept people where they are, even if we don't like it, and not require them to change?

Barb: I've seen us do that. Remember that woman who came to group who was pregnant? She was in inpatient treatment for drug abuse. And she said, "I really hope this baby is healthy because I want to be able to get some money." My husband and I were really offended because children meant so much to us and here was someone for whom they just meant monetary value. But we didn't not accept her. I know I felt really hurt by what she said, but she had a right to be there and a right to get the support.

Kathryn: Did she stay in the group?

Barb: No.

through the failures of thought in a time that disrupts our structures of knowing (Haver, 1996).

There have been other plagues, and AIDS is not the only plague of our time. The one in eight women who get breast cancer and the millions who have died of influenza in this century attest to that (McNeill, 1976). But the specificities of AIDS, its linking of sex, blood, drugs and death, its mutability that pushes us against the limits of medical science, its exacerbation of social differences, its very untimeliness: all contribute to the symbolic force that invests the disease so that it is both a measure and a mirror of the times in which we live. What are we able to say about AIDS that is beyond promises of rescue, whether from God or heroic medicine or communities of care (Duttmann, 1993)? What are we able to

say about AIDS as it alters the very code of the cells it occupies toward a doing based in the very limits of our knowing?

Conclusion 1: Out of Place

[From Feb. 10, 1995 e-mail to research friends]: We're getting close. The women's self-writing is trickling in, the artist permissions are trickling in, the desktop publishing woman is hot to trot, the member checks with the women are going swimmingly. They have given us rich and fabulous words in terms of their reactions to what we have written, widely varied responses to what they like and don't like. They also keep getting sick and breaking my heart, which is, thus far, motivating in terms of moving the book along, but it also makes me so keenly aware of why I needed the angels to do this. And, really, why I needed Nietzsche and Rilke and

Chris: I somewhat disagree with Barb. I don't think collectively we did extend out to her. She had terrible body odor and it was hard to even sit by her.

Barb: I think we all drew in to ourselves, but you can't stop that. When someone says things like that I can't say "That's great." I mean, I was shocked.

Lori: I don't think we have to say, "That's great." We can say "that's offensive," or "children mean so much to me." Isn't that part of therapy, the interaction, that we can express anger if we want to? I'm not saying everybody should hug each other and we should all be best friends and have tea parties together. But if someone walks in the door here, they deserve the same chance, the same experience that everybody else does. And if we can't do that, then we are not a support group. We are a social hour and we should call it that and quit lip servicing that we want new women, because we don't. It's out in the community not to come here. I think it's about vibes, we sit around and chit-chat and we don't know the new person and it's quite obvious that we all know each other well.

Barb: But that's part of coming to a new group. When I came, I remember, people were standing in the hallway talking and I just stood there and didn't know what to do and felt very uncomfortable. I said is this Dr. Chris Smithies' group? They said "yeah" and just kept on talking. So I went in and I gave

Benjamin, too. So I'm feeling much less burdened by how very long it's taken and more respectful of the process and its unfolding. For a while I was thinking that I was the wrong woman for the job, that they would have been better off to find some "realist" researcher to do the task, but the women's feedback has buoyed me that I'm quite the right woman for the job, that the book that only Chris and I could write is a book that will do the work for them that we all wanted. Of course, most of the women might well have been quite excited with a realist tale, but there are other things going on here in terms of how the format we have designed works, effects that I will keep tracking, if only out of my own self-interest that I have not "ruined" their hopes for the book.

An early title for this book was *An Alchemy of Angels*, growing out of what I witnessed as a kind of living alchemy that produces gold from base metal in the women's struggles to make meaning of the disease in their lives. While I changed the title, I end by returning to the way it captures the movement of a weary world toward forms of community that respect differences propelled from the very breakdowns of our usual frameworks of meaning in the face of traumas such as AIDS. Kushner ends Part II of *Angels in America* with Prior's words after he has wrestled with the angel, followed her to heaven and refused her request to not want more life because it only means more suffering: "This disease will be the end of many of us, but not nearly all, and the dead will be commemorated and will struggle on with the living, and we are not going away. We don't die secret deaths any-

it a shot and it's the best thing I ever did. My doctor feels that the women who don't come to groups don't want to deal with it. They don't take care of themselves. That's sad to me, because I had the same kind of experience at first, but I gave it a shot and it worked for me.

Kathryn: But it's a different group now. It may not be the experience for a new person coming in now that it's as welcoming a group as it was then. Since I've been with you the two women I referred haven't returned. I think that's troubling and it worries me a lot. I think some people aren't going to come but there are at least 300 HIV+ women in this area. Why aren't they coming?

Chris: Things are different now. When most of you joined this group, the HIV epidemic was relatively new, most of you had fairly recent diagnoses, and generally, you had good health. And you had the abilities to find this group, get here, use it, and give to it. We were pioneers, committed to survival, and we bonded closely. Now, all of you here this evening have been living with HIV for quite a while now. Some of you now have AIDS. It takes more effort to keep yourselves emotionally and physically healthy. And I think it's difficult to always have the leftover love and energy and time to really respond to someone. And some of these women coming in are really needy. Of course they deserve help and love and support, but they're really

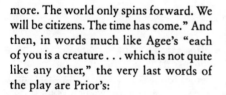

more. The world only spins forward. We will be citizens. The time has come." And then, in words much like Agee's "each of you is a creature . . . which is not quite like any other," the very last words of the play are Prior's:

> Bye now.
> You are fabulous creatures, each and
>   every one.
> And I bless you: *more Life.*
> The Great Work Begins.

Here the "gold" that we make from AIDS is not so much redemption into some Paradise as it is movement toward thinking our way out of rather than into the angel in our very having to do it for ourselves and one another. Here, the hope of a hope is the very alchemy of body, mind and spirit that AIDS demands of

those upon whose bodies it writes its lessons, those who are HIV+ and those who are, as I have learned to say, "not yet to my knowledge HIV+."

Conclusion 2: The Book as Ruin

> Courteous myopic angel, how
> you press upwards in me
> to light these humble bits
> of you I cook the books with.
> Stand now: be spilled, unmade.

(Terry Eagleton, "Homage to Walter Benjamin," 1981)

This book is an effort to find a structure that corresponds to the ever-changing, many-layered, many faces of HIV/AIDS. In writing, we have drawn from the tensions and powers of a profuse (dis)array: the changing nature of the vi-

needy, and they may not know how to do the give and take of a support group.

Kathryn: It's hard to sort out the impact of stuff outside of our group from inside stuff.

Chris: Yes. Women who are IV drug users, who work the streets at some time, who are poor, or a member of a minority group, who don't have formal education, face huge obstacles and social stigma in addition to being HIV+. These problems of prejudice and poverty and unequal advantage are not just here in this group. Most of us in this group are white and from middle class backgrounds, more or less. CR, I don't want to put it all on you, but why has this group worked for you? You are black, you had children very, very young, you've been poor, and you had little formal education. And how can it work for other women like you?

CR: For me, it was women like you who helped me to see my self-worth. Before I ever had the virus, I went to workshops and I read and went to conferences that made available to me other resources that women like Lorene never had. And I have to say for a fact that if I hadn't had some of those experiences, I would not feel that I could be a part of this group.

Chris: Yes. Some of the women who come to this group offend or alienate us because they don't know how to "behave." They don't know how to participate in this kind of talk, how to share the time, and so on. We have rules, but we don't make them clear. We forget that their self-esteem is in the

rus and its cultural meanings, the existential issues involved, the relations of co-researching, angels as an object of study, and most importantly, the movements in the lives of the women whose stories we have heard and shaped and re-shaped. I have learned to lose my way in this journey.

But one example is my phone conversation with Iris as we work to get her "new" story into the subtext of the book. She thinks, again, of pulling out because "it's too personal . . . I don't want people to gawk at me . . . now I know how the movie stars feel to have everyone looking into their business . . . maybe now is not my time to help. I just want to live a quiet life with my

girls. I don't want to be in the spotlight with stuff that is no one's business after so long when I was using drugs and alcohol and my life was an open book, fair game. I don't want all the attention." Committed to neither charming nor guilt-tripping her into keeping her words in the book, I go over with her what she has recently said, cutting, cutting, cutting. I read back to her this latest version, letting go of my "science" commitments to the "data," heart sinking as I face the possibility that she will still not feel comfortable with being included, guilt budding that I have cajoled her against her own best interests, in spite of myself and my deepening understanding of and gratitude for what

gutter, that they have good reasons to be distrustful, to not give a damn. CR, you made it easy for us to embrace you. Besides just being the beautiful person that you are, you could be what the group needed you to be. You're from a different place than a lot of the people here, but you could bridge the differences. I didn't have to leave my comfort zone. Once you came here and knew how to "behave," you were accepted as much as anyone else. But a lot of people with your background, with how you've lived, haven't figured their way to get here and be part of us. I think tonight we're talking about *our* responsibility to build some of the bridges.

CR: I'm a Lorene.

Chris: How does group fit for you now?

CR: This is the safest place I have that I can relate to other women. So, I generally get what I need. I have a great friend in Linda, so I feel like I'm just tagging along until the dam breaks.

Chris: It's a lot easier to ask questions then make answers, but once a woman gets here, how can she be helped to feel that this could work for her over time, and simultaneously, how can the group still work for you as the group experiences changes? And what about Lorene? Is there some way to attempt to correct that situation? I hear a lot of regret about how that went and I think we have some understanding now of why it went that way. How could you make peace with yourself about it?

Lori: I was going to drop her a note.

it means for these women to put their lives on such public display.

What can possibility be gained from such intrusion? Bill Haver (1996) writes "In the time of AIDS, we are all of us vampires." And I wonder about what Chris and I have contributed to what will have been said about AIDS and the possibilities of thinking our way out of the exhaustion of our usual ways of thinking about the shocks of history.

As we wrestle with last-minute re-orderings and face our own fears of finishing, we hope for a book that says more and something other than our own best hope: a book that is as much about futures as pasts, as much about beginnings as endings in some place of "non-stupid"

optimism that has heard all the "truth" we could handle and be grateful. Positioning ourselves to the side and below, it may not be the book we dreamed of, ruined from the start in terms of the limits of representing lives spilled, unmade, even lost, constantly changing information, and our own desire to "ride with the angels and raise a little critical 'hell'" (Sefcovic, 1995). One-winged, perhaps, ground-tied as we attempt to give wings to words; but it is the book it is: too near, too far, too late, too early, an ensemble of fragments waiting for the alchemy of response from readers who have ears to hear "a singing from within the burning of a knowledge" (Felman and Laub, 1992).

Barb: What if some of us asked her if we could come over and bring her some dinner and just talk?

Kathryn: She didn't come to the Xmas party, so CR and I went over and took her some clothes and some food. She said it was the only thing she got for Xmas.

CR: It would probably be better to take her away, out of the house, away from that husband.

Lori: Whoever plans it, count me in. I have some things I want to say to her. The argument was between her and me because I was the one who responded.

Kathryn: I think you were saying what others were feeling, you weren't speaking alone. You were the courageous one to speak up.

CR: I felt bad and I was embarrassed but I had this urge to go and sit next to her, even when she was blaspheming us. And then I just, it was bad, I mean sick inside me and in my head. She was a woman and she was a black woman, and I relate to her. And I feel like a traitor that I didn't.

Kathryn: I think what that says is that we can make mistakes in this group. If we reach out, we're not gonna lose somebody. We can say something, or not say something, as long as we call up later and say, "Gee, I felt like such an ass. I wanted to come over and put my arms around you and I felt bad that I didn't." There's room to make mistakes.

In addition to the support group for HIV+ women that we have talked about here, communities across the nation have developed programs to deal with AIDS that include a variety of support groups. For example, in Austin, Texas, Project Transitions is a residential AIDS hospice that opened in 1989 which offers HIV support groups and bereavement recovery groups for those who have lost someone to AIDS: families, partners, caregivers. Groups offered in the Los Angeles area include: positive teens and twenties drop-in, women alive, HIV+ heterosexual men, HIV– partners, coping with the loss of a loved one, gay partners, positive 30's, hospice, long term diagnosed survivors, educators, over 50's, Asian Pacific, mothers of AIDS patients, newly infected, women at risk, Positively Sober (HIV 12-step), and inter-faith exchange. To find out about support groups in your area, call your local AIDS service agency.

19

"Seize the Day": Lori

World AIDS Day, December 1, 1994

Greetings! As you have heard, this is the seventh commemoration of the AIDS fight around the world. In America alone, more people have died of AIDS than the last three wars combined. Women, teens, and people of color are the fastest growing demographic groups becoming infected. The face of AIDS is . . . Me.

I grew up in a Cincy suburb, went to college, worked my way up the ladder of one of our largest corporations. In 1984, I was transferred to Houston, Texas, where I fell in love with one of my co-workers. We thought our biggest problem would be in trying to keep our personal life out of the office. We married and moved back to Cincy, bought a house, then tragedy struck. My husband got sick and went through months of testing before finally being tested for AIDS. We tested positive in June of 1989, and he died a year later.

For many years, I led a "normal" life after his death. I dated, changed jobs, bought a new house, and traveled. I looked like you, I lived like you . . . I was you. But, there was a secret. My life changed dramatically last winter when I was diagnosed with my first AIDS infection. I was no longer just HIV positive; I now had AIDS! I have had to stop working as maintaining my health is now a necessity with some days being better than others.

I spend a lot of time speaking to groups about living with AIDS and trying to educate our city about prevention. It's amazing to think that this is the only one of all deadly diseases that is 100 percent preventable. Research shows that the strongest incentive people have to change risky behaviors is when they become aware of someone in their life who is infected. Isn't it funny that we don't think it could be us.

I realize that this is an enormously overwhelming problem in the world, and you may feel powerless to make a difference. But, there are a few things you can do:

One: Go home and discuss with your family what you read today and why it's important for them to know. Two: Create the environment around you that it's "OK" and necessary to talk about AIDS. Your children, dating friends and siblings, divorced or widowed parents—everyone needs to be informed. Three: Educate yourself and those around you. Four: Think about your own attitude about PLWA's (People Living With AIDS). We are all around you, and you won't know who we are. I am in my tenth year of infection and did not know I was HIV+ for four and a half years.

I don't speak for everyone who is infected, but I hope that you will not look at me and say that I'm not like you—that AIDS is never going to be a part of your life. I wish that were true. I'm often asked, "How do you get through your day?" My response is that I get through this the same way that people have been getting through tragedies for decades. I have always believed that every family has a tragedy at some point, and that this just happens to be mine. I have adjusted to the fact that my life tragedy is "AIDS." It's everyone else that needs to do the same.

This is a *disease*, and it should be handled in society just like other diseases—cancer, heart disease, etc. When you hear of someone who had a heart attack, your first thought is probably not, "I wonder if they ate steak and eggs every day" or a diabetic, "they must have pigged out on chocolate." This is a disease, and the people who are struggling with this want to be treated like anyone else who has an illness.

Cincy is very lucky to have a wonderful AIDS support system. You should be proud to know that we have a world class research and medical facility at the University of Cincinnati that is sponsoring clinical trials on the drugs that are helping to prolong and enhance our lives. We have a residence home, a parent and child center, a hospice program just for PWA's, and the support of AVOC (AIDS Volunteers of Cincinnati). We even have some fun!

As we stand here together on World AIDS Day, let's remember that letting AIDS into your life is a 365 day a year prospect. This day is a memorial day

Chris: When I first met Lori in 1988, I would never have dreamed that one day she would speak so powerfully at such a public event. For many, the support group became a support base for stepping out when they were ready for a more public activist role. For Lori, as her health declined, public speaking became an increasingly important avenue for finding meaning in AIDS.

I was so proud of her family for publicly commemorating Lori as an AIDS activist in her obituary after her death on August 8, 1996. Lori gave so much to this project; I wanted her to hold this book in her hands.

for those who have died. Together, let's make today and all days a celebration of life.

From Lori, February 17, 1996

I have just returned from the final group interview conducted after reading the book. We were asked at the session to give a final "wrap up" that would allow the reader to get an update on us and to close the chapters we have written. I could not put my thoughts into words at the meeting. How do you summarize the physical and emotional changes of the past few years into a paragraph or two?

I have been battling several AIDS illnesses on and off for two years. Although my health is not good, it's not too bad either, but I have suffered many losses of my old life. This continues to be the hardest struggle that I have had with the disease. To my surprise, many wonderful people have fought to stay in my life and be there for me. This has been the best revelation for me.

I get quite a bit of pleasure from being in the "AIDS community"—educating, prevention planning, support, etc. Since I am no longer able to work, this has become my new career and has been rewarding to me. The people I have met in the past seven years since diagnosis are the most important people in my life. However, I have learned that this is a very personal struggle and each person's experiences are truly unique. Although the love and support of the women in "group" and others in the community have helped me through my journey, I feel that *I* have to be the one to see myself through.

An Ache of Wings: The Social Challenge of AIDS

> And how bewildered is any womb-born creature
> that has to fly. As if terrified and fleeing
> from itself, it zigzags through the air, the way
> a crack runs through a teacup . . .
>
> —from Rilke, The Eighth Elegy, *Duino Elegies*

This final angel intertext is a moment of determined sociology in this book on HIV/AIDS and women's lives that foregrounds the certain power that outside forces have over our lives. It is also a moment of determined policy talk, a moment of what it is that can be done.

AIDS intensifies social problems. The list of social programs needed by PWA's includes: increased funding for research, extended insurance benefits, housing, emotional support, support for children, hospital and medical services, hospice care, and increased educational programs in safer sex practices. Culturally sensitive education in safer sex is needed among communities at risk for HIV: men who have sex with men, youth, intravenous drug users, and girls and women, particularly in communities of color.

As the incidence of AIDS continues to spiral among injection drug users, prevention and treatment programs, and harm-reduction efforts, especially needle exchange programs, become key. Newly approved therapies are by no means affordable and accessible to all who need them. Sexuality education for girls and women needs to be about much more than promoting the use of condoms that often leaves sexual relations of power intact in not dealing with the constraints on women's negotiation of their sexuality. Women continue to be under diagnosed and misdiagnosed. Women also live differently with AIDS than men, especially around issues involving pregnancy and child rearing. In the United States, all of these services are needed in cultur-

Interested in how socioeconomic and cultural factors increase women's vulnerability, the Women and AIDS Research Program at the International Center for Research on Women (ICRW) is conducting seventeen action research programs in thirteen countries to address how behavioral change requires addressing socioeconomic and cultural factors. ICRW, 1717 Mass. Avenue, NW, Suite 302, Washington, DC 20036. 202-797-0007. icrw@igc.apc.org

ally sensitive forms, and among the poor whose access to public services is limited. And all of these services are global needs.

Many current interventions pay inadequate attention to the broader social, economic and cultural context in which high-risk behavior takes place, constraining the adoption of behaviors recommended worldwide by prevention program (e.g., reduce the number of partners, practice mutual monogamy, use condoms, and seek treatment for sexually transmitted diseases). Crowded housing in polluted environments, underemployment or jobs with substandard health and safety conditions, the stress of living with violence: all of these affect the ability of immune systems to withstand viral attacks. Economic oppression and its effects on gender relations, substandard healthcare, the frequency of IV drug use, high rates of untreated venereal infection: these are typical poverty-related conditions that exacerbate the effects of unsafe sexual practices on the rate of HIV transmission. Access to treatment depends much on where one is located in the global maldistribution of resources. HIV+ women in Africa, for example, have little access to the AZT that can diminish the likelihood of bearing an HIV+ child from 33 percent to 8 percent.

To turn to social policy issues is to foreground the diminished life prospects of millions of poor people, undereducated, ill-served by governments and international agencies. CR talked at a lakeside retreat of how, since having AIDS, she has the social services she has needed all her life: adequate housing and medical care, community support, even, speaking of Chris, "her own personal psychologist." One thinks of the story of young Cubans deliberately infecting themselves with HIV in order to gain better social services. One thinks of the story Chris tells of "HIV impostors" who create an HIV identity in order to access social services. One wonders what such stories have to say about how people get their needs met in a social order increasingly marked by the maldistribution of social resources, including the "AIDS industrial complex,"[1] the institutionalized social-service bureaucracy that administers and delivers AIDS programs.

The AIDS crisis goes beyond a crisis of health, touching issues of sexuality, social inequalities, discrimination, the limits of science and the meaning

Several Cuban youth deliberately infected themselves with HIV in order to access the higher standard of living available at the quarantined AIDS sanitarium set up by the government. In a video smuggled out of Cuba, 80 young people are said to have shot up infected blood between 1989–1991. Sanitarium life offers far more comfort than most Cubans ever see: three full meals a day, air conditioning, no power outages, the absence of police (*Newsweek,* May 16, 1994).

In *Let Us Now Praise Famous Men,* James Agee wrote of the damages sustained by "the people at the bottom of the world": "each is a new and incommunicably tender life, wounded in every breath, and almost as hardly killed as easily wounded: sustaining, for a while, without defense, the enormous assaults of the universe." Such words are about what we might be and are cheated of, how we lose power to meet possibility, how, via "bonebiting traps . . . equations of destruction . . . [and] graves of angelic possibility . . . murder is being done . . . one's life is made a cheated ruin."

of human mortality. Whether it will result in increased self-determination for global populations or in increased regulatory social practices is precisely the question. This is the "epidemic logic" that Linda Singer (1993) addresses in her efforts to think against and toward death, the way it troubles and stalls our thought. Her hope was an unreasoned affirmation, an ungrounded hope, a wild hope that the very proliferative capacity of the disease might outstrip regulatory means and serve to force new relationships toward reinventing ourselves and our social relations. AIDS doesn't just happen to individuals, she argues; it is socially produced and demands social action and policy that addresses its multiple causes and effects.

Much is at stake in making sense of AIDS. Knowing the facts saves lives, but the facts we need to know are as much about a redistribution of social resources as they are about safer sex practices. What kind of knowledge or wisdom can we look for here? As we face the force of what we do not know, easy consolations lose face and the resolutely inspirational and piously sentimental fall flat. Romantic melancholia appears as limited a response as both reformist zeal and hope for divine intercession, as the plague-weary seek to break through the darkness of loss and fear. When the dying is by no means over, how are we to see so much suffering and death as anything but a waste? What new social logic might we seek out of the ruins of what has gotten us

What Do HIV Positive Women Need?

The following statement was created by the International Community of Women Living with HIV and AIDS (ICW) before the 1992 International AIDS Conference in Amsterdam. The list is important because it represents a united view of HIV infected women from all over the world who came together to identify their needs. These are the critical issues women want support organizations to address and include in their objectives.

To improve the situation of women living with HIV and AIDS throughout the world:

1. WE NEED encouragement, support and funding for the development of self-help groups, and local and international networks of women living with HIV/AIDS.
2. WE NEED the media to realistically portray us, not to stigmatize us.
3. WE NEED equitable, accessible and affordable treatments, and research into how the virus affects women, including psycho social and medical aspects, and both conventional and parallel treatments.
4. WE NEED funding for services and support for women living with HIV/AIDS, to lessen our isolation and meet our basic needs. All funding directed to us (HIV+ women) needs to be supervised to be sure that we get it.
5. WE NEED the right to make our own choices about reproduction and to be respected and supported in those choices. This includes the right to have children and the right not to have children.
6. WE NEED recognition of the right of our children and orphans to be cared for and of the importance of our role as parents.
7. WE NEED education and training of health care providers and the community at large about women's risk and our needs. Up-to-date, accurate information concerning all issues about women living with HIV/AIDS should be easily and freely available.
8. WE NEED recognition of the fundamental rights of all women living with HIV/AIDS, with special consideration for women in prisons, drug users and sex workers. These fundamental rights should also include the right to housing, employment, and travel without restrictions.
9. WE NEED research into woman-to-woman transmission, with recognition of and support for lesbians living with HIV/AIDS.
10. WE NEED decision-making power and consultation on all levels of policy and programs affecting us.
11. WE NEED economic support for women living with HIV/AIDS in developing countries to help them to be self-sufficient and independent.
12. WE NEED any definition of AIDS to include symptoms and clinical manifestations specific to women.

Reprinted from *World* June 1996. To contact the ICW, write to: ICW, 2nd floor, Livingstone House, 11 Carteret St., London, United Kingdom SW1H9DL. Fax: (44171) 222-1242.

to this place: gross social maldistribution of resources, epidemics of social inequities that converge into AIDS, fictions of coherence, mastery, choice and intention in the mirror that is AIDS as it rewrites our lives and times?

Linda Singer (1993) writes of AIDS as a "world transforming moment as we face the limits of our present systems." The everyday looks different; fantasies of salvation fall apart. Rather than quick fixes, great crusades or grand gestures, our task begins to look like a long haul toward a different kind of power and pleasure in building communities built on recognition of the limits of present logics of response. Here, in the ruins of our historical space, the constellations of complications deflect any magic bullet of some one solution in the face of the very proliferation of AIDS, its non containment, its very roots in the mix of racism, misogyny, heteronormativity and global politics that so determine AIDS policies. Here, we live out a complexity of "the pure too little, the empty too much," an ache of wings.[2]

Notes

1. Irene Elisabeth Stroud, review of *Women Resisting AIDS: Feminist Strategies of Empowerment*, edited by Beth E. Schneider and Nancy E. Stoller (Temple University Press, 1995). *Women's Review of Books*, 12(9), June 1995.

2. Kathleen Komar (1987). *Transcending Angels: Rainer Maria Rilke's Duino Elegies*. Lincoln: University of Nebraska Press.

Paul Klee, *The Hero with the Wing,* 1905, etching. Used by permission of Kunstmuseum Bern.

EPILOGUE

20

Troubled Reading:
Our Bodies, This Book, This Fire

In most studies, the researchers take entitlement to apply their analyses and perspectives to data. Once the "subject" gives permission for her story to be used, typically she relinquishes all control over that story. At best, the actual research subjects, or "participants" as we prefer to call the contributors to our book, receive a copy of the article or book. Their reactions, evaluations, and feelings about the "data" and how it has been presented virtually never impact the finished product. Feedback and criticism usually come only from professional colleagues.

For this study, we promised the participants that *they* would be our editorial board. This meant getting a first draft to the women, meeting with them to hear their reactions, and then returning to our book, to revise in light of their feedback.

Chris: When I first considered a book about HIV-infected women telling their stories, I was overwhelmed with the responsibility of getting it right. I could have been paralyzed by this fear that I could misrepresent or dishonor the women I greatly admire and love. When Patti and I first discussed the design of our project, I was thrilled with the notion of a "member check." It was a huge relief to know that the women would have the opportunity to edit us and themselves.

Their feedback was useful: it produced updates, substantive changes (title change, shorter angel intertext chapters, a re-ordering of the chapters, a different cover). A few suggestions we did not use, particularly regarding the split text format, although we did make small changes in the hope it would be more reader-friendly. Most interesting were the reactions of the women to reading themselves: awareness of personal growth, attitude changes, losses, shifting relationships

So, in November of 1995, using small grant money, we self-published 400 copies of the originally titled *Troubling Angels: Women Living with HIV/ AIDS*. In December 1995, with a cocktail of feelings that included eagerness, apprehension, pride and curiosity, we mailed two copies to each woman in the study. In January 1996, we began setting up meetings with their support groups. We also sent the book to potential publishers.

In January and February of 1996, Patti met with three of the original support groups. The fourth group had dissolved, and the members had either moved or died. Chris was unable to attend these meetings due to a health problem in her family. Feedback was also collected from colleagues, students, friends and family. In September 1996, we signed a contract with our publisher and brought together the final draft, newly titled *Troubling the Angels: Women Living with HIV/AIDS*. This epilogue presents that process and includes feedback from the women in the order that we introduced the support groups in Preface I.

Support Group 1:
February 17, 1996, 12:30–3:00 PM, AIDS community center

Present: Barb, Lori, Linda B, Carol X, Tracy (who was visiting from support group 3), a new woman, and Kathryn, the facilitator. Rosemary and Robyn were absent and had infrequent contact with the group. CR was in the hospital; her comments are included from a phone conversation with Patti after Lori died on August 8, 1996. Rita had quit the support group, but was delighted when we found her. Her comments are from a September 1996 phone call.

---

since taping the interviews. And the member checks were affirming; the extremely varied responses told us that we had produced the hoped for mosaic of women living with HIV/AIDS.

This book has been a multi-layered process of collaboration. Patti and I have been the core collaborators, finding for ourselves that two strong and opinionated women can share the process of envisioning, organizing, writing, critiquing, and changing in a way that shapes a loving and respectful relationship as well as a better book. Reflecting on how we did this, the key was that we had different but complementary goals. Neither of us was needy. Both brought years of feminism, as well as some professional self-confidence to the project. We were both deeply touched with the process of collecting the stories, being privy to such personal experiences and feelings. We took hot tubs together, practicing what we called "naked methodology." And we

Patti: I call this a member check, where we go back to the women who gave us stories, and see what they think of what we did with their stories and the book. So, just tell me what you think of this book.

Linda B: We're in a fishbowl, we're in the inside looking out so we are going to see this book completely differently than anybody. I wanted MORE of each woman's story! I feel like there's more to me than is in the book, a lot more.

Lori: How can a book tell everything?

Patti: This is part of the dilemma of doing interviews or any kind of research.

Lori: Knowing that you had hours and hours of material, I was really happy with what got into the book. There was a good balance of struggles and happiness. It captured the full circle of what it is like, the testing, the delay, decisions, like "should I run up all my credit cards?" When my copies came in the mail, I remember having this really awesome feeling, like "I'm going to be in history." When I took it to my brother and sister-in-law in New York I remember I had tears in my eyes when I gave it to them. It was just really emotional, like here's a little piece of my life that you're going to have on your bookshelf. It still makes me feel very emotional.

Patti: A feeling that some part of you will—

Lori: —live on.

Linda B: My mom wants a copy of it, but because of my dad, she'll have to read it at my sister's house. It's hard—I was happy with what was in there. I guess my problem with it is I'm not there anymore. I don't even remember when we did the interviews if I had told my family.

Rita: I thought it was excellent. I read it from cover to cover in an hour and a half. Everyone was pretty honest, but I was shocked to see the way I just laid it all out. It's like seeing a different person. At first I wanted to deny. I

⁂   ⁂   ⁂   ⁂   ⁂   ⁂   ⁂

consistently applied the same openness and respect we had for the women's stories to our own, including the relational story that was being nurtured day-by-day through our research.

Early on we knew that each required the strengths, skills, contacts, and perspective of the other to even begin to have a book such as this. Mostly we agreed, or at least agreed to try the ideas of the other. I suggested we switch from individual interviews to group interviews.

Patti suggested the top/bottom text. I found the support groups, Patti negotiated with our publisher, and so on.

Our biggest, deepest disagreement? The title of this book! Early on, Patti proposed *Troubling Angels*. She loved it, and had a quick attachment to it. I was alienated by the title, believing that it implied that women living with HIV/AIDS were trouble, troubled, or troubling, depending on the perspective of the beholder. We discussed this at length,

don't want to be that person, I don't like that person. I struggled so hard to get where I am today, to get off methadone.

Patti: Good for you, girl, because I've heard methadone is harder to kick than heroin.

Rita: It is. It stays in your body longer. It gets in your bones. With the heroin you're sick for like five days, then it's over. But with methadone it's like months and months of the worst flu you ever had multiplied by a hundred. Now, many of my secondary infections, the yeast infections and shingles, I haven't had at all since I got off the methadone because it's such an immune suppressant.

Patti: Well, obviously, a constraint for everyone is the time lag between the interview and where each of you is now.

Barb: Yes, I think I've changed, evolved so much. I was at the point where I was feeling that I'd done everything in my life, and that I was ready to go. My husband had died not long before the interviews and I really felt like that was the final chapter in my life. It sounded like I was looking forward to dying to be with him, and I'm certainly not looking forward to dying now. There's much more to do in life before that happens.

Patti: How did you find yourself reading it, Barb? Did you read it from beginning to end or what?

🐚   🐚   🐚   🐚   🐚   🐚   🐚

Patti was not backing down, and *Troubling Angels* became our working title. Would this dispute define our work, shut us down, would either or both of us struggle for control? Foreseeing the member check saved us. We'd let the women decide. This was a growth edge, our leap of faith that the project could continue and that time and process would offer a solution.

Why such intellectual and emotional chasm over the title? The troubling title was the symbol of a fundamental difference between us: I am an emotional trouble mender, Patti is an intellectual troublemaker. As a psychologist, I write to synthesize, clarify, inform, support, stabilize. As an intellectual and academician, Patti writes to explore, expand, disintegrate, to provoke intellectual discomfort and disagreement.

By December 1995, the women had reviewed the self-published version of *Troubling Angels*. We were ready to begin the member checks when I was faced with a serious health problem in my family. This defined my life for awhile so Patti went ahead with the member checks. The project had already taken much longer than we had anticipated, and we didn't want to lose anyone else to death before having her feedback. I was especially worried about Lori.

When I read the transcripts from the member checks, I found myself scanning the pages for feedback on the title. How did they feel about it? And when I discovered that some of the women shared my dislike for the title, I felt affirmed as well as concerned: what could Patti and I do about it? The troublemaker in her still liked it, the trouble mender in me wanted

Barb: It took me a good month. It was very difficult for me. It was very emotional. It was really good to read, and really hard. I talked with Lori and two other people while we were all reading it around the same time, and I think everyone felt the same way. It was very difficult to look back, especially the chapter where Lori is speaking.

Patti: "Seize the Day."

Barb: Yes, and how after that she got sick. I felt like she had spoken for me and a lot of other women. It was really good to read. It was real hard.

Patti: What was the good part?

Barb: I could relate to everyone's struggle. I felt like we had all helped each other get to certain points and that this book can also help others get to the points that we were. And maybe that helps others to understand me.

Patti: Were there any parts of the book that you didn't like?

Barb: The format. I wanted to read it all from one end to the other, and it was hard to do because I was reading two different things. I would have liked to read one part or the other in sequence.

Patti: So the top/bottom split text was irritating. And it never got easier while you were reading along?

Barb: No.

---

to soften and clarify. Patti seemed willing to change if we could think of a new title. I thought about it on my walks, before sleep, while driving; nothing worked. And suddenly, I realized that a tiny, simple word, "the," inserted into the title, could make it work for me. *Troubling the Angels* clearly externalized the trouble from the characters of the women living with HIV/AIDS but kept the frustrating, over-whelming, burdening reality that HIV/AIDS is to this century and the next.

I call Patti on the phone, share my idea. She says "hmmmm," and in light of the feedback from the member checks, she'll seriously consider it. She travels for several weeks, I forget about it. She returns and we don't mention it. Finally, I bring it up. "Well, what do you think?" Patti says that *Troubling the Angels* will do "just fine." While it took several years

and a member check to reach this com-promise, that little "the" in our title is a marker of a remarkable collaboration that has stretched us both. Patti writes to expose and confound the complexities of HIV/AIDS; I write to make them more manageable. Ultimately, this book is a manifestation of both of us, and I believe, better for it.

Patti: The earlier self-published version of this book was no first faint draft. While re-orderings, updates and additions have been made, this version is no radical de-parture from its earlier incarnation. This is not out of some sense of the great suf-ficiency of what we have done, but rather out of our puzzlement as to how to pro-ceed differently. For example, in the case of our continued commitment to the split text format in the face of participant res-ervations, we encountered publishers who

Lori: You're following somebody off on a really deep thing and you need to turn the page and then something else catches your eye, like Chris talking about picking up her daughter, and yes, it's a distraction. I have the same problem with the newspaper. I thought the content was excellent, but the layout needs to be tied together. I've given the book to four people, and they all said they had a problem with the layout. Some people won't see a movie with subtitles.

Patti: Yes, this is definitely a movie with subtitles. And it's not linear. That's troubling, very troubling. This format does not fit the idea of how we are supposed to hear people's stories.

Rita: I liked that part where the bottom was a little story, alongside the top part. It made it more interesting, very much more interesting.

Lori: Patti, do you like the layout?

Patti: I am so devoted to the format that I don't know if I could get rid of it. Part of my attachment is this: this is a very complicated disease and people's lives are so complicated by it, and I want a way to put the text together that shows how complicated—

Carol X: Right, but maybe we could do something about when both the story at the top and the monologue at the bottom continue on the next page, so you don't know which one to stop first in order to continue. Is there anyway to at least—

🐚   🐚   🐚   🐚   🐚   🐚   🐚

also wanted us to get rid of it in the name of appealing to a broader range of readers. We tried other options. We knew we didn't want our commentary to come before the women's stories as we wanted to give pride of place to their words. We knew we didn't want our words to come after their stories as that set us up as the "experts," saying what things "really meant." We tried the idea of "asides," where we would put our comments in sidebars. But all of these efforts renewed our commitment to the kind of "underwriting" that we had stumbled onto in our efforts to find a format that didn't smother the women's stories with our commentary and yet gestured toward the complicated layering of constantly changing information that characterizes the AIDS crisis. Trying to find a form that enacts that there is never a single story

and that no story stands still, we practiced a kind of dispersal and forced mobility of attention by putting into play simultaneously multiple stories that fold in and back on one another. This raises for readers questions about bodies, places and times, disrupting comfort spaces of thinking and knowing.

Our charge was simple: get the story out. The deliberately discontinuous mosaic that we have settled on may be a case of putting style ahead of story and, seemingly, we could have found a publisher more easily without this complicated and complicating format. But we risked this practice in order to bring to hearing matters not easy to make sense of in the usual ways. Forced to deal with two stories at once, the split text format puts the reader through a kind of "reading workout," a troubling exercise of reading. It stitches

Patti: Compromise? A compromise would be to lay it out so that each part ends as much as possible on the same page.

Lori: And both the stories are so compelling that you don't want to miss them. So you're like "should I go ahead with that or the other?"

Patti: That compromise wouldn't be too difficult to do. Talk some now about your reaction to the cover image. [See page 237.]

Barb: Well, I think that the picture is beautiful, but I think that it also brings about feelings of shame.

Linda B: But she's hugging herself.

Lori: But she's not standing up or anything.

Tracy: But it's not necessarily a bad thing because I think we've all been ashamed at some time.

CR: I liked the cover; it was a female like us, good women troubled with this thing that's come into our lives.

Patti: You don't think it is too pitiful?

CR: I feel pitiful and troubled by this in my life sometimes. I feel different from four years ago when you first talked to us. Reading the book now is like looking at a high school yearbook. We've matured in the face of the devastation of AIDS. We were naive then. We were encouraged to live positively. But now I feel like I've been through a war.

---

together discontinuous bits and multiples of the women's stories through seemingly disconnected narrative worlds, angelology, e-mail and journal entries, letters, poems, interview transcripts, academic talk about theory and method, and autobiography. Multilayered, it risks a choppiness designed to enact the complicated experiences of living with the disease, layers of happy and mournful, love and life and death, finances, legal issues, spirituality, health issues, housing, children, as people fight the disease, accept, reflect, live and die with and in it.

As well, the work of the angels in this text has remained a problem right down to the end. Chris' story of how we came to add the "the" to the title captures how she and I worked with and around my stubborn insistence on keeping the angels in the book. Knowing we would submit

what we were writing to the women in a member check worked as a safeguard for our own process and kept us from power struggles. When our interests and investments clashed, we would talk it through as best we could and then let it ride. With some aspects, like the split text, Chris eventually formed her own attachments. With some, like shorter angel intertexts, I eventually found my way. But I would not let the angels go, even in the face of resistance to their presence in the book.

Part of this was my very personal need to negotiate a relationship to loss. Over the course of this project, I broke down badly twice. Once was in transcribing Lisa's story of the death of her son, the last data story that we collected in this project. Recovering, I wrote in my research journal, "I have just broken down, crying. This is the first tape I've

Lori: How did you come up with the title "Troubling Angels"?
Patti: First I'd like to hear what you think.
Lori: My initial impression was who am I troubling? I had a real hard time with the title.
Kathryn: It bothered me immediately. My first experience with HIV/AIDS was this group of women. And I don't see them as troubling at all. I couldn't relate. These are not the women I know.
Linda B: Which part bothers you? The "troubling" or the "angels"?
Tracy: AIDS *is* a troubling situation. It's like cancer. You see a kid with leukemia, it's troubling. It's not like we're causing a problem, it's more like a psychological troubling, a spiritual troubling; it's not like "Oh, you're getting on my nerves." It's more like a story that we should not be hearing. We shouldn't be hearing of a mother dying when she has four kids. That's troubling.
Kathryn: What you're saying is that illness is troubling, not women with the disease.
Carol X: I found the title "troubling"! Being part of this group and some of the experiences of my spirituality, while from time to time it's troubling, it's more living with a challenge versus something that's definitely going to get the best of me. "Troubling" has a negative connotation that could be softened.

---

transcribed that I didn't know if I could get through it or not. It *is* cumulative; it does get worse with each death and, of course, a child, a child and a mother talking like this about her child's death." A second time was reading Chris' draft of the acknowledgments and seeing Rex's name, my long-time friend cut down by AIDS in the prime of a life well lived, a friend who gave me every encouragement in this project while still holding me to the fire of responsibility. Two bad cries in such a project testifies to the work the angels did for me, their cooling comfort that let me get on with the book.

This past July, Chris called to tell me of Lori's impending death. "I need to talk to someone. This is going to be a hard one. I've known her and her family for seven years. Her husband was my first

AIDS death." I listen. We talk of the protease inhibitors and how, for some, they are too late. The weight of luck and conjunction and timing and being caught in history's web asserts itself once again. I mention Tracy saying that she had read from the desktop version of the book at Danielle's funeral about Danielle's relationship with her father, and we wonder how many more stories like that we'll hear or whether the new treatments will end this funeral parade. And I think, again, of my stubborn attachment to my "necessary angels."

A recent article on Tony Kushner's play *Angels in America* helps me articulate why the angels worked so well for me within the context of this project. The author, Charles McNulty, writes that Kushner was not so interested in the place of AIDS in history as he was in what of

Patti: My attraction to the title is that the angels are many things. The angels are troubled by you, by your lives, by AIDS in our lives. We like to think of angels as powerful creatures who can mediate between us and the higher ups. But these are angels who are so troubled by AIDS in the world that they can't say the same old same old any more. It's like the old stories are kind of exhausted in the face of the global crisis of AIDS. So, like in the Tony Kushner play *Angels in America*, the angels turned to the people with AIDS for guidance, instead of the people with AIDS looking to the angels for guidance. The angels are astonished by people's ability to keep on living, in seizing life in the face of AIDS.

Rita: It was really interesting, but I had a hard time with the middle part about angels. It's just a little bit above me, I think.

Lori: I'll be honest, I skipped a lot of the angel stuff. I didn't get why it was in there and I was really into the stories about the women. I was enraptured by the women's stories, and I didn't want to waste my time at that point with the angels. Now that I've seen the play *Angels in America*, and I'm oriented to it, I'm going back to read it cover to cover. But at the time, it did not captivate me at all.

Carol X: I, too, didn't get the connection at all, and I was more interested in the stories.

history can be learned from the experience of gay men and AIDS. This, I think, was what I was trying to do here: use the angels to think how we think about the movement of history in the crucible of AIDS in women's lives. Cholera, bubonic plague, syphilis, leprosy, malaria, smallpox, polio, tuberculosis, cancer, as well as AIDS: across time and place, the stress of an epidemic raises problems of divine justice and social obligation. Each of these epidemics has had its moments of stigmatization of carriers, flight of the healthy from responsibilities of care and policy, conspiracy theories, flight to and from religion, and exacerbation of social inequities. Late medieval/early modern Europe, for example, was hard hit by plague and lost as much as twenty percent of the population (Ranger and Slack, 1992).

Poised at the end of our own century and "millennially challenged" as some wit has put it, the AIDS epidemic links global and local in unevenly devastating ways across class, race, sexuality and geography. Within this social and historical context, Kushner tries to rethink a history that can do us any good as we approach the next millennium. Recognizing the deeply political nature of what we think are our private troubles, Kushner uses split scenes, ghosts, "and a flock of dithering, hermaphroditic angels" (McNulty, 1996) to break up our usual ideas of the real. Pointing to life's unexpected interrelatednesses, Kushner's play is an homage to Benjamin's ideas about the debt owed to the past, the connections and responsibilities that we carry with us into the future. The untimely mourning that AIDS has brought can bring social

Lori: You're getting into a whole big thing about angels and in a selfish way, I think it takes away from our stories.

Patti: You felt that the sixty pages that went to the angels was sixty more pages that could have been your stories?

Linda B: Yeah, because I feel like there's a lot more to me than is in the book, a lot more. I had trouble keeping up with who is who! It was like we go out to Hollywood and everybody changes your damn name! I mean, there's not one person who would pick up that book and see "Linda B" and know that's me.

Tracy: That's the problem. If people identify a name with a certain person, then the story does not seem a universal. Do you know how many people have no story? Do you want to read the book and see people saying things and you've felt them too?

Linda B: Yeah, but it's like, will they ever really understand what I'm feeling? You can't put your true feelings on paper. Your feelings go up and down and they change minute to minute and day to day. You can't even get anybody to understand what it's like to be really happy and everything is really cool, and then just out of nowhere this problem that you have is there. And it's hard to put on paper to get anybody to understand.

Support Group 2

Louisa died in 1993 and this group broke up shortly thereafter. Sandy's phone has been disconnected. Copies of the book sent to Geneva were returned, although Tracy has heard that she has had major health problems. Ana's phone has been long disconnected and Maria never provided any contact information.

---

change: this is Kushner's hope in the play. We cannot keep going on with our separated lives, governmental back-turning, moral categories of "innocent" and "deserving" AIDS "victims," drug company greed, the AIDS Industrial Complex: the particular state of emergency that is our condition of living in history.

McNulty goes on to criticize Kushner for Part II of his play for "the soothing story of the healing angel" that falls into "a future that seems garishly optimistic" and "a poetics of apocalypse," a new mysticism into which history and politics disappear. Sensing a diminishing sense of crisis around AIDS and a lack of public response, activism, and medical advances, Kushner sought "the cover of angels." This is understandable, McNulty argues, but such "celes-

Patti: Here's something I wanted to ask you. We want to give a third of the royalties from the book back somehow to women living with HIV/AIDS, and we want to ask for your ideas of where that money should go, whether it is a little or a lot.

Lori: I wouldn't care if you and Chris keep it and use it for further research.

Carol X: I agree as far as utilizing it for more books about women and AIDS. As far as using it within the AIDS community, any cause within it is a worthy one.

Kathryn: I think if there is a little money I would like to see each of the women's groups that were involved in this get some money, that would be for women who are in need. We have women who can't come to our support group because they don't have money for childcare, or they can't pay their phone bill, or they have nothing for Christmas. It troubles me that we don't have money to be able to help out in these situations.

Patti: I like that in the sense that it would give back to the groups that made it all possible to begin with. Do you have any questions for me?

Carol X: When's the next book coming out?!!

Support Group 3

We met with this group three times to get feedback, first in early 1995 as we were making decisions about the desktop version, again in November of 1995 when the desktop book was literally just off the press, and finally two months later after group members had a chance to read it. The field notes from the first two meetings are in the subtext on the next page.

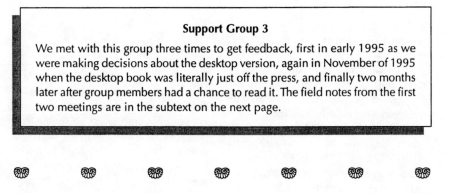

tial shenanigans" have to be resisted. If not, we lose Benjamin's insight into history as trauma, as "events that cannot be fully perceived as they occur." McNulty calls for a certain kind of vigilance against such "easy comforts" as we try to understand the force of AIDS in our historical moment. This raises great cautions about the angels as a place of use in this book. The work of the angels is to serve as a mechanism for disorientation, an instrument of doubt that links local to global and disrupts our conditioned responses. The work of the angels is to make the text say more and other about something as absurd and complicated, as untimely as dying in the prime of life of a disease of global proportions, facing a too much, too soon grief, caught in the weight of

Patti: So what did you think of the book?

Lena: You don't want people to know too much, so you don't get hurt. I still don't tell my family everything and they think that's wrong. This book did open up some deeper conversations with my family. Most of the books out there don't have anything about the emotional side. My mother thinks she needs to know everything to help me more. She says I hide things. My sister, a healthcare worker, said the book lets you treat HIV+ people more human because you get inside their experience, so it's different than other books. At

a different stage, I probably couldn't have read it. Where you are at and how you look at your life makes a difference in whether you want to read it or not. My fifteen year old niece doesn't want to read it. My mom read a chapter that caught her eye and then read wherever she saw Diane's name because we are such friends. Mom said Diane was famous!

> **7:30–9:30 January 9, 1996, office lounge**
>
> Present: Alisha, Diane, Lena (new woman) and Tracy as well as Donna, co-facilitator. Joanna, while doing well, now attends a group for men and women and works at a local AIDS organization. Both Danielle and Holley have died.

🌀　　🌀　　🌀　　🌀　　🌀　　🌀　　🌀

conjunction, chance, timing: history's web.

Rainer Maria Rilke wrote of how "terrible angels" help us negotiate being plunged into death like a stone into the sea. And Benjamin helped me see early on how the angel could function somewhere "between theory and embarrassment" (Ellison, 1996) in this study, an index that lets us see how history happens as we attend to the line between the limits of where we are and what is gathering beyond. Grounded in our study of women living with HIV/AIDS, trying to think about and against our habits of mind in making sense of social crisis, I have put the angels to work in order to continue the dream of doing history's work in a way that is responsible to what is arising out of both becoming and passing away.

From Patti's research journal, February 7, 1995

Present: Alisha, Tracy, Holley, and Gina [Alisha's signer]. Chris is in Paraguay, coming into the final days of Elena's adoption. I join the group the last half hour, overview the table of contents, walk them through handouts from selected stories that particularly featured members of their group, and pass around the angel images which draw some attention, but not much. Tracy can't stop reading; she gulps it down, talking about how much she likes the format. She says the angel images are good, "not fat little white babies," but images that "fit the topic." She says the format caters to a general reader, but also breaks the conventional style, a different style that will get attention. A doctoral student, she notes that the split

Diane: My mother talks to Lena, but not me. She doesn't want to face my situation and my feelings. It's all too overpowering. I give people tidbits, but I want to protect my friends and family. The book might help them ask the questions I want them to ask. I liked the book, I thought it was enlightening, but I thought a lot about how much we've changed since the interview was taped. I've felt stagnant lately, but reading the book made me realize how I've become more open. I'll give my mom a copy and she might peek at it, but never admit she read it.

Tracy: What caught me most was Danielle's death. She had asked me to speak at her funeral last spring, so I read parts from the section on her father. It was emotionally difficult to read the book. I know almost everyone in the book. It's not about "everything is going to be OK." It doesn't make it easy to read, but it is the way it is. It's not linear, you don't have to read the chapters in order. So I jumped in where my interest was.

Alisha: I told my mom to read the book and tell me how she felt about it. The book is very sensitive. My mother usually holds everything inside. She liked the description of other mother-daughter relations, but denied parts where I talked about her and me. But we talked more than ever and it is a beginning, another chance. The book helps tear down walls. My mom cried for the first time. I now realize how much my mom loves me,

---

text is "postmodern" with its multiple voices, dialogue within dialogue, its "not presenting a master narrative." "It's not just one woman's story, but a playing back and forth across the stories, stories that break into each other, providing relief." I am struck with all the stories we're not telling, both the shifts in the lives of the women we have interviewed and the stories of women who have newly joined the group.

From Patti's research journal, November 7, 1995

Present: Chris, Diane, Joanna, Holley, Tracy, Donna (co-facilitator), Alisha and her partner, Gina (Alisha's signer), and two new HIV+ women. Diane, Joanna and Holley arrive first, get books, sit together on couch, reading intently. I tell Holley to turn to very last pages. I sit hardly breathing, watching her read what I never thought she would live to see, experiencing a kind of accountability. I barely know how to fathom. I imagine her nonplused by what I have written on the side of her poem, but say nothing while everyone reads quietly, avidly.

Others arrive, get books. Joanna talks of how unusual it is that anyone actually carries through with getting something to the people they have talked to. She speaks of a dissertation student from Kentucky who said he would get her a copy of what he was writing, the copy that never arrived. She also speaks of how she could help revise the resources section, based on her AIDS work.

A new woman to the group asks for a copy for her mother for Xmas, speaking of how out she is as HIV+ to her family

finally, finally. Her reading the book opened up a little moment; she's not going to change overnight, but now I know she loves me and over time we will talk more. It makes me a little nervous, but I feel safer now, although I have scars and am afraid to trust that she will be there for me. My aunt read it too, for a long time, and then sat and talked to my mom for five hours!

Patti: The book seems to be a good first start to understanding, and it seems to work in many different ways with many different people.

Donna: [Crying] It's very hard to read. I've lost so many people to this disease. It gets worse instead of better, like I'm rawer with each death and angrier at the untimeliness and the difficulties that women have to face. The awe-inspiring strength to go on living in the face of the hand they've been dealt, the assertions of dignity, the combined voices in the book communicate this.

Lena: I've had to let go of my anger about the weight of all the deaths. I've lost over seventy friends, especially mentors in surviving. I tried to kill myself and that was a good thing because I realized I wasn't alone. There were support services and I needed to come out of the closet with friends and family.

Donna: Women being positive is a totally different political animal, for example, having babies in a country that goes bat shit over women's right to choose, but when it comes to HIV women, they're seen as selfish to want babies.

and how they worry and how hard it is for them to talk with her about AIDS. She has tried to find books that would help, "but they don't deal with feelings." This book, she says, deals with the feelings that might help her family understand.

I speak of how this is one of the happiest days of my life and immediately cringe in horror that my happiness would come from the sorrow of their lives. "This is such an ugly disease," Tracy says. Donna starts crying when she turns to the first chart on the changing demographics of the disease. "I know this," she says, "but I forget how awful it is."

Another new woman speaks of how being HIV+ effects the nursing work she

is doing, what it is like to be so deeply closeted about her own HIV status as she does her work, how knowing would shake up the people she works with who continue to harbor such biases and stereotypes of the HIV+. She has a two-year old child, HIV negative. I see how much an issue childcare is in giving her a space to breath and participate in the group.

As the evening ends, we stand for a group hug and I thank them for all their help and speak of my sadness that the book has to come from such awfulness. Tracy says she'll try to write something about her reaction to the format, but cautions me to be very careful about any message I might leave when I call her.

Patti: In addition to a section on HIV positive moms and HIV positive babies, we're deciding how much more medical information to add.

Tracy: Be careful not to over-medicalize it. There are lots of books out there that have that information. Don't weight this one down. Just refer to other resources and beef-up the annotated resource listing.

Patti: Well, anything else?

Tracy: How have you been feeling, Patti, your reactions? Has it been worth all your effort?

Patti: It's been a fabulous learning experience and it feels pretty funny to be saying that about something so painful in so many lives. I've been doing academic research for ten years, but it's been the kind of work that is read by a very small audience. This one feels like it will get out, be of use. And it has opened up new doors with my mom and dad whereas my other work closed doors. My dad said he read every word of my first book and didn't understand a word of it! With this one, my mom and I have had wonderful conversations. This is the first thing I've written where I feel useful to a broader audience.

Tracy: Yes, everyday people can read this.

Patti: Part of what I'm hearing from you tonight is that the book can stand as it is, pretty much, and do the work we want it to do. We hoped to capture the everydayness of people's lives, that it is not only one thing and it's not one thing all the time. We hope to be realistic without being all dark and melodramatic or going the other way and being airy fairy. It's that tone thing.

🐚   🐚   🐚   🐚   🐚   🐚   🐚

I count: twelve women, all white except for Tracy. The co-facilitator, Donna, speaks of how this group is so different from the one she worked with in Toledo that was mostly poor women of color, how I will get a very different reaction to the book from this group than I would from that one. I count: twelve women, four of whom are "helpers" of one sort or another (Chris, Donna, Gina and myself), two new women I haven't met before plus five who participated in the book.

Overall, I am ecstatic. It is out. This part, at least, is done. I can sleep better now, out from under the delivery of this text of responsibility into their hands.

From Patti's research journal, November 4, 1994

Present: Amber, Sarah, two new women, and Heather, Family Services social worker who has taken Melody's place as facilitator, given Melody's health problems. The two new women are both African-American, one is 67, diagnosed in 1984, quite healthy physically, with great struggles to not be consumed with anger at her husband who infected her. The other new woman also takes issue with the point I make about how women "don't waste energy being mad at those who infected them" (in relation to Louisa's story): "I would have killed him if he weren't already dead."

We don't want this to be a victimology. Did we balance the tone so it is neither overdone melodrama and sensationalism, or on the other hand, cold and distant?

Diane: It wasn't all negative. It shows the situation as it is.

Tracy: It's funny how closely you followed the language of the people that I know. I could tell who was talking, even with their pseudonyms. It's not sensationalist or preachy. I think it's great. I'm proud of you. Who would have thought when we did the taping [for the interviews] that it was really going to be a book?

Support Group 4

We received feedback from this group twice, in November 1994, a year prior to the desktop publication, and then in January of 1996 after group members had a chance to read it. Patti's research notes from that first meeting begin in the subtext of the preceding page.

Heather: Can we add stuff on Amber's relations with the group now that she has found out she is not HIV+? Amber, is your life better or worse now?

🐚   🐚   🐚   🐚   🐚   🐚   🐚

I hand out table of contents and loose pages from the stories to which their group had contributed heavily. It takes almost an hour to get through the overview, with many questions and stories bubbling out, especially from the new women who seem sad to miss the opportunity to get their stories in the book.

Amber seems thrilled to find her own and group members' words being used, corrects some attributions, and comments on what a long way I have come, how I am so much smarter now than when she first met me at the retreat. Over and over, they "confirm" the pertinence of the major themes we had featured, and are much more interested in the sexuality section than the death and dying one. I ask what they think of the angels, and one woman answers, "It's what holds us. I think it's beautiful." Another says that spirituality is such a part of this, that it makes sense. One woman wants to know, "But why 'troubling'?" I say: because these are not the romantic ladies tripping around in nighties that are so popular right now. These are angels who trouble our sense that all is right with the world, that AIDS is something "out there," unrelated to each one of us, and from which we can afford to distance. The biggest learning of this trip for me is that they want to read the whole book, not pieces of it, and how much they trust that we will do the "right thing" by them. This underscores our earlier decision to do the desktop publishing in order to get a "real book" into their hands in a timely fashion. 🐚

Amber: My health is certainly not any better. After I found out I was positive, I had to take Prozac and blood pressure medicine and I became a diabetic. I lost two teeth because I had been afraid I would transfer the disease if I went to the dentist. My life isn't all that much better now that I've found out I'm negative. I have a very special person as a husband, but a new relationship is a lot of work, a lot of work. I don't think about HIV so much any more. I have a lot of other things going on in my life right now. One thing is having to worry about getting it! My husband and I were tested, but how can I be sure any test is right?

Patti: Would you call that the burden of being negative?

Amber: Part of why I got married was to not have to worry about getting it so much. It was a way to protect myself somehow.

Melody: I loved the book. Real good work. Tell Chris. Can I get two more copies, one for my Mom and one for my AIDS buddy? You hit it on the head in terms of the way you presented the stories, point-blank, not sugar-coated. I read it at a gulp and will go over it again. There are other books out there of people telling their stories, but this was different. I've never been better in terms of my health. My counts are almost normal. I got over the flu in no time. I'm doing lots of herbal medicines and my attitude

> **January 17, 1996, 6:30–8:30 PM, AIDS community center**
>
> Present: Amber, Sarah, Heather (facilitator), and Kristin who has been in the group for years, but did not participate in the study. Tommie has married and moved away; Iris is more involved with her sobriety group than with the HIV/AIDS group; Nancy has died. Based on phone calls, Tina is busy and healthy and Melody has had major health problems. Now better, she has not been much involved in the group. Her comments are from a January 1996 phone call. This group has had twenty-four members over the four years of its existence.

> While Amber's strategy of getting married to protect herself from HIV is not uncommon, the possibility that more women are infected by steady male partners than by casual sexual relations is suggested across several studies. Hence monogamy and "knowing" sexual partners may not be adequate safer sex practices, especially for women. The structure of gender relations makes it difficult for women to assert themselves in knowing the sexual history of a man or demanding either monogamy or condom use. Additionally, in a study of the use of lying in the negotiation of safer sex, 35 percent of men said they lied versus 10 percent of women (Sobo, 1995, p. 12).

has a lot to do with it, but I don't come to group much so I'm particularly thankful to the Family Services agency for sending us Heather to facilitate the support group.

Heather: The book is incredible. I left it on my coffee table hoping some of the teenagers who travel through my house might pick it up.

Patti: I've got my 17 year old niece reading it. I'm actually very interested in what teenagers think.

Sarah: Well I loved it. I just thought it was wonderful, so affirming and incredible to read. I really liked the commentary that you two put into the bottom and I thought the stuff about angels was really interesting, some things I'd never heard of, and I thought the art work was good too. I really liked the Laurie Anderson song and the Jim Morrison poem. I don't think I have a least favorite part.

Patti: How did you read it?

Sarah: I first looked for my name and read the stuff I said. Then I read the parts where our group talked a lot. Then I started at the beginning.

Patti: In a rush or over a week or two?

Sarah: Over a week or two.

Patti: Was it emotionally difficult to read it?

Sarah: It was a little provocative, yeah. It wasn't difficult, but I did talk about it with my partner and with my mom. I even talked about it with her, so you know it was provoking!

Patti: Has she read it, can you imagine that she might?

Sarah: Not yet, but I think she will. I gave it to her, but I think she left it with my sister. I wanted her to read it. My plan was that she would read it on her trip to my sister and they would talk because she has a hard time talking to me about this whole thing. But I don't know that she did it. I really loved it, I really did. It was a wonderful thing to read.

Patti: Name a couple of feelings that you had as you read.

Sarah: I felt excited during parts of it, and sometimes I felt sad. I could really identify with some of the feelings that were there and the issues that were brought up. The part I liked best was the quote about *Angelus Novus* and the Laurie Anderson song. And this angelology part was really interesting.

Patti: Laurie Anderson read Walter Benjamin and wrote that song. How about you, Amber?

Amber: As soon as I got it, I went right to the toilet and started reading it. I called everyone up and said did you get your book? I read it in a day. I looked for our group first, but it was kind of hard to go down to the bottom and start reading on that. It's a whole different thing, so you start reading that and then you have to go back and see where you were. That was interesting. I like that commentary and the story within the story. It was just distracting because I wanted to read it all.

Patti: Was it irritating?

Amber: No, not really. I mean I'm not slow or anything, it was just—

Sarah: I found at first it was distracting, but then I got a method so that I read what the support group members said first and then I'd go back and read the bottom.

Patti: One publisher wants us to take the book apart and make it more conventional. What would you say to them, Amber, if you were talking to them?

Amber: I think it's important to look at your audience and you want to appeal to the widest audience. There's so much stuff in here and it's so well written, you're wonderful. I didn't expect it to come out this good, I really didn't. I really thought "they're working on it, they're working hard," but when we saw all the papers and the parts of the book, I thought oh this isn't it. But this is really neat. The worst part is the picture of the naked female angel. I worry about what people will think.

Kristin: I just happened to glance at it, and it gave me a funny feeling. I've never seen an angel with a bush!

Heather: What I think is neat about the book is the format.

Kristin: I haven't even read the book yet, but I think that's going to be distracting for me. I'm a very very poor reader, and I don't read a lot. I'm going to want to read this and that all at the same time.

Patti: There's a lot of things going on at the same time. Heather, what did you like about the format?

Heather: Some people are just going to read the dialogue, maybe to begin with and maybe only. It's real free flowing and kind of titillating in some places for someone who's not into deep reading. That might be the gist of the book for them. Other people are going to read both [top and bottom]. I think it's going to appeal to people from all different levels of ability to read and comprehend. If you want a book that the general population can read, it needs to be at grade three level, but the women's dialogue is readable no matter what.

As of January 1997, the Ohio AIDS Coalition has sponsored thirty-five Healing Weekends. Concurrent workshops cover such topics as AIDS 101, Sex Positive, 12 Step "Humor Workshop," Exercise and Wellness, Living in the Possibilities of Healing, Preparing a Will, Mask Making, AIDS and the Law, Anger and Forgiveness, Medical Update, Building the Immune System, Reflexivity and Yoga, Spirituality, Flesh and Spirit, Long Term Survivors, and No Talent Talent Show. Drawing on a network of community activists and volunteers, the weekends provide a space to network, heal and grow, particularly for those who are often isolated in their own communities.

Amber: You just said that a lot of people won't read the bottom part and there's a lot there for people to just overlook.

Heather: It's a smorgasbord that people can choose to read what fits them or read part now and go back and read other parts later. Some people might just look at the pictures!

Patti: Amber, you wondered if we'd ever pull this off and now it's a better and different book than you thought it would be. How's it better and different?

Amber: It just didn't seem like it was coming along. You'd say well I'll be there to talk to you guys in November, then it would be January or February and we'd hear, well they're still writing the book, they're still doing it. It's really great that you got it done!

Patti: Kristin, I know you just got a copy and haven't read it, but . . .

Kristin: I just feel bad that I wasn't in the study. I could have added a lot, but I heard [mistakenly] that you were videotaping, so I didn't participate. There's so many situations with this disease, like running into people who know people I know at the Healing Weekends, like my favorite aunt that I haven't told. The person I met wrote me a note, "Don't deprive yourself or her of the support." But the whole thing is my parents and how they view this as a shame based thing. I'm thinking about driving home and just telling. We have cousins in prison and in trouble with the law, and mom and dad view me as worse? I got AIDS, I'm sorry, but I'm sure I've not done anything worse than anybody else has ever done. And mom and dad just act like this is such a shameful, god-awful thing, without saying it.

Patti: How did the angelology stuff work in terms of trying to make some points about AIDS?

Sarah: Oh I think it did. I thought it was real effective. To me it was just interesting to read about these things, to know about angels in our culture and different cultures, and then to tie it in with the struggle with the disease and how we think about it. I learned some things I hadn't heard before. For people who aren't familiar with HIV, they'll be learning from what the women have to say, but if you've got it, what the women say is confirming, but I felt like I learned some things from the intertexts.

Amber: I liked the poetry, especially Linda B's poem about Los Angeles.

Patti: My last question is to Amber and Sarah: What did it feel like to read yourself on the pages?

Sarah: It just felt familiar. Like gee, I do say sort of a lot, don't I!

Patti: Is it kind of like a mirror, to see yourself reflected back to yourself at some level?

Sarah: Yes, but I felt compassion for myself. I thought, yeah, you have those kinds of issues.

Amber: I didn't realize there'd be so much about me. There's a whole chapter on me! It was like I can show my family if I want to. There's a few things that are not exactly straight, but it's all there.

Patti: We all change all the time, but it's important to us to feel like what's in that book is the story that you felt at the time, the spirit of where you were at.
Amber: I still feel a lot like that! I mean I'm not healed, or better or anything [laughter].
Patti: Any questions you have for me?
Sarah: I want to make a comment. I really appreciate you and Chris's integrity with this. I feel like you have a lot of integrity. And even in the interviewing process, you didn't interpret, you just asked and asked and asked to clarify. And the way you both pulled things out of people, you're just very respectful and really were just trying to understand. And that came across really loud and clear. You know, I learned some things about interviewing in reading this book too! It was wonderful. And how well intentioned you were and how you saw us. So I really appreciated that.
Amber: You really respected people's lifestyles and you didn't make judgments on anyone. You didn't even leave it open for anybody to make a judgment on anyone. I just felt like anybody could read this and have compassion for the people involved.
Heather: A lot of times research subjects feel abused. Just watching you with the women, and reading the book, this is a seminar with peers, this isn't about research specimens. There's a lot of respect in the book. I really appreciate that. We opened the group up to a Ph.D. student who interviewed the group and she gave us excerpts from her dissertation. It was more clinical, but she got her doctorate out of it, so we helped another person along.
Patti: That's wonderful to hear because part of what we wanted to get across was that we weren't here to interpret and say this is what this really means. We were here to try to figure out how to put a book together that would let you speak your own stories, that would include Chris and my stories of telling your stories in a way that people could hear all the different layers of what this book is.
Sarah: I hope that if you get it published, they don't massacre it!
Heather: It has to have angels in it. That's the whole context. I usually don't buy into such stuff, but as I do this AIDS work, it's a feeling.
Patti: Maybe when we get a contract and have copies of the book, we'll have a book party!
Sarah: It could be an angels' slumber party, angels causing trouble, angels from hell!
Patti: That was one of the titles of the book for awhile. I was so afraid that it would end up slurpy sentimental sweet, because angels lend themselves to that. So at one time we were trying to figure out how to mess it up, like hell's angels.
Heather: The angels have so much energy, angels are so intense. There's not enough books about women and AIDS. There's not much to help profes-

sionals learn how to deal with all of this, how you add the HIV factor into helping to support all these people. I think it's a work of art.

Amber: I hope this takes off and they make a little mini-series about it.

Patti: You could be the consultant.

Sarah: I think she wants to be the star!

The title of this Epilogue is taken from Michel Foucault, "My Body, This Paper, This Fire," that deals with the problems of history and writing. From Foucault: "I am here, wearing this dressing-gown, sitting beside the fire, in short the whole system of actuality which characterizes this moment of my meditation . . . the moment which mustn't be allowed to slip past has come" (p. 21). To doubt where we are, the place we have come to when we put our truths under examination, to risk thinking about how we make sense of the world: this, Foucault argues, is what it means to do philosophy, in this place, these bodies, this time.

Ben DeVeny, *Untitled,* design for *Angels
in America* (Aarhus, Denmark production, February 1995). Used by permission of the artist.

Appendix: Demographic Data (At Time of Group Interviews)

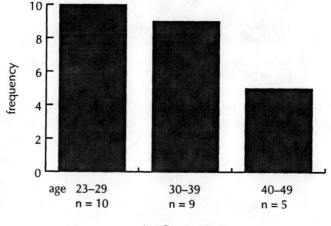

FIGURE A.1 Age Distribution (one participant did not report her age)

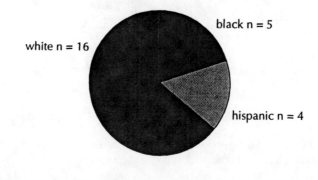

FIGURE A.2 Race Distribution

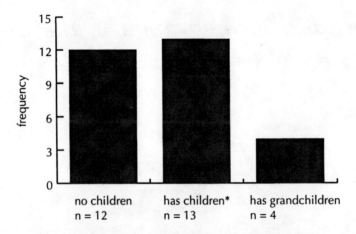

FIGURE A.3 Children and Grandchildren. *Included in this count is one woman whose child died of AIDS and one who placed a child for adoption.

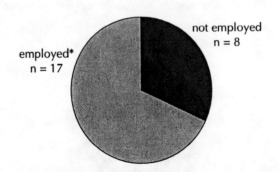

FIGURE A.4 Employment Status. *One woman who responded that she is on sick leave is included in this count.

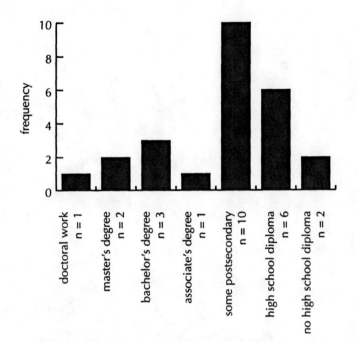

FIGURE A.5   Highest Education Level Completed

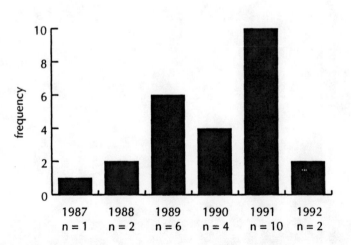

FIGURE A.6   Year Diagnosed HIV. Year of infection data is very difficult to represent given the range of response. See Table A.1.

TABLE A.1 Demographic Information Summary

Name, Age	Race	Children/ Grandchildren	Employment	Education	HIV Infection Date	Diagnosis Date
Nancy, age not given	white	1/0	yes	13 years	unsure when	7/5/91, died 1993
Geneva, 23	Hispanic	1/0	no	14 years	unsure when	6/21/91
Louisa, 24	Hispanic	1/0	no	HS diploma	before 1987	11/88, died 6/93
Danielle, 25	white	0	yes	B.S. degree	1984	4/90, died 7/95
Barb, 25	white	0	yes	B.S. degree	August 1990	8/91
Robyn, 26	white	0	yes	HS diploma	unsure when	8/91
Carol X, 26	black	0	yes	M.S. degree	1986	1988
Tina, 26	black	0	yes	15 years	1990?	6/12/92
Tracy, 28	black	0	yes	working on Ph.D.	1984–1985	Summer 1991
Tommie, 29	white	1/0	yes	HS diploma	1986 or 1987	1/6/90
Sandy, 29	Hispanic	1/0	no	13 years	1983–1985	11/6/91
Amber, 32	white	0	no	1 year short of B.A.	1985?	4/91, HIV– 3/20/95
Iris, 32	white	2/0	no	10 years	Summer 1987 or 1989	4/26/90
Lori, 34	white	0	yes	Associates degree	early 1985	7/89, died 8/8/96
Alisha, 36	white	0	yes	B.S. degree	unsure when	11/91
Diane, 37	white	0	yes	HS diploma plus	1987 or 1988	12/91
Rita, 38	white	1/0	no	HS diploma & 2 years vocational	1984?	1989
Maria, 39	Hispanic	0	yes	HS diploma & some college	1985	1987
Sarah, 39	white	0	yes	M.A. degree	1990	12/91

Melody, 39	white	1/0	no	14 years	1984–1985?	1989
Ana, 40	white	3/0	no	HS diploma	1989	6/14/90
Joanna, 42	white	3/2	yes	HS diploma & 2 years college	1983–1985	1/89
Linda B, 44	white	2/1	yes	HS diploma	end of 1986	9/89
CR, 47	black	4/6	yes	HS diploma	August 1987	1989
Rosemary, 48	black	4/7	yes	HS diploma	1987	1992

References and AIDS Resources

General Audience and Provider Books on HIV/AIDS

Andrews, Laurie and Laurie Novick (1995). *HIV Care: A Comprehensive Handbook for Providers*. Thousand Oaks CA: Sage.

Barouh, Gail (1992). *Support Groups: The Human Face of the HIV/AIDS Epidemic*. Huntington Station NY: LIAAC.

Bor, Robert and Jonathan Elford, editors (1994). *The Family and HIV*. London/New York: Cassell.

Brown, Marie Annette and Gail M. Powell-Cope (1992). *Caring for a Loved One with AIDS*. Seattle: The University of Washington Press.

Burkette, Eleanor (1995). *The Gravest Show on Earth*. NY: Houghton Mifflin.

Callen, Michael (1990). *Surviving AIDS*. NY: HarperCollins.

Cantwell, Alan (1988). *AIDS and the Doctors of Death: An Inquiry into the Origins of the AIDS Epidemic*. Los Angeles: Aries Rising Press.

Dietz, Steven and M. Jane Parker Hicks (1989). *Take These Broken Wings and Learn to Fly: The AIDS Support Book for Patients, Family, and Friends*. Tucson: Harbinger House.

Duh, Samuel (1991). *Blacks and AIDS: Causes and Origins*. Thousand Oaks CA: Sage.

Fisher, Mary (1994). *Sleep With the Angels: A Mother Challenges AIDS*. London: Moyer Bell. Addressed 1992 and 1996 Republican conventions.

Glaser, Elizabeth (1991). *In the Absence of Angels*. New York: Berkeley Books. Addressed 1992 Democratic convention. Co-founded pediatric AIDS organization.

Kloser, Patricia and Jane Craig (1994). *The Woman's HIV Sourcebook*. Dallas TX: Taylor Publications.

Richardson, Ann and Dietmar Bolle (1992). *Wise Before Their Time: People from Around the World Living with AIDS and HIV Tell Their Stories*. London: HarperCollins.

Rimer, Robert and Michael Connolly (1993). *HIV+: Working the System*. Boston: Alyson.

Rudd, Andrea and Darien Taylor, eds. (1992). *Positive Women—Voices of Women Living with AIDS*. Toronto: Second Story Press.

Shilts, Randy (1987). *And the Band Played On: Politics, People and the AIDS Epidemic*. New York: St. Martin's Press.

Squire, Corinne (1993). *Women and AIDS: Psychological Perspectives*. Thousand Oaks CA: Sage.

Weenolsen, Patricia (1996). *The Art of Dying: How to Leave This World with Grace and Dignity*. NY: St. Martin's Press.

HIV/AIDS Organizations and Newsletters

AIDS/HIV Treatment Directory. AMFAR, 1-800-458-5231.

Being Alive: People with HIV/AIDS Action Coalition Newsletter. Published monthly in English and Spanish. 3626 Sunset Blvd., LA CA 90026. Sliding scale.

Centers for Disease Control 24-hour AIDS hot line: (800) 342-AIDS.

CDC National AIDS Clearinghouse, Post Office Box 6003, Rockville, Maryland 200849-6003. 1-800-458-5231. Provides mid-year and year end *HIV/AIDS Surveillance Report* free of charge.

FCAN (Families' and Childrens' AIDS Network), 721 N. LaSalle St., Suite 311, Chicago, IL 60610. 312-655-7360.

(In)Visible Women. In Spanish and English. 26 minute video, 1991. Video Data Bank, 37 S. Wabash Ave., Chicago, IL 60603. 312-899-5172.

Lesbian AIDS Project, GMHC, 129 W. 20th St., 2nd floor, NY, NY 10011. 212-337-3532.

Lesbian/Bisexual HIV Prevention Network, Lyon-Martin Women's Health Services, 1748 Market St., #201, San Francisco, CA 94102.

Lesbian Services Program, Whitman-Walker Clinic, 1407 S. Street, NW, Washington, DC 20009. 202-797-3585.

National Native American AIDS Hotline. 1-800-282-AIDS, for copy of Raven's Guide to AIDS Prevention Resources.

Pediatric AIDS Foundation, 2407 Wilshire Blvd., Suite 613, Santa Monica CA 90403. 213-395-9051 or 800-488-5000.

Positively Aware, 1340 W. Irving Park Rd., Box 259, Chicago, IL 60613. Since 1989, full of information on clinical trials and medical and social aspects of the epidemic.

The International Community of Women Living with HIV/AIDS, c/o Positively Women, 5 Sebastian St., London ECIV OHE, United Kingdom. FAX: (44) 71-490-1690.

The Positive Woman. In English and, in Spanish, *La Mujer Positiva*. PO Box 34372, Washington, DC 20043. 202 898 0372 and 202 529 5447.

WISE (Women's Information Service and Exchange), 125-5th St., NE, Atlanta, GA 30308. 404-817-3441. FAX: 404-874-9320. Wise Words is a treatment newsletter for women with HIV/AIDS.

WORLD (Women Organized to Respond to Life-Threatening Diseases), a monthly newsletter by, for and about women facing HIV disease. Spanish quarterly. WORLD, PO Box 11535, Oakland, CA 94611. Phone: 510-658-6930. FAX: 510-602-9746.

Angels: Popular

Davidson, Gustav (1967). *A Dictionary of Angels*. New York: The Free Press.

Godwin, Malcolm (1990). *Angels: An Endangered Species.* New York: Simon and Schuster.

Kushner, Tony (1992). *Angels in America, Part One: Millennium Approaches.* New York: Theatre Communications Group.

Kushner, Tony (1992). *Angels in America, Part Two: Perestroika.* New York: Theatre Communications Group.

MacGregor, Geddes (1988). *Angels: Ministers of Grace.* New York: Paragon Books.

Parisen, Maria, ed. (1990). *Angels and Mortals: Their Co-Creative Power.* Wheaton, Illinois: Quest Books.

Wilson, Peter Lamborn (1980). *Angels.* New York: Pantheon.

Angels: Academic

Adolf, Helen (1968). Wrestling with the Angel: Rilke's "Gazing Eye" and the Archetype. In *Perspectives in Literary Symbolism*, Joseph Strelka, ed. University Park PA: The Pennsylvania State University Press, 29–39.

Alter, Robert (1991). *Necessary Angels: Tradition and Modernity in Kafka, Benjamin, and Scholem.* Cambridge MA: Harvard University Press.

Avens, Robert (1984). *The New Gnosis: Heidegger, Hillman and Angels.* Dallas, TX: Spring Publications.

Benjamin, Walter (1968). Theses on the Philosophy of History. In *Illuminations*, Hannah Arendt, ed. New York: Schocken, 253–264.

Bloom, Harold (1996). *Omens of Millennium: The Gnosis of Angels, Dreams, and Resurrection.* New York: Riverhead Books.

Cacciari, Massimo (1994). *The Necessary Angel.* Translated by Miguel Vatter. Albany: State University of New York.

Clark, Stephen (1992). Where Have All the Angels Gone? *Religious Studies* 28, 221–234.

Crites, Stephen (1975). Angels We Have Heard. In *Religion as Story*, James B. Wiggins, ed. New York: Harper and Row, 23–63.

Culianu, Joan (1981). The Angels of the Nations and the Origins of Gnostic Dualism. In *Studies in Gnosticism and Hellenistic Religions*, R. Van DenBroek and M. J. Vermaseren, eds. Leiden: E.J. Brill, 78–91.

Dunn, Steven (1989). *Between Angels: Poems.* New York: W.W. Norton and Co.

Encyclopedia of Early Christianity, Everett Ferguson, ed. New York: Garland, 1990. "Angels," pp. 38–42.

Forche, Carolyn (1994). *The Angel of History.* New York: HarperCollins.

Komar, Kathleen L. (1987). *Transcending Angels: Rainer Maria Rilke's Duino Elegies.* Lincoln: University of Nebraska Press.

Maritain, Jacques (1959). *The Sin of the Angel*, trans. Wm. Rossner. Westminister Maryland: The Newman Press.

McHale, Brian (1990). *Constructing Postmodernism.* New York: Routledge.

Rilke, Rainer Maria (1989). *The Selected Poetry of Rainer Maria Rilke.* Edited and translated by Stephen Mitchell. New York: Vintage International.

Ross, George Macdonald (1985). Angels. *Philosophy* 60(#234), 495–511.

Schneiderman, Stuart (1988). *An Angel Passes: How the Sexes Became Undivided.* New York: New York University Press.

Scholem, Gershom (1988, originally 1972). Walter Benjamin and His Angel. In *On Walter Benjamin: Critical Essays and Recollection*, edited by Gary Smith. Cambridge MA: MIT Press, 51–89.

Serres, Michel (1995, originally 1993). *Angels: A Modern Myth*, trans. Francis Cowper. Paris: Flammarion.

Other Works Cited

ACT UP/New York, Women and AIDS Book Group (1990). *Women, AIDS and Activism*. Boston: South End Press.

Agee, James and Walker Evans (1988, originally 1941). *Let Us Now Praise Famous Men*. New York: Houghton Mifflin.

AIDS Education and Prevention: An Interdisciplinary Journal. Guilford Publications, 72 Spring St., New York, NY 10012. Toll free: 1-800-365-7006.

Baker, Rob (1994). Alchemy and Angels in America. In *The Art of AIDS*. New York: Continuum, 213–221.

Bezemer, W. (1992). Women and HIV. *Journal of Psychology and Human Sexuality*, 5(1,2), 31–36.

Britzman, Deborah (1992). The Terrible Problem of Knowing Thyself: Toward a Poststructural Account of Teacher Identity. *Journal of Curriculum Theorizing*, 9:3, 23–46.

Bury, Judy, Val Morrison and Sheena McLachlan, eds. (1993). *Working with Women and AIDS: Medical, Social and Counseling Issues*. London: Tavistock/Routledge.

Duttmann, Alexander Garcia (1993). What Will Have Been Said About AIDS? Trans. Andrew Hewitt. *Public 7*, 95–114.

Eagleton, Terry (1981). *Walter Benjamin: Or Towards a Revolutionary Criticism*. London: Verso.

Ellison, Julie (1996). A Short History of Liberal Guilt. *Critical Inquiry*, 22(2), 344–371.

Farmer, Paul (1992). *AIDS and Accusation: Haiti and the Geography of Blame*. Berkeley: University of California Press.

Felman, Shoshona and Dori Laub (1992). *Testimony: Crises of Witnessing Literature, Psychoanalysis, and History*. New York: Routledge.

Foucault, Michel (1979). My Body, This Paper, This Fire, trans. Geoff Bennington. *Oxford Literary Review* 4(1), 9–28.

Game, Ann (1991). *Undoing the Social: Towards a Deconstructive Sociology*. Toronto: University of Toronto Press.

Greenblat, Cathy Stein (1995). Women in Families with Hemophilia and HIV: Improving Communication about Sensitive Issues. In *Women Resisting AIDS: Feminist Strategies of Empowerment*, Beth Schneider and Nancy Stoller, eds. Philadelphia: Temple University Press, 124–138.

Hammonds, Evelynn. 1990. Missing Persons: African American Women, AIDS and the History of Disease. *Radical America*, 24(2), 7–23.

Haver, William (1996). *The Body of This Death: Historicity and Sociality in the Time of AIDS*. Palo Alto CA: Stanford University Press.

Henriques, Julian, Wendy Holloway, Cathy Unwin, Couze Venn and Valerie Walkerdine (1984). *Changing the Subject: Psychology, Social Regulation and Subjectivity*. London: Methuen.

Hollibaugh, Amber (1995). Lesbian Denial and Lesbian Leadership in the AIDS Epidemic: Bravery and Fear in the Construction of a Lesbian Geography of Risk. In *Women Resisting AIDS: Feminist Strategies of Empowerment*, edited by Beth Schneider and Nancy Stoller. Philadelphia: Temple University Press, 219–230.

hooks, bell (1990). *Yearning: Race, Gender, and Cultural Politics*. Boston: South End Press.

Ibañez-Carrasco, Francisco (1993). *An Ethnographic Cross-Cultural Exploration of the Translations Between Official Safe Sex Discourse and Lived Experience of Men Who Have Sex With Men*. Unpublished MA thesis, Simon Fraser University, Burnaby, British Columbia.

Kayal, Philip Hayal (1993). *Bearing Witness: Gay Men's Health Crisis and the Politics of AIDS*. Boulder: Westview Press.

Marcus, George (1993, July/August). Interviewed in "Inside publishing." *Lingua Franca*, pp. 13–15.

McNeill, William (1976). *Plagues and Peoples*. Garden City: Anchor.

McNulty, Charles (1996). *Angels in America:* Tony Kushner's Theses on the Philosophy of History. *Modern Drama* (39), 84–96.

Meeks, Linda, B. Meeks, P. Heit and J. Burt (1993). *Education for Sexuality and HIV/AIDS: Curriculum and Teaching Strategies*. Blacklick, OH: Meeks Heit Publishing.

Michaels, D., & Levine, C. (1992). Estimate of the Number of Motherless Youth Orphaned by AIDS in the United States. *Journal of the American Medical Association*, 268, 3456–3461.

Patton, Cindy (1990). *Inventing AIDS*. New York: Routledge.

Patton, Cindy (1994). *Last Served? Gendering the HIV Pandemic*. London: Taylor and Francis.

Ranger, Terence and P. Slack, eds. (1992). *Epidemics and Ideas: Essays on the Historical Perception of Pestilence*. Cambridge: Cambridge University Press.

Sefcovic, E.M.I. (1995). Toward a Conception of "Gonzo" Ethnography. *Journal of Communication Inquiry* 19(1), 20–37.

Silin, Jonathan (1995). *Sex, Death, and the Education of Children: Our Passion for Ignorance in the Age of AIDS*. New York: Teachers College Press.

Singer, Linda (1993). *Erotic Welfare: Sexual Theory and Politics in the Age of Epidemic*. New York: Routledge.

Smith, Paul (1988). *Discerning the Subject*. Minneapolis: University of Minnesota Press.

Sobo, E.J. (1995). *Choosing Unsafe Sex: AIDS-Risk Denial Among Disadvantaged Women*. Philadelphia: University of Pennsylvania Press.

Taylor-Brown, S., & Wiener, L. (1993). Making videotapes of HIV-infected women for their children. *Families in Society: The Journal of Contemporary Human Services* 74 (8), 468–480.

Treichler, Paula (1988). AIDS, Gender, and Biomedical Discourse: Current Contests for Meaning. In *AIDS: The Burdens of History*, E. Fee and D. Fox, eds. Berkeley: University of California Press, 190–266.

Visweswaran, Kamala (1988). Defining Feminist Ethnography. *Inscriptions*, 3/4, 27–46.

"Time to Go Home": Holley

I don't think angels should have the last word. . . . They're only angels.

—*New York Times*, January 5, 1994,
quoting actress Ellen McLaughlin
in a review of *Angels in America*

Patti: Holley reads this poem at what we think is her final meeting with her support group. Sitting with an oxygen tube in her nose, she explains why she has chosen to not get treatment for the galloping cancer that came out of nowhere. At first she says that she won't publish this last poem, written a few days ago. She talks of how this is a time for finding who will stand with her and how she understands those who cannot walk with her for these final steps. Her friend Diane talks of the gift of these last days—going to the Arts Festival, taking photos, talking of friendship and death and how this time makes her so much more accepting than when Debbie died, going downhill so quickly. Her friend and hospice caretaker, Allison, a nurse from Guyana, sings every verse of the song, "Amazing Grace." We stand for a group hug, and Holley agrees for her poem to be used as the "last words" of the book.

As I listen to the poem, I think of how, for me, God is an available discourse. For Holley, God is the Father she is ready to come home to. Standing together, across such differences, I am, once again, struck with sadness: to lose such people in untimely ways, people gone, sparks on the coals of this moment that they so mark and register into a future once only, yet again, a burning point that freezes a moment of our danger in the display of lives in which truth and hope rest in the folds of a fragile witness charged with history as passage and threshold.

Chris: Holley was delighted at her first support group meeting; she had moved to the city specifically to find other women living with HIV/AIDS. With a history of rocky relationships and painful memories, she seemed to thrive with new friends, a job, and eventually, a marriage. She spoke on AIDS panels and wrote poetry. It seemed that AIDS had brought Holley more stability and companionship than ever before experienced in her life. She must have realized this, because she had the graciousness to really say good-bye to all of us in her support group. It seemed she would die within days. But Holley liked performance, the unexpected twist, the "last" last word. Her disease went into remission, she took herself off all drugs, and stuck around for another eight months. My last photo of Holley was taken at our Christmas party. She died on February 12, 1996. 🌸

Time To Go Home

I always knew that this time would come
My Father is letting me know it's okay to let go and come home.
Feeling special because time is given to say good bye,
Love me, be happy for me and don't cry.
My life here has been so complete, my job well done, as they say,
Changing from within became easier, as I approached it day by day.
I never imagined I would meet so many people on this journey,
Moving here was what was meant to be, allowing me to be free.
I wanted to make a difference and speak out,
So people not in the HIV/AIDS spectrum could learn what it's all about.
I'm just learning how many people's lives I've personally touched,
But I had the ultimate backing me up so the road was never really rough.
Even now, knowing my time is short here, I have total inner peace
My Father's mercy is more than I ever dreamed possible,
Letting me know and understand it's time to go home.
Opening up His arms to welcome me for eternity.

—Holley, June 1, 1995